WWII:
Through These Eyes

by

Frank "Lindy" Fancher

author HOUSE™

1663 LIBERTY DRIVE, SUITE 200
BLOOMINGTON, INDIANA 47403
(800) 839-8640
WWW.AUTHORHOUSE.COM

First published by AuthorHouse 04/26/05

ISBN: 1-4208-3310-3 (sc)

Library of Congress Control Number: 2005903774

Printed in the United States of America
Bloomington, Indiana

This book is printed on acid-free paper.

Prologue

I lived in the Mason City area until I started high school. My mother was very ill with cancer, so I had to quit school to help my dad make a living. In those days of scant work, it took both of us to make ends meet. No steady jobs were available. We did farm work, cleaned chicken houses, repaired wells, pumps, and cut wood for people who were fortunate enough to afford it. One year we shucked corn for a half cent a bushel and our noon meal. We had to walk about five miles because we couldn't afford to buy gas for our Model T Ford. We worked from daylight until dark, and could shuck as much as 100 to 110 bushels a day, which paid as much as fifty-five cents for the day.

As jobs were hard to find in our area, I finally found a job in a Shell service station in Peoria. The man who owned the station also owned several apartment buildings. I received ten dollars a week at the station, and on the side, received fifty cents for cleaning the apartment windows and screens on the second floor of the apartments and twenty-five cents per hour for the screens and windows on the first floor, so we were able to get by.

A hotel was built above the station, and I was able to rent a room. The recent widow who owned the hotel had a new car and owned a house on Peoria Lake at Rome. She said if I would drive her there when I was off work I could have my room free. I said yes even though I had no driver's license. I think I was only fourteen years old, and I would have done it for nothing just to get to drive that new Chevy. I kept that job as long as I was there. She was a wonderful lady and often times even fed me.

With no car, it was hard to get back and forth to Peoria, so after I walked thirty of the forty-five miles home to see my mother, who was still desperately sick, I started looking for another job.

I found work as a painter for Mike Dutz in Lincoln for a short time and later got a job with George Stoll's "Radio and Amusement Service" as a service man on juke boxes and pinball machines. I was on the road driving day and night, and was paid ten dollars a week, which at that time was a good wage. I was also able to sneak rides back and forth to Mason City on the Illinois Central freight trains.

I don't remember exactly how long I worked there, but it was for some time. We finally had a disagreement when I asked him for a raise. I was doing the same work as the other three guys and they were receiving twenty dollars a week. Another amusement operator in town, "Speedy Electric," offered me twenty-five dollars a week for just an eight hour day. I jumped at the chance. He was an electrical engineer and taught me how to rebuild and rewire electric motors and to wire houses, so it turned out to be a great thing for me. Being that I had to quit high school, this was a good opportunity to learn a trade that would enable me to make a good living. During the year I worked there, Carl Maurer and I became very good friends.

When the war scare started and it appeared that a draft was eminent, Carl and I talked it over. If you were drafted, you were obligated to a four year term. However, you could enlist for only one year. Carl said that if I enlisted, by the time the draft started, my enlistment would be up and I could have my job back and probably have the choice of many more. I decided to enlist in the Army and get my military service out of the way.

I enlisted in the 106 Cavalry, Illinois National Guard on the October 6, 1940 for one year. The 106th was inducted into the Federal Service on December 6, 1940 for one year. Since Pearl Harbor was attacked on December 7, 1941, it turned out I got to go early and stay late. After enlisting in the 106th Cavalry, I thought I was lucky. I'd be able to get my year over and I would be with people I knew.

What I didn't realize was that the 106 Cavalry was a "Good Old Boy's" outfit, and that all the good jobs and promotions would go to the old buddies of the established group. As an outsider, I didn't have much chance of picking my job or of advancement. Looking at the jobs that were left, I found only one, and that one was with the "Pioneer and Demolition Team," which for some reason, no one seemed to want. It was a job in which one had to work with explosives. I found out later there had been an accident with dynamite. The Table of Organization for this job called for a NCO to head the team, so there was a great chance for advancement. The job called for: the building of bridges, blowing bridges, laying and clearing mine fields, building roadblocks, installing booby trap and work with chemical warfare.

To me it sounded like a good deal, although, with my limited education, it would require me to do a lot of studying. As NCO, I had to use and operate the equipment listed: armored cars, Jeeps, motorcycles, tanks, 6X6 trucks, rifles, machine guns, mines and booby traps, and radios. I also had to be proficient in radio codes, demolition, and hand-to-hand combat. Along with all the military regulations, this was a pretty heavy load. I had to do a lot of homework while the other guys played. Failing to qualify in any of the above meant you lost your rank, so it was an incentive to work hard. Besides, with explosives, you don't get many second chances.

"D" Troop of the 106 Calvary was known at that time as 2nd or Down State Squadron of the 106th Calvary Regiment (Horse-Mechanized) of the Illinois National Guard. The 2nd Squadron or Down State Squadron was mechanized in the latter part of 1939. The unit was inducted in the Federal Service as a Horse-Mechanized Regiment and moved to Camp Livingston, Louisiana in late 1940. During the unit's stay at Camp Livingston, the Regiment participated in the First Army's maneuvers in the state of Louisiana.

Prior to the First Army's maneuvers, the 2nd Squadron made a reconnaissance of every bridge and culvert in Louisiana and the eastern part of Texas, mapping every road and cow path.

On Sunday, December 7, 1941, Pearl Harbor was attacked by Japan. The 106th Regiment was sent immediately to New Orleans as security for that city. The unit remained there for a few days, guarding bridges, docks, and other installations of military value.

We were replaced by an infantry unit and loaded on a boat and shipped to the Panama Canal Zone. The "D" troop then became "A" troop of the 27th. Later, after almost two years, when we returned to Camp Maxey, Texas, our unit was changed again to "A" troop of the 32nd Squadron 14th Cavalry Group. Later on we were sent to England and then to Europe.

Colonel Kenneth Buchanan, later promoted to Brigadier General in command of the 106th Regiment, bid the 2nd Squadron farewell. Under the command of Lt. Col. Maurice Peters, the 2nd Squadron sailed to the Panama Canal Zone where we spent the next twenty-two months guarding the Zone. In this move, Troop "D" of the 106th Regiment became "A" Troop of the 27th Cavalry commanded by Charles N. Greenup. A short time was spent at Fort Clayton and then a move was made to the Gorgona Beach area on the Pacific side of the Canal Zone. Later, Headquarters was moved back to Fort Clayton and "A" Troop went to La Chorrera to act as security for the Airacobra (Bell P-39) Fighter Plane Base located there. At this time, Sgt. Ed Burke (Springfield Illinois) and his Dirty Third Platoon was sent up to Aquadulce (Sweet Water) near Penonome to outpost a small air field located there. While at La Chorrera, the Troop worked with the 82nd Airborne on several field problems. More details on the Canal Zone stay are in the following accounts.

Frank L. Fancher WWII

Training began in Louisiana at Camp Livingston. Basic training was week days Monday through Saturday with reveille at 6:00 a.m., roll call at 6:25, calisthenics 6:30, and lineup for breakfast at 7:00. Then after breakfast, back to our tent to get into our uniform for the day, check and clean your tent, and fall in for inspection. At 8:00 a.m., we started our day, usually with close order drill, then to the motor pool to check and clean equipment. After that, depending on the schedule, it could be anything. Sometimes it would be a road march in the armored cars, Jeeps and motorcycles, or it could be weapons training class where we had to field strip our weapon until we could do it with our eyes closed. At 11:30, we were marched back to the tent area where we had lunch and then we were marched back to what was scheduled for one in the afternoon. This went on until 4:30, at which time we had dinner, dressed in our class A uniform, and stood retreat. After this we were on our own unless we had special duty. This could be guard duty, KP (Kitchen police), latrine duty, etc. The days were pretty busy.

After basic training, I was promoted to PFC (Private first class), which didn't mean much but it did give a little more pay than the privates' $21.00 a month. Every little bit helped. I thought things were going a little better. They took out $8.00 for insurance and $3.00 for laundry. Paying for dry cleaning, toothpaste, shoe polish, metal polish and razor blades left very little for pleasure. After basic training came advanced training courses, of which I will mention a few.

First there was the obstacle course. This course was a time limit course. At the start, we had to run about two blocks with full equipment. The first obstacle was an eight foot high solid wall. I didn't have much trouble with this, as I was used to walking and running everywhere I went. Believe it or not, with a little practice, you can run up a vertical wall one or two steps, grab the top and swing yourself over. We had to climb hand over hand up a rope to an eight foot platform and jump off, then hand over hand above a mud pit, crawl through culverts, jump over foot high logs, run through spaced tires, zigzag through trees, cross over a small stream on an eight inch log, then run four blocks to the finish line. I usually came in first. As I said, having no car or bicycle while growing up, I ran or walked everywhere I went so I was in pretty good shape. We had to do this course two or three times a week. I really enjoyed it as it took very little effort on my part.

The infiltration course was something that I was not used to. We started out running while shooting at some silhouette targets, then had to hit the ground and crawl under barbed wire strung only 2 1/2 foot above the ground, while live machine guns fired four feet over our heads. You also had to do this with all your guns and equipment. This course was always muddy due to the fact that they set off quarter pound blocks of TNT or nitro-starch in mud pits several feet deep and only twelve to fifteen feet from our position. This threw mud and water all over us. It was supposed to get us used to an attack on a fortified position. Believe me, I don't think one could ever get used to this, but we did learn to be able to move without freezing in position. If one quit moving, it was easy for the enemy to target mortar or artillery fire, which is much worse than machine gunfire.

The infiltration course wasn't done too often as there was a chance of someone getting hurt. In a few cases, someone would get frightened and attempt to stand up, but the people on the machine guns were on the ball and stopped firing. Some of these were at night. To look up and see live ammo with tracers just a few inches above your head can really shake you up.

In field problems, the Army was divided into two groups, the blues and the reds. The blues were the Americans and the reds were the enemy. The enemy would set up a defensive position and the blues or Americans would try to capture them. The group who got the most points on these problems got extra passes or didn't have to pull KP or some such thing. Our side went through this several times and lost each time, so I asked the CO if I could go out on an early reconnaissance mission.

A water tower stood a short distance away and since this tower was much higher than the trees, I thought that if I climbed it and used my field glass, I might be able to see all the opposing team's positions and weak points. Shortly before sunrise, I got to the tower and climbed up in the early morning. Everything was covered in frost. I climbed to the middle of the sloped area where the round flat spot was on the very top. As it started to get light, I stood up with my glasses to see if I could locate the enemy. My foot slipped and I went off the sloped top like a sliding board.

Thousands of things went through my mind. I was 96 foot up in the air. If I could catch the top of one of those pine trees, it would break my fall but those trees were at least fifty feet away. I know one thing: you can live years in moments in this kind of a situation. Anyway, I hit the ground. This I do not remember.

When I came to later, I don't know much later, I tried to move but couldn't. I finally realized that my feet had gone into the ground almost to my knees. My rear hit next and my head went between my legs, packing the dirt around my boots. I finally got myself out and made my way to the road. I faced the wrong direction. I knew our camp and aid station were in the other direction, but I couldn't make my body turn. I saw a man walking down the road toward me. I opened my mouth to ask for help, but a big glob of blood about the size of my fist popped out of my mouth. He threw up his hands and ran away. Shortly thereafter, someone came along and took me to the aid station. They checked me all over and found only a chipped tooth and a split between my legs. Although my neck was swollen to about the same size as my head, I had no serious injuries.

I think there were several things that helped save me. I was wearing cavalry boots that were laced up almost to my knees. Next, the tower was new and the ground freshly filled. Also we'd had a lot of rain, which made the ground soft. I missed only two days of duty but I was very sore for several days. They also put out a "General Order" not to climb water towers. I even made the papers. It said "Man falls 96 feet and lives." I once had a photo of my friend Tommy Depue standing in the holes that my feet made.

The operation of the armored car or scout car was another of our fields of advanced training. This was a 10,000 pound, four-wheel drive vehicle with a transfer case which gave it six speeds forward and two in reverse. I learned to drive this vehicle when I first enlisted. Growing up in a rural community and working on farms when I was young, I had gained experience driving tractors, corn pickers, plows, dump trucks, etc., so I had no problem with it. The scout car carried

3

eight troopers, had a 50 caliber machine gun with 750 rounds of ammunition, two 30 caliber machine guns with 8000 rounds of ammunition, and 540 rounds of 45 caliber ammunition. We also had a long range radio. Each trooper carried a 45 revolver and I, as car commander, carried a Thompson submachine gun.

This vehicle was to provide mobility and crew protection for reconnaissance under combat conditions. I had to teach the entire crew how to drive. This turned out to be a real job. Back then, people in the cities didn't have many cars like they do now, so with a few exceptions, this was completely strange to them. Driving a 10,000 pound armored vehicle with a straight transmission is a lot different than driving a car. Also, there was no power steering in those days, so we had to manhandle the thing around curves.

While I was in the process of doing this, I almost got busted down to a private. One trooper I was teaching got excited and failed to make a left turn. We were headed straight for a deep ravine. I was standing up on the passenger side. The only thing I could do to keep from going over the bank and into the ravine was to grab the emergency brake. In this vehicle, the brake was on the drive shaft. When you lock up the rear wheels on something with a weight like this, something has to give. In this situation, it was the transfer case.

I had to write a report and go to the commander's office to face the music. After I explained everything to them, they let me off but the poor driver got a month of KP (kitchen police working in the kitchen washing pots and pans, etc.). After this, they let me change the route so we could go straight ahead with no danger if a turn wasn't handled properly. I would like to add here that earlier, as a PFC (Private First Class), I received two weeks KP because I didn't remember my serial number. Today, almost sixty-one years later, I still remember the number was 20620603.

At this time, the United States' preparedness for military conflict was almost nil. The regiment (now known as the Mechanized Cavalry) participated in the First Army's maneuvers in 1941 in Louisiana and Texas. Prior to the maneuvers, we made reconnaissance of every bridge and back road in Louisiana and Eastern Texas. It was an interesting experience.

Since I was Pioneer & Demolition corporal, I was in charge of the group that was sent out to check bridges and roads in Louisiana and eastern Texas. This was to make sure they would support our tanks, trucks and other vehicles before the First Army used them for maneuvers. We had to check out every back road and cow path. A lot of these areas were so remote that you wondered how people could live there. In some of the remote areas and bayous, I don't think they knew that the Civil War was over. They were very unfriendly and I don't think they trusted our government. This was a little upsetting. As a whole, the rest of the people were friendly and it was an interesting time.

We had to enter all this information on our maps and then turn them in to headquarters. Some of these roads were under water part of the time. One rainy night we slept in the armored car. The next morning, when we woke up, water was up to the bottom of the doors. We were finished, so we pulled out and went back to Camp Livingston, where we spent the rest of the day washing and cleaning our equipment.

It was good to get back to the camp. We were able to get showers, clean clothes, and hot food. It really made you feel good.

Now that we were back, I had to hit the homework again, along with all my other duties. One more thing I had to learn was Morse code and radio operation. As a NCO, you had to be able to operate all the equipment or you lost your rank, so this first year was a real learning experience. As a corporal, I no longer had to pull KP or any of those things, but I did have to stand "Corporal of the Guard" duty.

I also had to qualify as a motorcycle rider. This was accomplished by riding down the road at between ten and fifteen mph as silhouette targets popped up along the road. When a target popped up, you had to spill the cycle, pull a Thompson machine gun from its boot, and get at least three shots into the target. It's hard to do, but with practice, it can be done. The little Indian Scout motorcycles we used were very easy to handle.

While at Camp Livingston, I was assigned detached service to a troop of "Horse Squadron," along with a scout car, eight men and two motorcycles from the motorcycle troop. Our job was to provide a Radio & Command Center for this horse troop. We also had to control traffic for a convoy of tractor trailers that stretched out for fifteen miles. For this, we used our two motorcycles along with twelve others. We had to ride down the center line of the road between the big trailers and the on-coming traffic in order to get to the next intersection to stop the cross traffic. It was a nerve-racking job, as the Louisiana roads weren't very wide and we had to ride our cycles almost wide open.

When we got to our destination, we set up our car as a "Command Center" and put out our perimeter guard, keeping the two motorcycles by the command car to run messages. The two motorcycle riders were twins referred to as the "Lane Brothers." It seemed that one or the other of them was always spilling his cycle and getting hurt. I was the NCO and the Car Commander, so I would have to replace them and ride the cycle, since I was the only other qualified rider. It seemed like something would get broken or damaged in all of their accidents, but wouldn't show up until I started to deliver a message. Then a chain would break or a front brake would lock up, and I took a few spills.

On one occasion, I was approaching a bridge and a 6x6 truck with a load of limbs was just leaving it. As it came off the bridge, it hit a bump and a limb about three inches in diameter bounced off. It struck me in the chest, knocking me flat and pulling my hands off the handlebars. I grabbed the saddlebags and steered with my feet hooked under the handlebars. I managed to get across the bridge and then sideswiped a fence before I stopped. Didn't get hurt badly, but I was very sore and black and blue for a week or so. I guess you might say I was lucky. Though I didn't like riding down the center of the road with traffic in both directions, this would have been easy duty for me if I could've kept the Lane Brothers on their cycles.

We were out there for two weeks, sleeping on the ground in pup tents, but we saw some pretty country. I would have really enjoyed riding the motorcycles, if they had not been damaged much of the time. That little Indian Scout was a mighty fine machine.

It was interesting to see how the horse troops really worked. Most of their training was in woods and timber where vehicles would've had a hard time operating. I think later in WWII, there was a time they could've used horses. The Germans did a few times.

Another interesting phase of my training at Camp Livingston was that of bridge building. As demolition Corporal along with the demolition officer, I was responsible for getting men and equipment across small streams that could not be forded with vehicles. This was accomplished by building bridges. We were not equipped to build across rivers or bigger streams—that was left up to the engineers.

Our equipment consisted of two-man chain saws, TNT or Nitro Starch, safety fuses, instantaneous fuses and number eight tetra blasting caps, number eight galvanized wire, axes, shovels and so forth. With my eight-man crew and as much extra help as we needed, we were supposed to build a bridge across a twenty-foot stream that would carry our 12,000 pound armored cars and tractor trailer trucks. As you can imagine, I was a little scared. First, we cut trees (about eight inches in diameter) using TNT, as this was much faster. We only used the saws to trim them to length. Next, we had to build an A-frame to hoist these logs up and across the water.

Guess who had to climb this A-frame and attach the block and tackle? I had fallen off that water tower only a short time before so I didn't know if I could climb or not, but once I got started, I was OK. Anyway, without going into a lot of detail, I got the pier built in the middle of the stream and we laid the tread way consisting of three logs wired together with number eight wire. This done, we leveled the approach with our shovels. I saluted the lieutenant and informed him that it was ready. He looked at me and replied, "Fancher, take that 12,000 pound scout car across and bring it back." It was probably ten feet from the bridge to the stream bed—a lot of time to think—I'd be in the Army for the rest of my life, I'd probably be court-martialed for destroying government property, I'd have to stay in until it was paid for. Fortunately, it worked just like the manual said it would. I did a lot of sweating on that one.

Remember, I had to quit school and go to work so my education was very limited and there were dozens of formulas for figuring the size of the logs and the weight they would have to carry. After this first one, I would go on to construct several more during my stay at Camp Livingston. It was a great learning experience for me, and after that first one, a lot of fun. Also, this was the first time I worked with explosives doing an actual job. Maybe I'm crazy, but I liked working with explosives. TNT and Nitro Starch are very stable explosives and very safe to work with.

After completing the first bridge, I thought I was done. The lieutenant called me over and said, "Corporal Fancher, you did a good job. We're on this side and the enemy is on the other. We need to delay him as long as possible. I think you should blow this bridge and leave no logs big enough to be used to rebuild it."

I don't think I ever had so much fun in my life.

Some of the replacement men had to train with broom sticks and wooden guns and trucks with tanks painted on them instead of real tanks. In spite of these deplorable conditions, the men went on training and soon our enlistment term was over. We were ready to go home and get on with our life.

Some of my buddies and I went into the nearest town, Alexandria, Louisiana, to work on a friend's car to get it ready for the return trip to Springfield, Illinois. While we were still in town the news came over the radio that Pearl Harbor had been attacked and bombed by the Japs. We were all to report back to camp for assignment, as a state of war now existed between the United States and Japan and Germany. Thus began several years of active duty in Panama Canal Zone, Central America, South America and the European Theater of War.

THE REST IS HISTORY.

The Words of Frank L. Fancher

Saturday December 6, 1941

Sgt. Graivet, Tommy Depue and I went into the town of Alexander, Louisiana to try to repair his car so we could go back to Illinois. This was the day we had completed our year of service. All our discharge papers were on the captain's desk to be signed on Monday, December 8th. We had a lot of trouble finding parts for Graivet's 1933 Plymouth, so we decided to stay in town. The next day, we finished with the car and went out to get something to eat. We had just received our food when the radio blared the message for all troops to report back to camp. Pearl Harbor had been attacked. We finished eating and headed back to camp. When we got there, we were surprised to find that our outfit was already gone. They had left a guard at the supply tent and he issued us each our 45 revolvers and a Thompson submachine with 250 rounds of ammo and a boot for the Thompson. We were instructed to report to the motor pool. There we were issued three Harley Davidson motorcycles and told to head for New Orleans without delay and meet the rest of our unit at the Huey P. Long Bridge.

After a 223 mile run, we arrived at the bridge and reported to Capt. Greenup. He ordered us to do dock patrol. After that, they assigned dock, beach, bridge, and government building patrols. We took over an Army camp by an amusement park near Lake Pontchartrian. This was where we spent our time when we weren't on patrol. That night it snowed about an inch and a half and the temperature dropped down to about twenty-nine to thirty-three degrees. Those four man tents had no heat. I don't think I have ever been so cold in my life. In the middle of these tents was a fifty gallon oil drum for garbage. Within twenty-four hours, there wasn't a wooden fence or tree within a half mile of this camp. The drum made a good stove and the smoke went right out the vent in the top of the tent.

We were informed that we would be replaced by an infantry unit as soon as possible and that we would be leaving the United States. We started getting our shots, etc. I don't remember how many day we were

9

there. In addition to our patrols, we repaired and serviced our vehicles and equipment. We were told our ship would soon be ready.

We were assigned to the *Algonquin*, which had been a coastal cattle boat. They had washed it all down and installed bunks, but it still smelled like cattle. We boarded early one morning and headed out into the Gulf of Mexico. Every time the propeller shaft turned over, our heads bounced about and inch off our bunks. This was a real "rust bucket." I think you could've kicked a hole through the side with your foot. We were four days and three nights going from New Orleans to Panama. Later we went from New York to Glasgow, Scotland on the Queen Elizabeth in the same length of time.

After arriving in the Canal Zone, we spent a short time at Fort Clayton, then moved to Gorgona Beach area located west of the Canal entrance on the Pacific side, where we set up a field encampment with tents a short distance from the beach. Off duty time in this area may not have been paradise but it was pretty close. The water was warm and the beaches were all white sand, so swimming just came naturally.

By this time, I had gained the title "Sgt. Fancher" (sergeant #2 combat team, 3rd platoon). In order to set up the camp, we had to dig latrines and a large hole for the kitchen ice boxes. The ground was rock hard after you got down about twelve inches, so I, as demolition sergeant, had to blast out the holes for the latrines and kitchen ice boxes at several different locations. The latrines were located about a block from our tents across a little ice cold rocky stream that came down from the mountains. Due to the difficulty of digging new holes, we poured them about 1/3 full of creosote to keep down the odor and covered them with a wooden two hole seat. An amusing incident happened one morning regarding these blasted out latrines.

I was pulling charge of quarters' duty and had just started my inspection tour. As I walked out of the command tent, I heard this boom so loud that I felt it. I looked up in the direction of the latrine and saw our commanding officer, Capt. Greenup, getting up off the ground with his pants down around his ankles and heading for the little stream where he stuck his rear end in the water. It seems he sat down on one hole, lit a smoke, and tossed the match down the other. The accumulated gas from the creosote exploded and blew him about eight feet, so he was an old sore—for several days. It was one of the funniest things I ever saw.

Our next move was to a new camp called Camp Pacora on the Pacific side of the canal at the Panama City entrance or the Colombian side close to Chepo River and Darien Indian (Headhunters) country. The troop outposted Juan Dias, Cheop and patrolled the shore line from one to the other. While patrolling this stretch of beach, my number two combat team spotted a Jap sub evidently stuck when the tide went out. We opened up with our 50 caliber and our 30 caliber machine guns, but they were having little effect, so I called the Coco Solo Navy base for air support. We, in the meantime, kept up our machine gun fire. While this did little damage, it kept them away from their deck guns.

While waiting for Navy dive bombers, I called for another combat team because we were running low on ammunition. The two Navy planes got there first and made short work of the sub. This is the only time I know of that a Jap sub was spotted along the Central America or Panama coast. I later learned that on September 23, 1942, a Jap sub shelled an oil refinery at Ellwood, California. June 22, another sub shelled Fort Stevens, Oregon, and in September an aircraft from a sub dropped incendiary bombs on Brooking Oregon. On September 29th, a plane from the same sub bombed another city in Oregon, the name of which I do not recall. This plane was hauled over on the Japanese sub and must have been a float plane. It would have been very interesting to see just how they managed this.

At this same time, Panama was the spy crossroad of the world. People from all over the world lived in Panama at that time, so it was quite a problem—but that was not our worry.

Our problem was with the small German radio stations that operated in Panama undercover. We had directional finders and it wasn't very difficult to locate those that were operating from a permanent location. The mule-pack radios that were always on the move in the jungle or mountains presented much more difficulty in locating.

One of the more interesting jobs was locating a station hidden only a short distance from our camp. We kept getting a reading from our directional finder that this radio was located nearby in a cantina or tavern called the "Sunny California." Though it was just a short distance from our camp, they would hear us coming every time and get the radio shut off before we could locate it. We finally parked our Jeep about a half mile away and walked. We found the radio concealed in the piano and

11

Author in the jungle near camp Pacora on the Pacific side of Panama. Lindy's unit patrolled the beach and jungle from Juan Dias to Chepo, two small villages along the coast.

traced the antenna outside to a hollowed out palm tree. We destroyed both. The higher HQ decided we should check this tavern several times a day, the last check being between ten and twelve at night. I took this duty several times a week.

One night, Lt. Lawton from Vermont, Bucky O'Brian from Springfield, and I were making the last check of the day. We finished checking and walked outside, standing around the Jeep talking. It was a lively place, and since Bucky was shy around girls, we decided to have a little fun. A beautiful native girl worked there as a prostitute. She didn't look native at all, just like she had a good suntan. She was always trying to get us to go to bed with her, but if you could have seen some of her clients, you would know why we always declined.

Lt. Lawton got her to one side and told her we weren't interested but that Bucky was a virgin and she should talk to him. She had been drinking and said, "I won't even charge him." She started after Bucky and he jumped in the Jeep. She went in right after him and Bucky went out the other side. She ran around the Jeep and caught him and gave him a big kiss. He got away from her and jumped in the back of the Jeep where she couldn't reach him. She ran to the back of the Jeep and grabbed him around the neck through the opening in the top and kissed him, which we thought was pretty funny. Our laughter caused her to look at us and he got away from her and took off down the road. We were still laughing, but she was really mad.

She turned to Lt. Lawton and grabbed his 45 and said, "I'll show you guys! I'll shoot him and screw him before he gets cold." I managed to get the gun away from her, but it was touch and go for a while. We were all real shook up. It could have turned out bad, but it sure made for an exciting evening.

At Sabanita, where we patrolled the Gatun Locks, Lake Madden Dam and a small fishing village on the ocean, we had a noteworthy experience with the MPs (Military Police Patrol).

We had a camp enclosed by a high chain-link fence containing troop and kitchen barracks, a caterpillar generator shed, and a garage for our vehicles. This was good duty and we had a kitchen crew that took care of all our food. The rest of us pulled shifts for our patrol work and check points. The check points were manned by

13

three men and two 50 caliber machine guns. First Lt. Sam Woods of Springfield, Illinois was our platoon leader and I was the sergeant.

Just north of our compound about 100 feet was a cantina or tavern. They also served good sandwiches. Lt. Woods told me that any of our men who were off duty could go there anytime as long as they were ready when their shift came. It was great to have a Coke or beer and sandwich as a break from Army food.

This arrangement was working out great until an MP came into the place and wanted to see their passes. They told the MP corporal that they didn't need passes and to check with their sergeant, who was next door. The corporal came over and I told him that since we were in our patrol perimeter and under our control, we didn't need passes. He left and returned in about an hour with a smart-assed 2nd lieutenant. He arrested our two troopers and took them into town to MP headquarters. There was nothing I could do.

When Lt. Woods returned from a meeting at headquarters, he was mad as hell. He said, "How did they get past our checkpoint? I didn't sign any passes." Passes to our area had to be signed by the commanding general and countersigned by our immediate commander. The reason for this was security for the Canal Zone. He then told one of our corporals to take over the compound.

He said, "Sgt. Fancher, get your Thompson Submachine gun and Jeep." I got the Jeep and he got his submachine gun and said, "We'll take care of this situation right now. Let's go into town to MP headquarters."

On the way in, we stopped at our number one checkpoint, where he instructed our men to open fire with the 50 caliber if anyone tried to go through without a pass signed by him.

When we got into town, Lt. Woods stalked into MP headquarters and asked for the officer in charge. It turned out to be the same smart-assed 2nd lieutenant.

"Lieutenant," Woods said, "you have two of my men and I want them released immediately or we will take them by force. You have caused me enough trouble." He turned to me and said, "Sergeant, take your safety off and you, Lieutenant, go get my troopers. NOW." They were brought out and Lt. Woods instructed them to go get into our Jeep.

Turning back to the Lieutenant, Woods said, "You pass the word along to all your people: when you come to our checkpoint in your MP uniforms and MP Jeep and a proper pass, we will let you pass as a courtesy. But we also have a second machine gun position concealed a short distance farther along, just in case someone gets past the first gun. From now on, you will have the proper pass signed by the Commanding General and countersigned by me or my officer in charge, and if you fail to stop, I have given orders to my men to open fire. As soon as I get back, I will issue a written order to that effect. Another thing, we are responsible for the security of all Panama, not just the Canal Zone. The rules we work under were set by the Commanding General. If you have any questions, I suggest you contact him."

When we arrived back in camp, Sam Woods said, "Lindy, let's stop over at the tavern and buy these boys a drink. Unless you are sergeant of the guard, you and I will have one too." I replied, "Sam, I'm off duty tonight, so that sounds good."

Thus ended our problem with the MPs.

We had several camps scattered around Panama, and we moved from one to the other when we were not out in the jungle with our "Guerrilla Warfare Training."

While in these locations we led a pretty quiet life when not on duty in one of our checkpoints or roadblocks. These were manned twenty-four hours a day. One camp was located on the road a little way from Madden Dam close to Gatun Lake.

In every outfit you have your screwballs; some are pains in the ass while others are just funny. While in this camp we had a trooper named Finfrock. He was a good guy, he just had trouble getting things right. I spent a lot of time helping him and showing him how to do his job. He did OK with everything except our 45-S&W revolver. I happened to be an expert with this gun, so I spent a lot of time teaching him how to shoot. He got to be a good shot, after which he would run around telling the men what a great sergeant I was. "I would trust the sergeant with my life," he said.

The guys came back. "You wouldn't do that, would you?"

"I would even trust him to shoot a cigarette out of my mouth," he said.

15

This went on and on, and it was getting tiresome. One day things were quiet. He walked over about twenty feet away, lit a cigarette, and said, "Sergeant, show them how you can shoot this out of my mouth."

"I can't," I said. "I don't have my gun."

"Here, use mine," he said.

I thought I'd teach him a lesson. I took his gun and aimed about a foot in front of his head and fired. The cigarette disappeared. I don't know who was more shocked—me or the men watching. I looked at his gun, which had a high front sight. Somehow he had bent it, and it was off a foot at that distance.

I thanked my lucky stars that I'd aimed that far ahead of him. You live and learn. I don't think Finfrock did, though, because he still ran around telling the men, "See, you have to trust your sergeant. If you do, he'll take care of you."

He eventually left our outfit, but he did come through the war OK. I saw him later when he got home. He was a car salesman, and he was still telling the cigarette story.

I learned my lesson. I never shot close to one of my men again. Finfrock was still smoking. I didn't ask him if I could try again, afraid he'd say yes.

THE INTERNATIONAL DIVIDE, PANAMA

While we were stationed in Panama, we spent every other six weeks living in the jungle, training in guerrilla warfare. The other six weeks, we ran our beach, dock and road checkpoints and lived in Fort Clayton or Fort Davis or one of our outposts. These were mostly fun times when we were off duty, but as I said, Panama was the spy crossroads of the world at that time.

I seemed to pull a lot of extra duty when we were in Fort Davis. I'm not sure why, but it may have been because I liked it and was good in the jungle. At any rate, we got a report that a native village just over the international divide which ran down the center of

Panama, needed to be checked out. The village was between forty and sixty miles from where the nearest road ended, so I decided to take three Jeeps and six men.

We loaded all the extra gas we could carry and extra food, along with hundreds of feet of rope, and, although the higher mountains had plenty of springs, extra water. We started out and reached a town (I think it was Santa Fe). This was where the road ended, but we still had another forty to sixty miles to go. A mule trail ran out of the village, so we were able to use it until it "petered out." By this time, we were in the higher foothills, which were pretty bare except for some sparse grass, so we had to use our compass to proceed.

Some of the hills were pretty steep, but as everyone knows, that little Jeep was a great little vehicle. As our journey progressed, we had to drive up some dry stream beds. Then we ran into some trouble. One hill was so steep that I thought the Jeep would have gone end over end had we not tied rope to the back and let it down like they used to do when going West with the old covered wagons. We got all the Jeeps down, and after a few more miles, reached a half-way level spot where we found the native village.

I don't think that the natives had ever seen a vehicle before because they all ran away. They seemed to be more Indian than anything else. After much coaxing, we finally got them back and talked to them, mostly through the use of sign language. When they settled down and became friendlier, we gave them some candy bars and I think we made friends for life.

Leaving the village, we tried to go on over to the other side to get to Misquito Coast, which was on the Gulf of Mexico. To do this we would've had to have let our Jeeps down a thirty foot vertical cliff and then cross several streams. Beings that I didn't want to take the chance of having to stay in the Army for several more years to pay for a Jeep if the rope broke, we started our return trip to camp.

On our return trip through the village, we stopped again and gave the natives more food and candy. They were really grateful. The rest of our return trip was great. We camped a few miles this side of the village and proceeded on the next morning.

I know my brother Dale would have loved this part of the trip. The first part of it was along the International Highway (it was unfinished

17

then) that he had always wanted to travel. He had already traveled the northern stretch of the road. When the road was completed, it would stretch from Fairbanks, Alaska in North America to Santiago, Chile in South America.

One reconnaissance operation was to check along this road from Panama City to a small town just inside Costa Rica in Central America. This check was to see if it would be possible to move a large army of troops and vehicles along this road to meet an invasion of Japanese forces, if such should occur. This trip was between 360 and 400 miles one way. Aside from a few muddy spots, the road was pretty good until we were about sixty miles from Costa Rica. There, we had to lay down some corduroy roads (logs laid across the road to create a firm road bed) for several yards in a few locations. We had some problems with gas due to having to operate our vehicles in low gear most of the time. The problem was not too great, as we were able to send some vehicles ahead to our next stop and return with enough gas to get the others through. We did make it into Costa Rica, but I can no longer remember how long it took or the name of the town at our destination.

The town was in a pretty remote location and the main way into it was by sea. The people were very friendly and wanted to feed us, but the only place that was big enough was an exclusive all-girls school. They made arrangements with the nuns for us to use their dining room. The school had a stone fence (probably twelve feet high) with gates that were locked at all times. The nuns counted all the troops as they came in and again as they went back out. The food was good, especially after eating cold food for most of the trip.

To shed a little more light on this unique situation, these girls were from very rich families and some from as far away as Santiago, Chile. Their ages were probably anywhere from sixteen to twenty-one or twenty-two years old, and none had been away from their homes or this school without a female chaperon. These were all beautiful Spanish girls, so you know we had our hands full. You can understand why the nuns counted and why our Commanding Officer and NCO were on pins and needles the whole time we were there.

Later, after dark, we found some of the troopers trying to get over the wall. I'm not sure, but I think the girls inside may have been trying to help. They kept telling the boys to be quiet. We put guards on patrol around the wall and they had to report every fifteen minutes to the sergeant of the guard. Just to set the record straight, I was not one of those trying to get over the wall. The thought never entered my mind. (I know you believe that.)

The next morning, we started the trip back, which seemed much easier than the trip down. We had taken care of most of the problems and carried extra gas. We had found that with a little work by several engineer troops, the road could handle the troops and vehicles to repel an invading force, should it be necessary.

The El Valie was a high mountain valley that we also had orders to check out. The only entrance to this valley was by one road over the first mountain and then down a very steep narrow road with such sharp turns that we had to start around then back up and then go forward to get our big armored cars around the turn. To make matters worse, there were no guard rails on these drop offs of anywhere from fifty to five hundred feet. We kept the cars in low gear and took it very easy.

When we finally got down, it was well worth the anxiety of the trip. There were only two houses in this beautiful valley, which was about eight or ten miles long and probably only three to four miles wide and was completely surrounded by mountains except at the lower end. I think that the families who lived here must have been very rich. It was a paradise with lush grass and with a small rocky stream running through the center and out the lower end. It contained orange, grapefruit, pineapple and banana groves. Where the houses (very large) were located, the temperature during the day time was a constant 70 degrees with a fairly heavy rain from 10:45 to 11:45 a.m. and again in the afternoon from four to five p.m. The families who lived here informed us that this was true most all year long and was due to the mountains and the ocean being so close to the outside mountain range.

These were friendly people who, due to the horrible road, did not have many visitors except for the few natives that worked for them. In fact, I was concerned about getting our 10,000 pound cars back up the road. As we were getting ready to leave, these wonderful people loaded us down with all kinds of fruit. We had stalks of bananas with basket after basket of fruit. As I have often reminisced, this was a real break from regular Army life.

Just before we left, they took us down to the lower end of the valley where the little stream ran out. Down a little way, it turned into the jungle. I don't think you could have left that way, even on foot, unless you went down the stream bed, and even then, there seemed to be several water falls a little farther down stream. We did go down to where the jungle started again. It was so lush and thick that you'd have had to cut your way through. It even contained an abundance of wild orchids.

We went back to the house and the people told us good bye and begged us to stop back any time. As it was getting close to the time for the evening rain, we wanted to get on our way as soon as possible since the road out of the valley wasn't paved. I don't think we could have gotten out if it had been raining.

These were just a few of the things that took up our time besides the constant beach checks and road blocks, manning check points, guarding trains and our "guerrilla warfare" training during which we had to carry 75 pound jungle packs in addition to our gun and ammo. In spite of all this, this was one place (besides the United States) that I think I could have lived happily ever after.

The time spent in the Canal Zone was not all work. Spare time was spent exploring the jungle and visiting the Indian villages. Most of the natives in this Central America area were headhunters and still practiced their art, but our troops were on good terms with them and stayed out of their hunting areas. While in Panama, "A" troop was sent up to La Chorrera to act as security for a Fighter Plane base. My 3rd platoon of A troop was sent to another air base located at Aquadulce to provide security there.

When we were off duty, we could do pretty much as we wanted. A very short distance away was another small town called "Penonme." In our off time, we discovered a nice store that belonged to a Chinese man named Tuck Chanc. He had several stores and also had seven daughters between seventeen and twenty-seven who helped run the stores. The two daughters who ran this store were very friendly, so

Tom and I spent a lot of time there. There was a large courtyard behind the store enclosed by a large wall. In this enclosure, they had tables and a big family bath tub. As you probably know, Chinese families all bathe together. After the store would close, we spent a lot of time back there. The girls would cook food for us, and it wasn't long until we were all bathing together.

That is where I learned that the Chinese girls weren't built any differently than American girls. Since the weather was very hot, they slept out there in hammocks. We ended up trying to get them inside to bed but they said no because it was too hot. We were ready to give up, but the older of the two girls (about 21) said, "You stay. I'll teach you to make love in a hammock." That was one wild night.

Needless to say, we went back every chance we got. One night we had too much to drink and while heading back to base, we ran our Jeep in the ditch. We walked back to the store to enlist the aid of the girls to pull us out. They got their car and pulled us out of the ditch, then one girl drove the Jeep and the other drove her car. They took us back to the Air Base, went through three security posts, parked the Jeep in our spot in the motor pool, took us to our tents and put us to bed, and then they returned home. It sort of makes you wonder about security.

When we finally left Panama to come back to the States, we went by in a convoy and couldn't stop, but they were standing in the door waving and crying. What I hadn't mentioned, was that they changed girls around in these stores. The rest of the girls were just as friendly as the first two, but only with Tom and me. The other stores were closer in and the parents watched them much more closely.

We adopted a couple of wild animals that we allowed to live with us in our barracks. The first was an ocelot that we found when it was just a kitten. The beautiful yellow cat with black spots grew up to be a very large animal several feet long from nose to tip of tail. It would sleep in the rafters of our barracks most of the time, but if it got too cold, it would join one of us in our bunk. This was fine until one night he jumped down in bed with a new replacement that knew nothing of his habits. After all the turmoil subsided, all was peaceful the rest of the night.

Another of our animals was a marmoset (a small monkey). It didn't take long for him to become one of the family. He rode around on the back of the ocelot and they became close friends. The monkey would accompany one of us most of the time we were in base.

He developed a taste for beer and when we were having a little respite, he would always be there begging. We taught him to take a steel wool pad and scrub out our mess kit cup, which had a small top that was easy for him to get his small hand in. He would be rewarded with a little beer in his own mess kit cup. It was not long before he learned to take our empty bottles and drain what was left in them into his cup. There was not a selfish bone in the little fellow's body. He would always share his beer with the ocelot.

We served as guard for installations on both the Atlantic and the Pacific sides of the Canal Zone including the Gatun Locks, Lake and Dam and the Madden Dam. While in Panama, stationed at Fort Davis, I was assigned to a detached service unit (I still don't know what kind) that was headed by the FBI, who were in charge of most security problems at that time. This was before the CIA was formed.

German subs were sinking many ships in the Gulf of Mexico (one even in the mouth of the Mississippi River). This got so bad that something had to be done about it. To keep these subs on station, they had to be refueled and supplied. They used German supply ships in the remote inlets along the Central and South American coast to do this. Big German radio stations in Colombia and Ecuador, both of whom were supposed to be neutral, coordinated these efforts.

Since I was Pioneer and Demolition Sergeant and trained in working with explosives and in Guerrilla warfare, I was chosen by the FBI to take a fire and demolition team into these countries through the jungle and destroy these stations. We had to remove the serial numbers from our weapons and had to wear civilian clothes. The unit was headed by the FBI. The United Fruit Company supplied a large ship because they had lost so many ships to the subs. We landed on the coast and went in through the jungle. Most of the stations were in Colombia, so it was much easier that way. Our orders were to destroy these stations without killing, if at all possible. Once we were on the beach, we were on our own, and were informed that if we were caught, no one would help us. To make a long story short, we got the job done without any casualties, but I'm afraid the enemy was miserable for a few days.

We then returned to our regular duty, but were told not to talk about this operation to anyone. As a remark: it must have been effective, as the sinking by German subs in the Gulf dropped greatly. Of course, there were still some sinkings, but with most of their supplies cut off, they were unable to do the job they were doing before. This was a very interesting interlude in my life. There were several interesting experiences I had while still in Panama. In going through old pictures, I ran across a picture that reminded me of another experience.

As you will remember, we were running down German radio stations, some of which were on mule packs so they could keep moving them continuously. We kept getting readings on our directional finder and finally had orders to locate where it was coming from and silence it. In our Jeeps, we had to follow mule trails and small streams to make our way through the jungle, but we finally ran one down and destroyed the radio operator. We gave the mule to some of the natives.

On the way back, we were driving along a stream and had to cross over to keep going. We would never put more than one of our Jeeps in the water at the same time just in case the engine drowned out. That way we could use the other to pull out the disabled one. We had also been doing a little target practice with our 45s on the way back. I had just crossed this little stream and pulled up on the bank, and turned to check the Jeep on the other side, which had just entered the water to make the crossing.

One of the guys in the Jeep yelled, "There's a big snake over our head in this tree. Why don't you shoot it, Sergeant?"

I looked over and said, "Watch your head." With that, I shot. Crashing down through the tree from above came an iguana about six feet long. For those who don't know, the iguana is a large tropical lizard (very good eating).

The guys laughed, razing me about shooting a lizard instead of the snake. About this time, sliding down the tree, came the boa constrictor. It was about twelve feet long and landed right in the middle of the Jeep. The guys went in four different directions into the water. What happened was that the snake had swallowed a portion of the lizard and when I shot it behind the head the lizard popped out and fell to the ground.

Needless to say, four wet guys were no longer laughing. They finally got themselves dried off and we made our way back to base camp, satisfied we had accomplished our mission. We had destroyed one more vital link in the German radio communication and supply system.

After more of these same types of missions, our tour of duty in the Canal Zone, Central America and South America came to an end in November of 1943. We sailed from Balboa, Canal Zone and spent a pleasant, uneventful ten days on the Pacific before docking in San Francisco.

An overnight trip by ferry put us in Stoneman, California, and another week by rail put us at Camp Maxy, Texas. The last part of the year and the first of 1944 were spent reorganizing and training for the invasion of Europe. In May 1944, we sailed from New York on the Queen Elizabeth past the Statue of Liberty for Glasgow, Scotland. Many of us wondered if we would ever see the great lady holding up her arm in freedom again.

CAMP MAXEY NOVEMBER 1943

Before getting into the English stay, I think a brief run down on our outfit would be in order.

While stationed at Camp Maxey, the 32nd Calvary Reconnaissance Squadron became part of the 14th Calvary Group under the command of the spit and polish West Pointer, Colonel Mark Devine. The 14th was composed of the 32nd and 18th Calvary Squadrons and a small headquarters group. The 32nd, as well as the 18th Calvary Squadron, was formed from a headquarters troop, three reconnaissance troops (lettered "A", "B", and "C") and assault gun troops (lettered "E") and a light tank company called "F" Company.

Each reconnaissance troop had a headquarters platoon and three reconnaissance platoons. Each reconnaissance platoon was divided into three combat teams. Each team consisted of an armored car, a machine gun bantam, and a mortar bantam. The armored car mounted a 37mm Cannon, a 30 caliber machine gun in a movable turret, and was equipped with two powerful radios. The machine gun bantam was armed with a 30 caliber machine gun mounted on a pedestal mount and carried a voice radio of limited range.

The assault gun troop had six assault guns. These were 75mm Howitzers mounted on light tank carriages and capable of direct or indirect fire. These six guns were divided into three platoons of two guns each.

The light tank company was equipped with M24 tanks (powerful brutes) that carried a 37mm cannon, two 30 caliber machine guns and a 50 caliber machine gun. The light tank company was the heavy fist of the squadron. It had seventeen tanks divided into a headquarters platoon with two tanks, and three combat platoons with five tanks each.

These elements, the reconnaissance troops, the assault guns and the tanks worked together as a team. A reconnaissance troop on a mission would usually have an assault gun platoon and a tank platoon attached. At times, especially in static situations, all six assault guns would be used as battery. Most of the time, the group was assigned a cub plane from Corp's artillery for observation missions.

A cavalry reconnaissance squadron was trained, equipped and armed for one purpose only—reconnaissance (to seek out information as to the location disposition and composition of the enemy forces). This was accomplished by hit and run tactics, by stealth or by fire. Most important was to get the information back to higher headquarters. The reconnaissance unit was in effect the eyes and ears of the corps, division or unit it was attached to.

At Camp Maxey, Texas, I was promoted to staff sergeant and transferred to the 1st platoon. As an additional job, I was designated "platoon sergeant" of the pioneer & demolition platoon for the whole squadron with Capt. Striker as C.O.

Under this heading we were to build bridges, destroy bridges, lay and clear mine fields, instruct on booby traps, and instruct on chemical warfare and small arms—both ours and the enemy's. So with my duty as platoon and demolition sergeant, I had little time for pleasure. My job was to make everyone aware of the danger of booby traps, gas, etc. To do this we used training devices that produced harmless but effective explosions.

Capt. Striker said no one was to get out of this training. "I want you to make sure this includes the first sergeant." We were using eight inch firecrackers on these "training" devices, and to make a long story short, if the sergeant went to the head, it exploded; if he opened a desk drawer, it exploded. If he sneaked into his room for a nap, a tear gas bomb went off. Without his gas mask, he cried awhile. I don't think he appreciated me, but when I was done everyone was aware of the danger, including our group commander, Col. Devino. I made a lot of people cry, but later this probably saved a lot of lives.

Also at Maxey we had several "Table of Organization" changes. They took away our S&W revolvers and issued us M1 Carbines. We got new M8 armored cars with a 37 mm anti-tank gun in a movable turret, with a coaxial 30-caliber and a 50-caliber on a ring mount. We also had 80-rounds 37-mm—400-rounds carbine—1500-rounds 30.06 machine gun—750 rounds 50 caliber—16 hand grenades—4 smoke pots—6 anti-tank mines. The M8 armored car was a very fast vehicle. The only problem was if we had to rise up out of this movable turret, we couldn't get our M1 carbine up where we could use it.

They told us we could have a side arm if we wanted to buy it, so on my way to New York from Camp Maxey, I stopped by home and bought a gun from Coonhound Johnny's. Since I was in uniform, Coonhound, the owner, looked at me and said, "Son, doesn't the Army trust you with a gun?"

I explained the problem. He said, "My son is in the Army. I'd give the gun to you, but that's bad luck. You give me $4.35 for this Colt-45 and I'll throw in a shoulder holster and fifty rounds ammo."

I carried this gun with me in European campaigns, to the hospital in England, and back to Paris with the criminal investigation division. I STILL HAVE THIS GUN ALMOST SIXTY YEARS LATER. IT SAVED MY LIFE MORE THAN ONCE.

NOW BACK TO ENGLAND

After four short days aboard the great ship, we anchored in the Firth of Clyde near the city of Glasgow, Scotland. During the war, the ship was never docked on the European side of the Atlantic for fear of bombing raids against her. She was kept mobile. The squadron was barged ashore and boarded a train that was to carry them across Scotland and England. Their destination was the beautiful seashore resort town in Southern England called Bournemouth.

Here the squadron was billeted in splendid homes that had been evacuated by townspeople because of the V1 and V2 bombs. While most of the people had evacuated, next door to the house where we stayed, an old woman still resided. Engaging her in conversation, she informed us that she had lived in that house all her life and that no fancy bombs where going to drive her out. As all the men and able-bodied people were doing something for the war effort, the old lady could get no one to do anything to help take care of this big old house.

Since we were just playing a waiting game at that time, we offered to help her out. After we had everything repaired and in ship-shape, she wanted to pay us for our services, but we declined to take any compensation. The next evening, she called us over and fixed a wonderful home-cooked meal for all four of us. We found out later the poor soul only got one fourth of a pound of meat a month. We went to the mess hall, got some meat and tried to give it to her, but she was too proud to accept it. Trying a different tack, we told her that our mess sergeant couldn't cook as well as she could and would she please cook us a good meal before we went across to France. She agreed to do so and in that manner we paid her back a little and at least she got one good meal.

For the next two weeks, "A" Troop spent some time in special training, radio and vehicular maintenance, and waterproofing their equipment. In the evening the men were allowed passes to go up town. When going on pass, we had to make a mental note of our routing, remembering different landmarks, for in returning in the pitch black, we had to use the Braille system to feel our way back

27

home, as the whole town and the rest of the country were totally and completely blacked out. While spending this brief time in England, "A" Troop drank its beer or ale warm, settled for fish and chips in the restaurants, rode the double decked buses, drove on the wrong side of the road or street, played darts in the local pubs, and in general found that a good time was had by all.

After a short two weeks' respite, the squadron moved to an assembly area near Southampton and loaded aboard Landing Ships Tanks, better know as LSTs. That night, we crossed the English Channel and landed the next morning on the Omaha Beach Head. When the 32nd Calvary landed in France, it was the early part of June 1944. The war had already by-passed the beach heads and was ready for the great sweep across France.

EUROPE

The next week was spent bivouacking in a marshaling area in Normandy near the Cherbourg Peninsula, where mud was master.

Since we slept in pup tents and it rained constantly, it was very miserable. Capt. Striker, our commanding officer, called me into his tent and said, "We have to do something to get these men off the wet ground!" (There was no such thing as plastic ground sheets.) He also stated that we needed to do a recon and see if we could find some wood to make floors for our tents and also find a German ammunition dump. We needed to get all the enemy guns, mines, booby traps, mortar shells, etc., so we could teach these men what to be aware of.

First, we noticed a partially destroyed train station and elevator just a short distance way. We sent a crew over to haul the boards and sheeting over to our camp. In a short time, we had floors in all our tents. In the meantime, Capt. Striker and I located a German ammo dump loaded with almost every kind of enemy equipment that existed. Also, there was an empty prefab building which we sent a crew to tear down and reassemble in our area so we would have a place for our training school. I started disarming all this enemy equipment and it turned out to be quite a job but well worth while. We really concentrated on the operation of enemy small arms and automatic weapons. This, later on, proved to be quite an asset in saving our lives when we had to use the enemy equipment when we were cut off and out of ammunition during the "Battle of the Bulge."

After we had made this camp almost livable, as usual, we got orders to get ready to pull out. In one town, which we liberated on the way, we had a small fire fight but no one was hurt. I received a round through a tire, so I had to pull off the road and wait for Squadron Maintenance. The mayor (or Burgomaster) was so happy that he wanted us to come to his house and eat. He went out in the backyard and dug up a bottle of Calvados (a very potent French liqueur) while his wife was fixing the meal. We had a couple of drinks, and to make a long story short, the maintenance crew missed us. I was a little concerned so I had my radio operator call them and they were already about twenty miles on down the road. They asked if it would be possible for us to get the tire repaired where we were. I asked the Burgomaster if they had a tire repair shop to which he replied, "No, but we do have a cycle repair shop." To get on our way, we used bicycle tire repair to fix our tire and it worked.

My driver, who I could never get to drive fast enough, had only one shot of the Calvados and I couldn't get him to slow down. He ran away from our two Jeeps before I finally got him slowed down. A short time later, we caught up with the rest of our outfit and headed on for the Mosel River in Luxembourg.

After two weeks, the squadron ended the road march through France, (St. Lo, Fontainebleau, Paris) and up to the front lines along the Mosel River in Southern Luxembourg. Here the squadron set up a counter-reconnaissance screen with outposts in the small villages along the river forward of Burmerang. The troop was in the middle of wine-making country. The river was terraced on either side with vineyards. In Burmerang, the homes were not only for living quarters, but also part of the wine-making industry. One would have a machine shop attached, another a winery, and still another, a bottle and label area, etc.

In a town like this, the men were given to scrounging when the lines were static. For instance, one day four men were seen coming down the street carrying a baby grand piano. When asked what they were up to, they answered, "We don't have a piano in our house." Jerry Redding collected clocks. In his room he had the walls covered with clocks of all sizes and shapes. That was a lot of tick-tock. Sgt. Murphy collected smoking pipes (the Germans later recollected them).

The town of Burmerang was occupied by my 1st platoon of A troop. The sister town across the river was occupied by Germans forces. The main street ran straight through both towns, but the bridge between the towns had been destroyed.

We were there for some time and in a holding position. No one shot at anyone on either side, unless we deliberately exposed ourselves. So, until about the fourth day, being constantly on alert and with nothing happening, we were becoming rather bored UNTIL we discovered a large building containing a winery down close to the river. There was no way of getting to it without exposing ourselves. After some deep thought, I used my skill as a demolition man to open a wall protected from the view of the enemy troops across the river. In checking out the building, I found that besides being full of wine (enough for the whole squadron), it was also filled with sugar. I backed two 6x6 trucks up to the building, one for the wine and one for the sugar. From that time on, I was known as "The Mad Dog" or the "Bomber." They gave me these nick names because of the way I had to run to place the charges. Needless to say, with a truck load of sugar and one of wine, we had a lot of friends.

While in this town, I also found a great machine shop. With all this equipment at hand, I converted my semiautomatic carbine to fire either full automatic or semi-automatic. This was done by building a new sear and reworking the safety. It worked so well that I started converting carbines for my whole platoon. On full auto, it would fire between 800 and 900 rounds a minute. Later on (in the Korean War) they converted all these carbines to this and changed the name to 30 caliber carbine M2.

While still in this town, I also was able to check out some of my favorite German weapons. I will go into a little detail to give a reason for this.

With our American Bazooka, the penetration was only a little over three inches. This was good only against the lighter German armor or tanks. As an example, the German Panzerfaust would penetrate eight inches of armor, which made it effective against anything the enemy had. It was also smaller and very easy to handle.

The German anti-tank rifle grenade and regular grenade was much more accurate than ours and would penetrate five inches of armor, while ours only penetrated about 1 ½ inches. With the German rifle grenade, I could put a grenade through a window a block and a half away but with ours, I would be lucky if I could hit the house.

Another weapon they had that was very good was the MG-42. This was probably one of the finest machine guns of WW2. It had a quick change barrel and the next belt of ammo could be attached without shutting down the gun. The rate of fire was 1200 to 1400 rounds per minute. This has rarely been exceeded today by a single barrel gun. Today, one of our main machine guns is the M-60, which has a lot copied from the MG-42. This gun fired so fast that it was demoralizing to hear. It sounded like the sound you hear an old coon dog make when a coon is treed. I carried one of these on my armored car and used it often. We had to be careful where we used it because our own artillery would often target on the sound of enemy guns. I also carried on one or two cases of German rifle grenades and at least four to six German Panzerfausts.

While in these holding positions, the squadron suffered heavy casualties in men wounded and killed in one major encounter, the taking of Stromberg Hill. I lost my mortar gunner and radio operator, Tech Sgt. Walter Kobialka of Springfield, Illinois, along with a full mortar battery crew (all killed in action). Radio Operator Anthony Nigro of New York City was badly wounded by a tree burst while on radio watch in an observation post.

The basement of the house "A" Troop used as its command post was like a butcher shop. The medics used it as their aid station. These men were doing a great job under very adverse conditions.

As you can see, this is just a general overall picture. I'll try to go into more detail of what happened to me as platoon sergeant of the 1st platoon of A troop.

It was here on Stromberg Hill in Luxembourg that I received what is considered by many the second highest honor that our country can bestow on a soldier, the "Battlefield Commission." The following is my description of this action.

STROMBURG HILL – LUXEMBOURG

"A" Troop, 32nd Calvary Recon Troop, pulled into a small village located on a horseshoe bend on the Moselle River. Stromburg Hill overlooked this town and the down river section with a commanding view of both the town and the river. The hill was still occupied by the enemy. General Patton's 3rd Army was crossing a short distance downstream. As the enemy had artillery and mortar observers on this hill, Captain Striker was ordered to take the hill. In the meantime, we had taken a pillbox just outside of town and cleared the town, killing an enemy artillery observer and a sniper located in the church tower. We used this pillbox, which having walls several feet thick, made a good place to watch the hill and still be protected from the mortars. It was about a half mile from the base of the hill. The road into town was sunken and provided easy access to the pillbox and the town. We could move along the sunken road for a good distance without being seen.

The hill was heavily fortified on the reverse side, so we were having trouble. As dark was approaching, we planned our attack for the next morning. Early the next morning, the CO ordered 3rd platoon leader Lt. Sharp to attack the hill. Lt. Clark, of my 1st platoon, took my mortar gunner along with those of the 2nd and 3rd, to set up a mortar battery to give them support. They were doing great until they received a heavy counter-battery barrage, killing all six men and wounding Lt. Clark so badly that he had to be evacuated to the States. As a result, this attack failed.

That night, I volunteered to take a patrol up the hill to recover the bodies of the dead. We didn't leave our buddies if it was at all possible to recover them. I also managed to clear several mines. We got back down without any losses. One of the dead was my mortar gunner, Walter Kobialka of Springfield, Illinois, who had been in my platoon since the start of the war. Capt. Striker was wounded by a mine and evacuated to England, so I had no platoon leader. I had lived and fought with most of these guys for the past two or three years. As a result, I guess you know, I didn't sleep well that night.

Being short, our commanding officer and XO, Lt. Reppa, took over as CO, and Lt. Sharp took over the remains of the 2nd and 3rd platoons. Early the next morning, they sent a tank up a trail leading to the top of the hill to try to knock out a machine gun emplacement. I still had no platoon leader, so I put my men on the sunken road below the pillbox for flank security, and with a squad, moved along the road with the tank for security. It was really more of a trail than a road, very narrow.

The tank took out the first machine gun but just past it, hit a mine and was completely destroyed, blocking the trail. It blew the driver and bow gunner out of the tank and badly wounded the rest of the crew. I had the driver in my arms. He had both legs cut off about mid thigh and both arms cut off half way to his elbows. I tried to get tourniquets on to stop the bleeding until an aid man could get there. To this day, I'll never understand. This man continued to talk to me as if nothing was wrong but died in my arms from loss of blood. With help, I got the rest of the crew back down to the aid station.

Again, as I had no platoon leader, I was sent back down the sunken road with the pillbox as flank security. Lt. Sharp took over the remains of the 2nd and 3rd platoons again and we started the attack, but the whole unit was pinned down in a cabbage field about half way to the base of the hill. From my position along the road, I could see this and also where the fire was coming from. They had protection from the machine gun fire between the cabbage rows, but then they started receiving mortar fire and this was really tearing them up.

From where I was on the road, I couldn't get a clear shot, so I jumped up on the bank, thinking that I could take out both the mortar observer and the machine gunner, but my gun failed to fire. It wouldn't do anything, but I did draw the attention off the 2nd and 3rd platoons when the gunners saw me. I jumped back down on the road and discovered that someone had taken my gun and left this one in its place. I ran back to the pillbox and tried to get someone to give me his gun, but no one would. I grabbed one of the 30 caliber machine guns off a tripod along with two 250 round belts of ammo, and took off back down the road to my former position. This time, when I jumped up, I took out the mortar observer and then the machine gunner. I was running forward all this time and didn't realize I was halfway to the base of the hill. When I ran out of ammo, I looked around and managed to find a little cover. I had a terrible time trying to load another 250 round belt in a gun that was supposed to be fired off a tripod.

I yelled for the 2nd and 3rd for support, as they were no longer pinned down. Again, I looked around and found that there was no way I could get back to cover without exposing myself to the remaining machine gun farther up the hill. The only way I could go was forward. I took off, and with a little support from 2nd and 3rd platoons, I managed to take out the last machine gun. From then on, it was an easy trip on up to the top. As I looked back, the rest of my men were following me and we soon gained the top and set up positions.

The only problem I had was the holes burned into my gloves from the hot machine gun barrel. We got our positions set up but couldn't drive the enemy off the back side of the hill, which wasn't too important, since their artillery observers could no longer adjust fire on Patton's river crossing.

The top of this hill was a mostly flat, oblong plateau. We tried to dig in for foxholes, but the soil was only about six inches to a foot deep and then solid rock, so we had to scrape and pile the soil up for a little more protection. We had a shortage of men, so our holes were too far apart. Since it was getting close to dark, we were concerned that the enemy might sneak in between us. We tied string to our fingers and ran it from one hole to the next so we could keep each other awake. This was a wise precaution because we held the hill for four days and three nights.

I called in our own artillery fire, which was coming closer to us than the enemy artillery on the back side of the hill. They were afraid they would hit their men on their side of the hill. This went on for four days and three nights without let up. During the constant incoming and outgoing artillery (beside all the noise), we hoped and prayed that the two would not meet overhead and wipe out the whole unit. We were scared but could only lay there and shake and pray. I called for relief, but was told that they couldn't get through the enemy. Among our other worries, we were afraid our radio battery would give out and we also needed water.

Just to show how bad or good things can get, no one could relieve us, but on the second night, our mess sergeant, Tony Brian from Springfield, Illinois, got through the enemy and brought fresh hot bread, hot coffee, meat loaf, baked beans, and most importantly, water. The sergeant and his men got back through to HQ without losing any men, so I don't know why we couldn't get any relief.

On the last day, Patton had a major force across the river. The enemy on the back side of the hill, to keep from getting killed or captured, pulled out about mid-afternoon. Then as it got close to evening, we got orders to report back to HQ. We went back down this hill, which didn't seem nearly as large as when we were going up. We had held the hill for the four days and three nights without one of our group being killed or wounded. We were lucky, but a lot of bullets whispered in our ears. That is a sound that you will never forget. Again, we were lucky. As a result of this action, I received the coveted "Battlefield Commission."

The squadron was later pulled out of these positions and moved to the lovely castle town of Clervaux, Luxembourg. Squadron Headquarters, "A" Troop and "C" Troop, along with the assault troop, set up a counter reconnaissance screen, out-posting a seven mile front along the Our River and Sky Line Drive a few miles forward of Clervaux.

"A" Troop billeted in a castle once belonging to the ancestral family of President Franklin D. Roosevelt's mother, Sara. The castle was the focal point of this quaint storybook-like town. Here "A" Troop spent Thanksgiving Day, November 25, 1944, with turkey and all the trimmings. That Thanksgiving weekend, "A" Troop relieved "B" Troop and outposted two villages on the Sky Line Drive, Heinerscheid and Fishbach.

I had my first platoon and part of the second platoon of A troop set up a defensive position in these two villages. I located my headquarters in the larger of the two (Heinerscheid). The second village (Fishbach) was located about two miles to the right of Sky Line Drive.

I started setting up my outpost with my number one located at the Main Street and Sky Line Drive and my number two to the left on Sky Line Drive at the edge of Heinerscheid. My number three was located across the road in Fishbach. I got the men posted and we then started setting up our radio and telephone communications. Next were our machine gun positions with interlocking fire. Then back at my command post, we set up a 50 caliber machine gun on an antiaircraft mount just to the right of my CP. Just behind my CP was a small courtyard in which I set up a battery of three mortars.

Across the river and about three blocks away, were three German heavy concrete pillboxes. These were located at a slightly higher elevation than we were at, so we were under German observation at all times. We were about 1/2 mile on this side of the river, and on our side, three wooded draws ran almost up to our positions, so should the Germans attack, they would have concealment to within 75 to 100 yards of our positions. First, I zeroed our mortars in on these draws, then after dark, I mined the approaches coming out of the draws. I tried a little different set up on the mines in the way the arrangement of the trip wires were set and it proved to work out well. The next thing was the road barricades. We used rolled barbed wire and a daisy chain of anti-tank mines, which we could remove easily since we would have to use the road to take supplies to our number three outpost (more on this a little later).

Also, this was the town where they sent a replacement first lieutenant to learn the ropes. The only thing he had done before in the Army was office work, so the teaching turned out to be a pain in the neck.

After getting everything set up, I thought we were in good shape, so we settled in for the night. We stood radio and telephone watch with each outpost reporting in every fifteen minutes. I slept in the office next to our radio and telephone and I always took the three to six a.m. watch because I had to check our number three outpost and deliver them food and supplies, and this had to be done before daylight.

We were just settling in for the night when I got a call from Capt. Reed at troop HQ, informing me that Col. Devine, the group commander, was coming for an inspection the next day. The captain seemed upset, as Col. Devine was very strict. They all called him "The Great White Father." Capt. Reed wanted to know if everything was OK, and I informed him that as far as I knew, I didn't think he could find anything wrong.

I lay down in the office to try to get some sleep until they woke me up for my three to six watch. It turned out to be quiet. I went out back as I came off shift and sent three mortar flares into each of the draws. Everything seemed to be OK, so about ten minutes before daylight, I called my number one OP to have them pull the wire and mines so I could get through, and told them that I was on my way. I had to make this run without lights to avoid drawing enemy fire. I went screaming down Main St. and around the corner onto Sky Line Drive. I spent no more time than necessary, as I ran a gauntlet under enemy observation.

Everything was great until all of a sudden, I thought the world was ending. There was an ungodly screeching and fire flying all over and the Jeep came to a screeching stop. It lit up like a Christmas tree. By this time, I thought I'd had it. I made a flying leap into a ditch and culvert just as the Germans scored a direct hit on the Jeep, completely destroying it. What had happened was that this dumb >@*#* pulled the daisy chain of mines out of the road but didn't remove the rolled barbed wire, which tangled on the drive shaft and undercarriage of the Jeep, stopping it.

The next day, due to my pure heart, I was still alive but my poor Jeep was in heaven. Now, all I had to do was to make it through another day, which was difficult. I got a call from our CO, Capt. Reed, that Col. Devine, "The Great White Father," would be up soon to make his inspection and that I should start getting my command post in order. I checked all my outposts and warned them to be on the ball but, of course, I didn't have to worry about OP number three, since I didn't think Col. Devine would want to run the gauntlet down Sky Line Drive.

At eight a.m., Capt. Reed and Col. Devine walked into my CP and called everyone to attention. Capt. Reed said, "At ease. I want to see your maps and drawings for the defense of these two towns." I put the replacement lieutenant in charge of the CP and started explaining everything to Capt. Reed. When I finished, Capt. Reed said that Col. Devine would like to inspect the OP positions. (Of course, you know that there is some element of danger in this).

Capt. Reed said, "Sgt. Fancher, get your Jeep and when you are ready, get Col. Devine and we will go with you." Turning to address Capt. Reed, Col. Divine said, "Capt. Reed, you stay here in the office and I will ride with the sergeant. It appears that your platoon sergeant has done a good job and he seems to be the only one who knows what is going on. I also want to see this new system that he has on the trip wires on the mines."

I showed him how the system worked. We had to look through field glasses since we couldn't get too close without coming under enemy fire. Anyway, he seemed very happy with the system. We returned to my CP and the colonel said, "Reed, let's go. I need to get back to headquarters. I'm happy with everything here and don't let anyone change his defense setup."

As they were getting ready to leave, he turned to the replacement first lieutenant and said, "This is the way an outfit should be run. Try to learn your lesson well!" Now that the inspection was over, all we had to do was just sit there and wait to be shot at.

Behind my CP and a little courtyard was a machine shop similar to the old blacksmith shops back home. It had a jack shaft running across the top of the room with long belts running down to each machine to operate them. This jack shaft was operated by an enormous electric motor. Also, in case of a power outage, it had a large, one-lung gas engine. I got a bright idea. As I had worked for an electrical engineer and had learned a little about motors, I rewired this motor as a generator and using the big old gas engine for power, and we were able to have electric lights.

Also, on a slight hill behind the village was a water reservoir that was, of course, empty. The pump house was down on the river almost under the German's noses. Unless you've been there, you can't imagine what it is like to attempt to bathe out of a steel helmet. Since we had not had a bath for days and days and the prospects looked like we would be there for several more days, I called a meeting and asked if anyone would be interested in having a bath in a real tub. I guess you know what the answer to that was. That night I took two troopers with me and we made a recon patrol down to the river with three five gallon cans of gas. We filled up the pump engine and got it started and then got the hell out of there. We got the reservoir about half full before the Germans realized what we were doing and hit the pump house. Anyway, it was enough for all of us to have a bath, even though it was with cold water. With the lights back on and using black out curtains, our stay was more comfortable for the people during off-duty time.

After the inspection, we were left alone. Things were quiet after the pump house engine was hit. There was some mortar and machine gun fire from both sides, but mostly just to keep each other on the ball. There would be more to come, but for a while, it was quiet.

All of this made for fun-filled days in Heinerscheid. Things were great. We had lights and water for baths. We got to enjoy all this and got paid for it too. All we had to do was sit there and let the Germans shoot at us. So what? They weren't very good shots anyway.

I had only one problem. I had a platoon leader from our days in Panama named Sam Woods from Springfield, Illinois. Sam was a little older than the rest of the guys, so when we went to Europe, they promoted him to captain and made him "Squadron Motor Officer" to keep him off the front lines. This was not to Sam's liking and he would always be finding some excuse to get away and come up to see me at the front. I was showing him around my number one OP one day and let him use my field glasses. As he looked across the way, I saw his eyes light up as he saw some Germans walking out of the pillbox. I should've known right then that I was in trouble.

I had to get back to my Command Post so Sam asked if he could hang around for awhile and I told him OK. When I got back to my CP, they informed me that I had a message. It was from my number one OP and the trooper told me that Capt. Woods was up in the observation post with a Springfield rifle and scope, shooting at the

Germans around the pillbox. It was a long way over so I didn't think he could hit anyone, but he did and that is where my trouble began, for you know they were going to respond in kind. We were still OK, but had to stay under cover.

Sam went back to headquarters, but he always found some kind of excuse to get back out here. He would come with his old Springfield, get up in the observation post and start shooting when any of the Germans were outside the pillbox. I don't know how many hours he would've spent there. I would receive a call from the squadron inquiring if Capt. Woods was there. I'd say, "I'm in my CP and I don't see him." After several phone calls, they would send some officer, usually Major Krake, and he would look him up and take him back. (That was after Krake took a couple shots with Sam's rifle.)

This turned into an ongoing thing and it wouldn't have surprised me if Col. Devine himself had showed up for his turn. The problem for me was that when they got lucky and hit someone, we got return fire and had to be very careful for a few days and stay under cover. I think that might have been the high point of Sam's life in Europe. It was sorta fun for me too and it made the days go faster.

I don't remember exactly how long we were there, but once in a while things got exciting. I'm not going to go into that right now, but I do know we didn't get any men killed or wounded while we were there and we were able to sleep in a bed when we were not on duty. I, myself, always slept on a couch in my Command Post. I never undressed or took off my shoes except when I left the replacement lieutenant in charge when I took a bath. I think they were about ready to send him to the 2nd platoon and I had gotten to the point where I liked having him around, and he did give me a little break so I could work on our electric and water systems, but I didn't like leaving him alone too long.

There was one more interesting thing that happened during our stay in Heinerscheid. Things had been going rather smoothly for quite awhile—just a few rounds of machine gun fire and very little mortar or artillery fire (which we returned in kind). I really think they were trying to save the town with the expectation of recapturing it.

I had just started my morning duties when I received a call from my number one OP. A large German combat patrol had crossed over the Our River under the cover of darkness and was headed for our positions. They said that it appeared to consist of between one hundred thirty and one hundred fifty men. Our total strength was only forty-six, so I was concerned that we wouldn't be able to stop them with only our machine guns and small mortar battery. They'd have cover from our machine gun fire until they were within 100 yards of our position.

I immediately called troop HQ and had them put me through to Division Artillery. I got through and I had my maps out and all the while, I am still talking to my OP and trying to keep track of the enemy troops. The artillery command came on the line asking a lot of questions, which made me pretty unhappy. I had my finger on the map and asked the replacement lieutenant to read me the coordinates, which I relayed to whoever I was talking to at Artillery. I was still getting the run around and I finally lost my cool, and after some very foul language sprinkled with some choice cuss words, another voice came on the line.

"This is General So and So (I no longer remember his name). Who am I talking to?"

"This is Platoon Sgt. Fancher," I replied.

He said, "Sergeant, what are the coordinates of your number three OP?"

To which I replied, "Hold it, Sir." That stupid lieutenant had given me the wrong coordinates. He gave me the ones for my number three OP—we would have been bombing our own OP. I made the correction, giving the coordinates of the enemy instead of our own OP and got the artillery fire on the way. With it and that of our mortars, machine guns and mine fields, we turned back the attack and inflected a heavy loss to the enemy in killed and wounded. We had some minor damage to equipment, but had no one killed or wounded.

I guess you know that I had to eat some "humble pie" over this, but the fact that the lieutenant admitted that it was his mistake and that we did turn back a major attack kept me from getting busted. It didn't hurt matters any that I had a friend in "the Great White

Father," Col. Devine. It still scared the hell out of me. If they had fired the artillery at the first coordinates, it would have wiped out my number three OP.

You can see how easy it was to make a mistake. I should have double checked everything myself. A lesson well-learned, but you must realize that I was talking to about ten different people and coordinating artillery, mortar and machine gun fire. This was a real embarrassment to me as all this conversation was on an open line and everyone from platoon up through division heard every word. After this, I was very careful to double check everything. What most people do not realize is that these calls have to be made very quickly. In this battle, a wait of just a few moments would have resulted in all or most of us being killed, wounded or captured. I guess in the long run, I shouldn't feel too badly. Had I made the mistake instead of the lieutenant, I would probably have been court-martialed.

I don't remember just how long we remained in Heinerscheid, but aside from the normal back and forth fire, we had no more major battles. I did take one small combat patrol across the river just to check out their defenses. We managed to get over and back without any trouble and we pulled out of these villages a short time later.

In the early days of December 1944, the squadron was relieved by Col. Hurly Fuller and his 110th Regimental Combat Team and moved on to the town of Vielsalm, Belgium. In Vielsalm, the squadron was held in reserve for the 18th Cavalry, the other squadron of the 14th Cavalry Group.

The squadron, being in reserve in this so-called quiet sector of the Ardennes, was planning on a lot of rest, a little Schnapps drinking and some hell-raising. Instead, all hell broke loose all around us and we caught the brunt of German Field Marshal Von Rundstedt's counter offensive mounted by three German Armies in a tremendous two-pronged attack. One was toward Bastongne and the other toward St. Vith, our area. The bloody Battle of the Bulge was on. Massive artillery barrages preceded the attack. Poor intelligence on the part of our higher Commanders resulted in not having seen the tremendous German build up. Our lines were spread thin with only a group or regiment holding where a division or more should have been.

This poor intelligence resulted in the following account by Eugene Murphy ("A" Troop Communications Sergeant):

WORDS OF SGT. MURPHY

Along with much confusion, in general along the front, these and other factors resulted in our capture by a spearheading tank element of the First S.S. Panzer Division of the Sixth German Army (the same outfit involved in the Malmedy Massacre). We were captured forward of St. Vith, Belgium early in the morning of December 17, 1944, in the small village of Honsfeld on the German-Belgium border.

It was later said that the valiant defense work of the 14th Calvary Group, commanded by the spit and polish West Pointer, Col. Mark Devine, slowed down the powerful armored Nazi spearhead during the early hours of the counter offensive. The Germans were driving to capture the important road center of St. Vith and this threw the Germans off schedule, thus gaining time for our forces to regroup.

The day preceding our capture, December 16, 1944, about 7:00 a.m., 1st Lt. Robert Reppa (Panama Canal Zone Commander of "A" Troop of the 32nd) assembled the troop in full battle gear and told us "C" Troop of the 18th was in trouble. Five enemy tanks were raising hell with them and they were being forced to withdraw from Krewinkel to Manderfeld. We were ordered to move up and give support. Moving up, our armored column twice was under heavy artillery fire, once in the village of Ander and another time in a wooded sector. We buttoned up and came through without any casualties.

On arriving at Manderfeld, we set up a defensive position on a hill to the west overlooking the town. More important than anything else, our squadron and group HQ was located in this town and we had to get them somewhere that it would be safer. It was almost dark, after seeing Col. Devine and his staff, escorted by an armored car and three Jeeps, on their way to his new command post in Poteau. I understand that they ran head on into a German tank.

A German sentry, standing close to the armored car, yelled "Halt!'" But an American officer, riding escort in the commander's position, shoved his 45 in the sentry's face and emptied the entire clip. The gunner in the armored car opened up with the 50 and 30 caliber machine guns and the light from the tracers illuminated between fifteen and twenty German tanks lined up along the road. The armored car and Jeeps were able to get their lights on and turn around and get away with only one anti-tank shell whistling harmlessly overhead.

Remaining in Manderfeld, as the afternoon wore on, the situation around us worsened. The 18th got information back to Group, and Col. Devine's Executive Officer called General Jones at his 106th Division Command Post at St. Vith. (We were now attached to the 106th Division).

In the meantime, Lt. Reppa, in a defensive position above Manderfeld, ordered Platoon Sgt. Fancher to take the first platoon and do combat patrol to the north, east and south of Manderfeld to keep the roads open between Lt. Ferrens' unit and Manderfeld. This he managed to do. A little later, "C" troop was ordered to pull back through Sgt. Fancher's first platoon and the rest of "A" troop, and then Sgt. Fancher was ordered to bring up the rear and join the rest of "A" troop.

They reported to him that Germans were passing southwest of the 14th's position and moving toward the Our River, and if he wasn't allowed to withdraw at once, they would be cut off from the rear. Permission was given and soon the 18th was evacuating Manderfeld covered by the guns of "A" Troop of the 32nd. We of "A" Troop were last to leave town. In departing, we could hear the lumbering of German tanks approaching the east end of town. Our troop then moved northwest parallel with our lines. In the gathering darkness, artillery duels were taking place all along the line with 30 caliber and 50 caliber tracers, buzz bombs and screaming meemies. It put Fourth of July celebrations to shame.

After several miles, we came to the village of Holzheim. Here we set up in a defensive position, as an anti-buzz bomb battery was pulling out. Later a young lieutenant in one of the outfits pulling by told us the "Krauts" had cut the road to Schonberg. They would be here any minute and if we were smart, we would follow them out north to Honsfeld. Lt. Reppa told him he didn't have orders from Squadron to withdraw, so we remained uneasily in the village. The villagers became cool and almost hostile as they began to clear their homes of signs of American occupation. Someone said, "Next they will be hanging out German flags."

After about two hours without hearing from Squadron, Lt. Reppa, without order or regrets, moved "A" Troop out of this unfriendly town. He prayed we would get to Honsfeld before the Krauts. It seems that about this time the Germans were as confused with the situation as the Americans and for the moment, we were unknowingly safe.

In Honsfeld, we found the town being used by the 349th Regiment of the 99th Division as a Rest Center. Here we found the officers and men placidly taking their rest and recreation. YES! They had heard there was some trouble up front, but the situation was now in hand. Lt. Reppa tried to impress a captain of the 99th in charge of the Rest Center that the situation was everything but in hand. The captain was not impressed and informed the lieutenant, "The good word here was to RELAX."

Lt. Reppa ordered us in Headquarters Platoon to set up the troop command post in one of the houses and to keep trying to make radio contact with Squadron. The "Krauts" were jamming the American frequencies, making radio contact next to impossible. Lt. Reppa then had Sgt. Creel and his 1st Platoon establish a road block at the east end of town. He then ordered Sgt. Pat O'Brien (Springfield, Illinois) and his dirty 3rd Platoon to set up a perimeter defense of the area.

On returning, Lt. Reppa was still uneasy and the 99th Division captain was amused by his nervousness. Lt. Reppa demanded to know, "Where the hell is everyone and how come I'm all alone?"

The captain explained by calling his regimental headquarters and connecting the lieutenant with a Regimental staff officer. Lt. Reppa tried to explain to the officer the situation.

In turn, he informed Lt. Reppa, "You have nothing to worry about. You are well behind the front lines and since you will come under my command at daybreak, I want you to prepare to make contact with the enemy."

45

"At daybreak," muttered Lt. Reppa to himself, "the Krauts will be here making their own contact!" The officer wanted to know what he had said. Lt. Reppa told him, "Nothing, sir," and bid him GOOD NIGHT!

Later a captain and his driver came into our command post, both hit with shrapnel, looking for medics. The captain was not badly hit but his driver was hit in the face and his complete lower jaw was missing. He was still walking, so the medics sat him down and shot him full of morphine, then took him, still standing, to a field hospital. I understood that later, this hospital, along with our two medics, was also captured. So under the circumstances, this fellow's chances were at best, real bad.

Once during the night, a full colonel with an antiaircraft outfit of the 99th Division with his heavy equipment, pulled back by us. He told Lt. Reppa that if he was smart, he would pull our unit out behind his. His orders were to withdraw and reform on a line a few miles back. Lt. Reppa told him that we had to await orders from Squadron. Later that night, we finally made radio contact with Squadron and received orders to move south-west at daybreak, so we awaited the DAWN!

About four a.m., American vehicles, trucks, armored cars, artillery pieces, antiaircraft units and half-tracks bumper to bumper, were still coming into and passing on through Honsfeld. As it turned out, not far behind this creeping column was German Obersturmbannfumer S.S. Lt. Col. Joahim "Joachim" Peiper and his spear-heading tank unit of the 1st S.S. Panzer Division.

In the early morning before daybreak at our troop command post, we had one man on guard at the outside door. Radio Operator Jerry Redding (Springfield, Illinois) was asleep in a chair, backed against the wall. Lt. Sharp (Texas) and Lt. Moynahan (Boston, Massachusetts) were asleep in other chairs. Lt. Reppa was lying on the floor. Radio Operator Goldman (Bronx, New York) was in the armored car outside on radio watch. Radio Operator Steve Bensack (Milwaukee, Wisconsin) and driver-gunners, Jacaway, Haensal, and Wangard (all from Springfield, Illinois) were in the building next door. Thus we waited.

The drone of heavy equipment moving by caused me to doze off. There was a deadly silence. Then more heavy equipment began moving by. I came awake fast, as did most of the other men. The sounds were different.

Lt. Reppa asked Lovelock, our motor sergeant for two years, what the engines sounded like. He listened and said they sounded like White engines. "White engines my foot!" exclaimed Sharp. He was interrupted by the outside guard bursting through the door and reporting, "There are tanks going by loaded with soldiers, and English, they are not speaking!"

I took a look and there stood a big German 60-ton Tiger Tank with my radio Jeep smashed under one of its tracks. Their turret gun was pointed at our window. Sgt. Goldman had been captured. I told the others the bad news, shook Redding awake and told him we were surrounded by Krauts. Jerry replied, "What a hell of a way to wake a guy up from a peaceful slumber!"

Lt. Sharp and Moynahan began to burn papers and maps. Lt. Reppa cussed the regimental staff officer who'd told him how far behind the lines we were and then to RELAX! His anger then switched to Sgt. Creel in charge of the South Road Block.

About this time Sgt. Creel walked in. Lt. Reppa wanted to know what he had to say for himself. Sgt. Creel replied, "I was in my armored car and a guy came walking down the road in front of a big vehicle swinging a flash light. Behind him was the biggest damn tank I've ever seen and it had a swastika on it!"

"Why the hell didn't you shoot?" asked Lt. Reppa.

Sgt. Creel replied, "I did, but our 37mm guns were about as effective as sling shot, so I thought I had best warn everybody, so here I am."

Outside, a voice in German shouted, "Come out!"

Lt. Reppa looked at the others and said, "We can't make it! We can't do a damn thing!" He went to the door, opened it and called, "Kamerad!"

So it was, RAUST MIT YAW. With hands on top of our heads, out we came.

The next thing I know, a young German soldier with a Shmeiser, or burp gun, jams it into my tender ribs demanding a pistol for a souvenir. The Krauts were as hot for our 45 automatics as we were for their Lugers. The crews of the Kraut Tank Company did the honors. They were equipped with the latest new 60 ton Tiger Royal Tank, the biggest cotton-picking tanks I had ever seen. In the lighter vein, if there could be one at this time, Mess Sgt. Tony Bryan (Springfield, Illinois) had a barrel of sugar and several cases of "D" bars in the mess truck.

When the Germans captured the truck, they lost their composure as soldiers and gentlemen. They were eating sugar by the handful and scrambling for the "D" bars. After the immediate preliminaries of being captured, we were unceremoniously lined up, gangster fashion, alongside of the buildings. According to Sgt. Binsack, who spoke and understood German, there was an argument between two German tank officers as to our disposition. Since they were a spearheading unit, their orders were not to take prisoners. So the debate was whether or not to shoot us, at that moment--a good question! I believe our unwashed necks and pure hearts were saved by a company of Kraut Doughfeet (Infantry) who were moving up and who agreed to furnish five men to escort us to the rear.

We were marched back, with our hands on top of our heads, several kilometers. After what seemed a long period of time, we reached a group of farm houses. Here a German officer with a Mouser rifle shoved it at us, and with much gusto and theatrics, put the safety on, impressing us as though he was taking it off. He then proceeded to dress us down in German. The only words I could understand were "Chicago gangsters and swine." Finally he allowed us to take our hands off our heads. With subfreezing temperatures and snow on the ground, my hands were frozen. I had to have help getting them apart. At this time, an artillery shell fell about twenty-five yards from us and we hit for cover—German officers included.

As we were marched back to the farm houses, German tank and combat units were moving up. Every now and then a tank would move out of line and try running us down. We also noticed one tank or truck would be towing another. They were that short on fuel. As these units moved up, the men relieved us of our personal effects, watches, rings, wallets, and etc. They also relieved us of our outer

48

garments, overcoats, overshoes, and gloves. I ended up with a knit cap, jacket, denim trousers and GI shoes.

While walking back, all around us in the woods and forest, we could hear small arms fire and some artillery. On the opposite side of the road from us, we saw two German soldiers crouched in firing position over their rifles, both dead and frozen in that position, looking like German soldiers. They always managed to look like German soldiers in their immaculate gray uniforms, even in death.

Leaving the farm houses, four of us were ordered to help carry a young, wounded German soldier. About a mile or so down the road, still struggling along with this fellow, we heard a swish and a thud. A mortar shell landed within ten feet of us. The shell was a dud. The wounded German sure got shook up, for we made a dive for the ditch, leaving him on the road. To this day, I say a prayer for the lunk head who fell asleep making a mortar shell, be he American or German. A German ambulance finally took the wounded man off our hands.

In the middle of the afternoon, still walking back into Germany, several units of United States' vehicles, armored cars, trucks and tanks all manned by German soldiers in American uniforms moved by us. While waiting for these units to pass, the skies above began to clear and we watched three United States Air Force P-38 Fighter planes engage three German Messerschmitt ME-109 Fighter planes in a dog fight. In a matter of five minutes, the three American aircraft were knocked down and their pilots hit the silk.

That night, we were herded and packed into a small village rail station, some in the cellar and the rest in the station itself. Thus ended the first day of a NIGHTMARE.

Our second day in captivity found us walking deeper into Germany toward the city of Bonn. This day we walked about twenty kilometers, passing through small villages and towns, by air bases, military and radar installations and big gun emplacements. That night we were billeted in the lofts of a business house in a small town in route. Our bill-o-fare for this day was any stray sugar beets we could find in the fields along the road. That night we were each given two small links of sausage-like meat.

49

The next morning we were rousted out of the lofts and walked a few blocks to a small four-room red school house. Here the Germans had set up an interrogation center. They relieved us of any overcoats and battle gear that the front line troops had missed. Then, one hundred men at a time were ushered into one of the rooms. Inside the room at one end was a low platform, and above it was a large blackboard. On the board was written:

"According to the Geneva Convention, all you
must give is your name, rank and serial number."

Standing on the platform were three German soldiers dressed in uniform, with more gold braid than Fort Knox. These three men were dressed like field marshals of the first rank and were most likely not above the rank of sergeant. When the men were all in the room and some order achieved, one of the men on the stage stepped forward. In a soft-spoken voice and speaking in English, he told us of our rights under the Geneva Convention.

After this fellow said his piece, one of the other men stepped forward and what followed blew our so-called training to the four winds. This overstuffed private in a general's uniform bellowed in a loud commanding voice, "Now all men from the 28th Division line up over here."

A shuffle of feet and the men from the 28th lined up. So it went. The 106th over here, the 99th over there. The straw that broke the camel's back was a man in the rear wanting to know where the 2nd Division went. At this, the Kraut on the platform almost broke a blood vessel, for he could hardly contain himself. After running out of divisions, Redding and myself, along with several others, were left still in the middle of the floor. He asked Jerry what outfit he was from. Jerry answered, "At the moment, we are unattached." Much to our surprise, he let it go at that.

They moved us on out of the school house and once again we started to walk. The pay off was that most of the men wore Army Division or Corps shoulder patches, so all the Germans had to do was look to determine who belonged where.

The next two days we spent walking and at night sleeping in barns and pig sties of small villages. In two days, we received one loaf of bread for seven men and each day, about two ounces of sweet, bright orange-colored candy-like substance on a piece of paper. It was good so I ate it, paper and all.

On the fifth day we arrived at a small village near Bonn where they had a Transit Stalag (prison). Here we spent the next two nights and days resting. Each day we were given a hot, thick bowl of barley soup. I believe this rest and food was the difference between staying alive and dying.

For the two days at this Stalag, the skies were clear of clouds but darkened by United States B-17 bombers headed into the Reichland. The antiaircraft flack was heavy around Bonn. As we watched, now and then a ship would blow up in formation or you could see one glide out of formation, hit and in trouble. When this happened, you prayed to see puffs of white trailing behind as the men hit the silk.

On the afternoon of December 23, 1944, we were loaded and packed into an unmarked freight car of a German train, seventy men to a car half the size of a standard box car. The car I was in had previously been used to haul coal. I was, until liberation and later, washing and cleaning the coal dust out of my skin. The days and nights were bitterly cold. While on the train, which was until early Christmas morning, we had no food, little water, no straw or bedding, no heat and no sanitary facilities. Most of the men suffered from dysentery and all of us suffered frozen hands and feet.

With so many men to such a small car, it was necessary to sit, lie or stand in shifts. The men not sitting or lying down, stood and bunched together, attempting to keep warm. At night the Germans parked the train in their railroad marshaling yards, which were prime targets for our Air Force. As can readily be seen, this was far removed from a comforting situation. At times, when the train stopped, through a small opening in the upper part of the car, we were able to beg a little water from the civilians. I traded my ID bracelet for a small can of sardines. There were seven little fishes for seven men. In this case, the biblical story of the fishes and bread did not work.

Christmas morning we arrived at Limburg, Germany. We unloaded at the depot and were marched through the town to the Stalag located there. Christmas Eve, the R.A.F. had bombed the town and accidentally dropped a 500 pounder in the middle of the compound, killing and wounding a number of American officers and men. On account of this, the Stalag Commander refused to take us in, so we were marched back through the town to the depot.

On the march back through the town, the town's people ridiculed us. Now and then they would toss a stone or so our way. In general, they let it be known that a Merry Christmas was not being offered. Of course, we were a fine example of clean-cut American manhood with coal dust ground into our skin and with the bitter cold and the state of hunger making us look like the "Bowery Bums."

Back at the depot we were made to stand alongside the train and spend the rest of the day waiting for an engine. The depot had an outside water faucet but the guards were ordered to shoot anyone going near it. I suppose if our towns were bombed out from under us, a drink of water might be too much to give to those who did the bombing.

The following day, December 26th, we arrived at Nuremberg, Germany, Stalag 13D. The first ten days, to say the least, were rough. Arriving at Stalag 13D, we were moved into compounds and housed 100 men to a barrack. Here we were issued one and one half of a thin blanket and a sack-cloth mattress filled with shredded paper. Our names and ranks were taken and we were given a shower of three minutes duration. Our clothes were deloused. This was the first of three baths that I was to receive for as long as I was a prisoner.

The Russian POW's were taking care of the delousing and bath station. Upon our arrival, they proceeded to give us the "Raspberry" or "Bronx Cheer." They said, "No wonder you got the hell kicked out of you. You are nothing but a bunch of spoiled playboys anyways." Since then, I have often wondered how come they were also prisoners. It looked like the Russians also had a few so-called playboys.

At Nuremberg, it was necessary for two men to sleep together to keep from freezing to death. Jerry Redding, my chief radio operator, and I shared a bunk. We used his combat jacket, zipped up, to put our feet in. My jacket was used to wrap around our shoulders. In the day time, we would spend hours rubbing each other's frozen feet and warming them against our bodies to bring back circulation and to keep gangrene from setting in. When our feet and hands would get warm, the pain made us want to scream.

The night of January 3, 1945, the Royal Air Force made a 500 plane bombing raid on Nuremberg proper. They used Lancaster planes with a blockbuster strapped under the plane and bomb bays loaded with incendiaries. The raid lasted three hours. With the blockbuster blowing up and the ack-ack firing all around us, I got to shaking so badly I almost shook Jerry out of the bunk. It wasn't that I was scared—scared could hardly describe the feeling. When one of those big bombs hit, it would pick the barracks up and set it back down again. There were 500 of those bombs!

During this January 3rd raid, Nuremberg suffered casualties of more than 10,000 killed and as many wounded. It took the Hun's almost three weeks to bury their dead. The Germans used the Russian, Polish and Serb prisoners to dig a common grave. A big ditch ten feet wide by twelve feet deep and about a city block long was dug. The bodies were wrapped in sheets, placed in the ditch, one on top of the other like cord wood, then covered with lime and later covered with earth. Our compound commander, or block fuehrer, a German master sergeant, lost his wife and two children in the raid. Strangely enough, his attitude toward us did not change for the better or for the worse.

For heat in the barracks, we were allowed eight briquettes of coal per day for two stoves. This was finally discontinued altogether. It was just as well for this amount of coal would hardly heat the stoves themselves.

The bill-of-fare during our uninvited stay as the guest of Reich Fuehrer Adolf Hitler was one bowl of hot ersatz tea in the morning. It was tea made from ground roasted barley. At midday, we were given a bowl of water soup. The men called it GREEN DEATH. One time, we were sure it had meat in it for there was a skeleton of a horse's head floating in the soup barrel. For five weeks this so-called soup was made without salt. In the evening, after count, we were given one loaf of Jerry bread to seven men. Later this was changed to one loaf for ten men. For anyone who wishes to reduce, this formula is highly effective. I went from weighing 150 pounds to 105. At one time you could play Rachmaninoff's Prolog in C-Sharp Minor on my ribs. While a prisoner, I had grown a goatee and mustache. With the loss in weight, it made me look like my head had been squeezed in a vice.

On January 15, 1945, we received one American Red Cross parcel to be divided among four men. On an average, we would receive these packages every fifteen days. The parcels contained a small can of American cheese, a #1 can of margarine, a small can of jelly, a small can of Spam, a "C" ration of meat and beans, a can of powdered milk, a box of raisins or prunes, a small box of "C" ration biscuits and five packs of cigarettes. While dividing the package into four equal portions, the prisoners had eyes like a micrometer—one slip of the knife meant trouble.

As a prisoner of war, our lot in life was the everlasting state of hunger and just plain boredom. Things to do were limited to talking about food and knocking ourselves out planning menus, most of which were far out. In times past and under different circumstances, when two or more GIs got together, the conversation would soon turn to women. Here in prison camp, this was far removed, for thoughts of food was the main topic. I spent some time each day playing solitaire with a deck of Red Cross cards till I wore them out. Part of the time, we spent gathering news of how the war was going and betting on the day of liberation.

As for the source of news that we received, there were at different times as many as four small crystal radio sets hidden in our compound. These sets were built by the British and Australians. Some of them had been prisoners for as long as five years. In that time, they had learned to speak the German language and had bribed, stolen and improvised these sets. Everyday someone would broadcast the news and repeat each word twice so it could be copied and distributed throughout the camp. Each barracks would get a copy. We would place a guard at the doors and windows and the rest would gather around and have the news read to them. The cry, "TALLY HO," was the signal that a goon was coming, so duck the news and spread out.

One day during news time, a guard walked in on us and the cry of "Tally Ho" went out. We made like nothing was taking place, but the guard came on into the barracks and said, "Tally Ho, your rear end. I want to know what the news is, for I can't find out anything in the way of news around the camp."

Another time, the Germans tore down a barracks, board by board, looking for a radio and found one, but the next day we had the news as usual.

One room in a barracks in the compound was set aside for use as the infirmary. However, there were no medical supplies or doctor. If you were sick, it was to have your T.S. card punched with the nearest Sky Pilot.

Here at the 13D, trenches were dug in the compound to satisfy the International Red Cross Inspector so that we had minimum protection during air raids. These were every night by the RAF and every day by the USAF. During the raids, the goons ordered us to stay in the barracks or be shot. This they did at 13D. In the middle of February, we were uneventfully moved by train from Stalag 13D to Stalag 13C at Hammelburg. Here the conditions were much the same as 13D. This camp was at one time a horse artillery post, so we were housed, 1000 men to an "Old Horse Stable."

Here at Hammelburg, the Russians were in the next compound from ours. These people were treated pretty badly by the Jerries. Less food and more work. When one of their men would die, the Russians took up the floor boards and lay the body under the floor. They then would continue to draw his rations until the odor got bad enough for the Goons to find the body, bury it and cut the rations.

The Sunday before Easter, we got up in the morning and found we were confined to the buildings. The detachment assigned to guard duty over the camp was in full combat regalia. Machine guns were set up at different points and a hustle and bustle in the camp said something was popping. Hopes were that liberation was near, but by later that afternoon, the camp was back to normal. So it was said the German Army wasn't much different than the American Army—dry runs!

The next morning, the popping popped for the civilians and German officers and their families were leaving the camp by wagon, auto, truck and on foot. The German guards around the compound were asking the men inside what they should do when the Americans got there. Around the camp, we could see young boys and old men manning antitank guns and digging holes where a young boy would get down into with a Panzerfaust (an antitank weapon like our bazooka). About 4:30 p.m., artillery shells began dropping in and around the camp. From our compound, we could watch the Germans bring up heavy antitank and combat units.

Later in the evening, on the road alongside our compound, three Sherman tanks came lumbering up. The Yanks were prisoners and the tanks were manned by the Huns. That night I talked with a young, blond-headed lieutenant, his sidekick, and a combat medic, all who were captured that afternoon. The lieutenant was in charge of Recon Patrol of Infantry Scouts from the 10th Armored Infantry Battalion of the 4th Armored Division. He told us they were a task force commanded by a Capt. Baum, consisting of one company of armored infantry, a company of medium tanks, a platoon of assault guns and a recon patrol.

In vehicles, they had twenty-seven half-tracks, ten medium tanks, six light tanks, three armored 105's assault guns and six Jeeps. All told, they had 292 fighting men. He said the B-Tank Company of the 37th and B Company of the Armored Infantry under the protective cover of three divisional Artillery Battalions, broke a hole for them out of the Main River Bridgehead near the outskirts of Aschaffenburg along the way. They made a mad dash for Hammelburg. Their orders were to liberate the officer lager, to arm the officers liberated and to return.

We in camp, as well as the German High Command, thought it was a spearheading outfit to split Germany. The Germans were so convinced that they moved their High Command Headquarters. On finding out for sure that no main body was following this so called spearhead, I cried like a baby. The lieutenant said the German commander surrendered the camp to them and then they were retaken by German combat unit. So I can say that I was liberated and recaptured all in one day!

General Patton later wrote in his book that the only mistake he made was not sending in a division behind these two companies, for he did have a fresh division held in reserve. He also said the Task Force was sent to create a diversion from the activities of the rest of the 4th

Armored Division farther to the North. It will be forever believed by the men involved that it was a sacrifice mission to free Patton's son-in-law, a prisoner in the camp.

The following day, the Germans began to move the prisoners out of the camp—British, Aussies, Poles, Serbs, Russians and Americans. I and several other men hung back and hid in the barns hoping our forces would catch up with us, but the Goons had other ideas. Saturday evening they brought dogs in and rooted us out. They walked us four miles to Hammelburg and the railroad station.

It was a beautiful clear Easter eve. Here we waited till about two a.m. Easter morning, when a train arrived with about twelve unmarked freight cars. We were loaded, forty men to a car. Much to our surprise, they had straw on the floor of the cars. There were two German guards to each car, one on each side of the open cars.

Then, lucky for us, about five a.m. with a low-hanging haze, we were jolly-well jockeying down the rails when two P-51 Fighters took a crack at us. They strafed the head end of the train and dropped two wing bombs, killing four men and wounding several others.

The train stopped, we unloaded and ran away from the train as fast as we could. One of the pilots came down to take a look, noticed we were POW's and moved on. After the planes departed, the guards ordered us back onto the trains. Almost all of us refused. The train commander got the guards together for a conference, and then there was a renewed effort to get us back on the train. The guard nearest me kept yelling in German to get back on, then in English told the men around him that if they did, they were NUTS! So they finally decided to leave those that wanted to walk and those that wanted to ride, ride. Most walked. They gave each one of us a Red Cross Parcel and we started to walk.

That evening we arrived at Schweinfurt, the ball bearing factory center that was a main target for our bombers. We were loaded back on the train. However, this time "POW" was painted on the roof of each car of the train. We arrived back at Nuremberg, Stalag 13D.

The next day, after each received another Red Cross Parcel, we were marched out of Nuremberg and headed south toward Moosburg Stalag 7A. This was a town approximately thirty kilometers slightly north and east of Munich. At this time, it seemed the Germans were gathering and moving Allied prisoners from all over Germany in a southerly direction towards Munich, the Bavarian Redoubt or Bavarian Alps. In the column, there were Allied POWs and many others. It seems they were toying with the idea of holding all as hostages to gain a better deal.

The afternoon of the first day out, which was a beautiful, sunny day, we climbed higher. Looking back at Nuremberg, it looked as if it were down in a saucer. At this time, the 8th Air Force was bombing the city and sound waves around the city looked the same as when you throw a pebble into a lake.

The first evening out, I joined up with six Limeys. These men had been captured in the ill-fated Dunkirk Landings early in the war. They came from the Piccadilly Circus area of London, which could be compared with "Hell's Kitchen" in New York City. They had worked in the mines of Upper Silesia (Schlelsien) and had been POWs for approximately four years and had learned to speak German very well during that time. Since they could speak German, we slept in German homes each evening along the route. I traded my coffee to some woman for a link of sausage about a foot or so long. The Limeys smashed up some pancakes, fried the sausage, and we had a GOOD BREAKFAST!

I traded my cigarettes for a jar of wheat. One home had a pretty good hot fire going in the kitchen stove, so I took the wheat, laid it out in a pan, put it in the oven and roasted it. After it was roasted, we took a coffee grinder they had hanging on the wall, ground the wheat, then cooked it like oatmeal. Good!

The seven of us started out near the head end of the column and we ended up dragging in close to the rear end. Some said that if you had stood in one place, it would have taken ten days for this column to have passed you by.

We arrived at Moosburg Stalag 7A a few days later. On April 29, 1945, a beautiful sunny Sunday morning in Moosburg, Bavaria, Germany, or to me, more correctly, Moosburg Stalag 7A- POW camp, there were a bunch of guys out in the compound with an Irish priest from the British Army saying Mass. The services were almost over when one of the men shouted, "Hey, man, is that a Sherman Tank on the hill?" BROTHER, IT WAS!! The good Father looked around and said, "God bless you. If you ever get to Ireland, look me up. Now get in the ditches!"

By noon the show was over. There was a lot of fire-fighting going on around us. Artillery shells landed here and there. The camp was taken. Several Sherman tanks were in the compound. By one p.m., the American flag was flying over Moosburg. The 14th Armored Division of General Patton's Third Army did the honors.

Early the next morning, General Patton, with his famous ivory handled pistols, came into the camp. Later on that day, Senator Brooks from Illinois was in the camp. On this day, I talked with war correspondent Hal Faust. I had known Hal at the Abe Lincoln Hotel when he was a newsman for the Chicago Tribune. He was able to inform my folks, ahead of the Army, of my liberation.

The next day some of the A Troopers, my old colleagues, came in with a truck load of rations. They had C-Rations, K-Rations, Ten-In-One Rations—you name it, they had it all. I got my six Limey friends and fixed them up with plenty to eat until they were satisfied.

The following day, we were loaded onto trucks and moved to Landshut, Germany. We were taken to what looked like a gigantic meadow. As far as the eye could see, there was nothing but green, green grass. The only thing useable in sight was a small gray building, which I understand was used as a control tower. We were unloaded in this big field. I mean there were hundreds and hundreds of POWs in these trucks. The trucks drove off and there we sat. Like I always said, the Army way was to "hurry up and wait." Boy, was I fooled this time because they were landing C-47s like---. I have never seen so many planes in one place in all my life. They landed one underneath the other and right underneath the other.

(As a side line comment, at this German Air Base at this time, there was nothing above ground. Everything was below—the hangars, machine shops and even the hospital. You could walk five abreast in the tunnel from the air base to Landshut, which was the town nearby.)

While all this was going on, here came two ME-109 Messerschmitts, which apparently came in from Czechoslovakia. They had their landing wheels down to signify that they wanted to surrender. So they landed all right, but one pilot, as soon as he hit the ground and was down good, pulled the landing gear up and smashed the plane up. They worked him over pretty good. The other pilot had a porker (pig) behind his seat in the plane.

In the meantime, they started loading us on the planes. I said I wasn't going to get on the plane, and about this time two guys grabbed me and put me on. After we were up, I noticed that they had one of these Kriegies (Ex-POWs) flying the plane. I wasn't too happy about that. They got right down on the deck and you could almost drag your feet right down on the ground. One could see where all the bridges had been blown all the way down and all that. As a radio operator, I got right up with the pilot, co-pilot, navigator and radio operator. They showed me around and whatever. It was really nice looking right out over them.

We were taken to Le Havre, France (Camp Lucky Strike), and in a day or so, loaded on the M.S. John Erickson. We left France on May 16, 1945 and the United Kingdom on May 19, 1945. I am going to say that approximately six to eight days later, we arrived in the U.S. They took us to Orange, New Jersey, shipped us home by Troop Train (GIs called them "cattle cars") to Camp Grant in Rockford, Illinois, which is near Chicago. We were each granted a 90-day furlough with orders to report to Miami Beach, Florida.

At Miami Beach, we spent a week and the entire time they tried to re-enlist us. I didn't play, so I was then shipped back to Camp Grant and discharged.

Thus ended the WWII POW nightmare of Sgt. Eugene Murphy. Though the POWs in the European theater of war were treated badly, I think they were treated even worse in the Pacific.

Certified account of Robert B. Reppa's surrender

1. This is to certify that about 100 on 16 Dec. 1944, I was ordered as Tr CO, to move Tr A 32nd Cav Rcn Sq [M] from the Sq rest area at Veilsalm (Rencheux, Belgium, to Manderfeld, Belgium, in order to cover the withdrawal of the following units: CP 14 Cav Gp [M]; CP. Hq, C, E, and F Trps of the 18th Cav Rcn Sq [M]; and CP and Tr of the 32nd Cav Sq. This mission was accomplished by holding, dismounted, the high ground South West of Manderfeld. About 1600, on orders from the CO 32nd Cav Sq., I withdrew Tr A to the town of Holzheim, about two miles South and West of Manderfeld,

where I requested additional orders for Tr A and information as to the position of the remainder of the 32nd Cav Sq.

2. A radio message was received from the CO 32nd Cav Sq to send the Tr Co or other officer to the Sq C to the Southwest of Holzheim. I was unable to comply with this order because no vehicles could travel against the columns of Cav, TD, and AAA units, which were retreating on the only available, one-way road between the two CPs. Cross country movement was restricted because of the deep snow and the darkness. I returned to my CP and radioed this information and the fact that retreating units reported this road had been cut by the enemy advance.

3. Neighboring units of the 18th Cav Sq and various TD and AAA units withdrew to the West, and fearing encirclement of the Tr A from the South, I withdrew the troops at about 2200 to road junction at Honsfeld, Belgium, as neither orders from troops nor information regarding flanking movement from the enemy coming from the East or South. Sq CP was informed when this move was contemplated, and after a lapse of two hours, during which time no answer was received, the troop moved to Honsfeld.

4. Troop was ordered into a perimeter defense, with Tr CP in center, and I observed further withdrawal of convoys through town. Informed that the town was the regimental rest area for the 394th Regt, 99 Inf Div, with direct telephone connection to regimental CP in a town just to the North, I contacted the Regtl Ex O and identified Tr A as a unit being with the 99th Div in the same camp in Texas. A platoon leader was sent as liaison officer to Regtl CP, where he was informed by Regtl CO that Tr A would not be in contact with the enemy since the 394th, plus units of the 9th Armored Div, would form both the OPL and MLR. The Regtl CP requested that elements of Tr A patrol two roads to the East of Honsfeld at daybreak.

5. Orders were received from Sq CO 32nd Cav Sq to assemble Tr A at a rendezvous to the southwest of Honfeld whenever traffic and weather conditions permitted. Because of the vehicle losses sustained by the troop in movement from Holzheim to

Honsfeld, it was decided to move the troop at dawn when light and traffic would be better. This information plus a route to be taken was radioed to Sq CP and approved.

6. Orders had not been given to mine the roads in Honsfeld because of the heavy traffic of Cav, TD, and AAA units. Also, as noted in paragraph 4 above, we had been informed by the Retl CO of the 394th that we were far in the rear of the MLR. Vehicles were not stopped for identification because many of the vehicles were unarmored, and as the town was being shelled and many casualties occurred. It was thought that requiring vehicles to stop for identification, would result in congestion and more casualties. Traffic continued to pour through the town until about 0415 17 Dec, at which time there was a lull for about fifteen minutes.

7. Vehicles began to move through the town again, and after a dozen or more of tanks and half tracks (with motor noise similar to American Lt Cav tanks) had passed, we discovered by the light of a shell burst that the vehicles were German Tiger Royal tanks and armored half tracks, carrying SS personnel. At this time the sergeant of the guard reported into the TR CP to confirm this information, and he also reported that he had not been able to stake out AT mines when the vehicles came through because he had heard no warning firing by the troops supposedly in the OPL and Mir positions to our front.

8. I immediately ordered a message sent to Sq C with an estimate as to the amount of armor in the breakthrough, and sent runners to all platoons to alert them for immediate withdrawal, by vehicle preferably, or by foot after destroying the vehicles. The Tr Hq platoon vehicles were parked in front of the Tr CP on the road that the enemy was using. I hoped to mount all Tr Hq plus 20 to 30 men of the 99th Div rest center and "sandwich" into a break of the German column until it was possible to turn off on a side road heading North.

9. This action became impossible when several more shell bust in town and by their light, the Hq platoon vehicles were seen by the Germans. Several tanks and flak carriers stopped to cover their dismounted investigating troops. When they

discovered our presence, it would have been possible to make casualties of possibly half a dozen enemy infantry (but not their vehicles), and failing to see how a breakthrough of all that armor could be halted, the loss of a few men in exchange for the probable death of 30 to 40 Americans in the CP house, I surrendered my HQ platoon.

10. We were searched, striped of all articles of values, and marched to the other side of the road opposite the house. Tentative orders to shoot us were being given, when a German infantry support battalion marched through town and an officer had us sent to the rear.

11. From information collected in POW camp and after my release, I found that my warning to the platoons and the delay caused the Germans by my surrender had made it possible for two platoons to make their way, dismounted, to the U.S. lines after inflicting light casualties on the enemy.

----Robert B. Reppa Captain, Cavalry Dec.1945

The Words of Sgt. Fancher

Sgt. Fancher: "Battle of the Bulge" or "The Battle of the Ardennes," the largest battle ever fought by the United States Army. A total of 87,000 casualties from the sixteenth of December 1944 to the twenty-fifth of January 1945. This involved a total of 600,000 men.

My start in this began about a week before when we were pulled out of the line in the lower part of Luxembourg, where we had taken heavy casualties securing a hill on the Moselle River. It was necessary this hill be taken before General Patton crossed the Moselle. After we were out, we ended up in a rest camp in the town of Vielsam, Belgium. We were stationed in a rest camp in a former SS barracks where we received replacements of men and equipment. While we were there, showers were available and also clean clothes.

After we had taken care of our needs, along with our armored cars, guns, Jeeps and ammo, we received passes for the town, so a great time was had by all. We then had to start training our replacements, most of who were not used to the Mechanized. Cavalry. Anyway, the C.O. said we should make up our teams (they consisted of an armored car and two Jeeps) and get them used to the procedures.

I was platoon sergeant of the 1st platoon, so I took my unit up close to the front lines so we could get the new men acclimated to the sounds of the big guns and being close to the fighting. We spent some time in the area, which at the time was pretty quiet. We went over to a firing range so we could check out our replacements on the weapons they would have to use. They seemed to catch on quickly, so I thought they needed a little break. In this reserve area, the civilians had moved back into the taverns and the eating joints were operating again. We found one that looked pretty good, so I set up a defense around this tavern with the armored car and three Jeeps on each corner. We took turns manning each and the rest of us proceeded to have a good time. (Although I thought it was a safe location, there was no point in taking chances.)

In a situation like this, with everyone having a good time, as anyone in a similar situation knows, the time passes all too quickly. To make a long story short, it got very late before I realized it. I looked at my watch and it was three thirty in the morning. I started to think that I might be in trouble. We went back to our motor pool and very quietly parked our vehicles and headed back to our barracks.

We got into our barracks building and I had just sat down on my bunk and taken off my shoes, thinking we were going to make it. In came the C.Q. He said, "The old man wants to see you."

I thought, boy, I've had it now. I will probably be a private by morning. I pulled my shoes back on and headed for the captain's office. By this time I was feeling pretty shaky.

He looked at me and said "Mad Dog, how soon can you have your platoon ready to go?" By this time, I would have done almost anything. He told me they were having some major trouble in the line and it may have even been broken through in some places. "Go get your men mounted up and ready to roll, and then give me a call."

This done, I gave him a call and he gave me a location to set up a defense position and to hold until relieved. This position was in an open valley and just behind the main line. We could not have withstood even a light attack, but those were orders. It was now starting to get daylight. I could hear a lot of big guns, heavy tank motors and lots of small arms fire. Then about two or three blocks away, an old German buzz bomb hit, making a hole you could drop a house into. I called HQ and asked if I could find a better position on the side of this valley, but the orders were to stay there. I never expected to see the sun set that day. (THAT'S HOW THE BULGE STARTED FOR ME.)

As the morning became brighter, I could see that my position was even worse than I had first thought. The location was on the side of a road running through a flat valley only about two miles wide. The entrance of this road from the enemy side was between two hills about half a mile from my location. Any enemy armor entering would be on top of me before they were in effective range of my guns.

I could hear machine gun fire and a lot of heavy guns and tank motors, so once again I called HQ and asked if I could find a better location for the armored car and Jeep. Again it was denied as all of our artillery was targeted by map coordinates, so we dug fox holes trying to get some protection so that we could at least make some kind of a stand. We could tell from the battle sounds and radio chatter that things were really going to hell. About mid-morning, I was becoming more worried. I heard the sound of tank motors coming ever closer and figured I might as well kiss my rear goodbye. (I would like to add that my gun was a 37mm, which wasn't very effective against enemy tanks.)

I alerted my men, all of whom were unhappy with our setup. We had our guns and mortar targeted on the entrance to the valley. As the tanks came closer, I raised my hand, ready to give the signal to start firing. Looking through my field glasses, the tank seemed to be one of ours. I flagged the two tanks down to try to find out what was happening. The tank commander said the enemy had made a major breakthrough and that all <u>hell</u> was breaking loose with only these two tanks being left out of his whole company and that he was getting the <u>hell</u> out of there. At this point, I would like to add, that these were T26 tanks with 90 mm guns that would stop almost any armor the enemy had. I would have given my left arm for just one of them.

I again called HQ to let them know what was going on and again requested permission to find a better defensive location. Again the answer was no. We tried to improve our fox holes, which at this spot was impossible, so it was just a waiting game. As the afternoon wore on, the sounds of battle were getting closer all the time. I had all my guns targeted on the valley entrance, but didn't want to fire because there might still be some friendly troops coming out that way. Just as I started thinking that I was never going to see the sun set or even see another pretty girl, I received a radio message to pull my eight men and equipment back through a battalion of tanks and men behind us and meet the rest of the troop on the hill above Manderfeld, Germany.

We made the trip without any casualties, although we came under heavy artillery and small arms fire. We set up a defensive position on a hill overlooking the town. Our squadron HQ was in this town and we had to get them moved to some place safer. We also had a sister unit, C troop of the 18th, who were in bad shape and badly outnumbered like 50 to 1, in the town ahead of Manderfeld.

After arriving at Group Headquarters in Manderfeld, Germany and seeing Col. Devine and his group started on their way to his new command post in Poteau, escorted by an armored car and three Jeeps, it was almost dark. I understand that on the way, at a crossroad in the darkness, they ran head on into a German tank. A German sentry, standing close to the armored car, yelled "Halt."

An officer riding erect in the commander's position of the armored car shoved his 45 in the sentry's face and emptied his clip. As the gunner in the car opened up with the fifty and thirty caliber machine guns, the light from the tracer bullets illuminated between fifteen and twenty German armored vehicles lined up along the road. The armored car and Jeeps were able to turn their lights on and then turn around and get away with only one antitank shell whistling harmlessly over head. They arrived at Col. Devine's command post around midnight.

In the meantime, Capt. Reppa, commander of A troop, set up a defensive position on the hills to the north and west of Manderfeld. Our sister unit, the 18th squadron, was located in the Losheim Gap area ahead of Manderfeld in several small villages (Afst, Kerwinkel, Weckerath, and Roth). In these small garrisons, there were between forty and fifty troops in some and only fifteen to twenty in others. In Kerwinkel, the commander of this little garrison of between forty to fifty troops, Lt. Kenneth Ferrens was attacked by the German 3rd Parachute Division (a parachute division has about 10,000 troops).

Lt. Ferrens waited until they were almost on top of the outer coil of barbed wire before opening fire. The first fusillade of fire did terrible damage to the German column, but those who survived, dispersed and pressed the attack. Several got inside the village where fighting raged at close quarters, but the vastly out-numbered Americans, firing from dug-in positions, had the advantage. "Surrender, Americans," yelled some of the Germans. "You're surrounded."

It was just about daylight when the Germans finally began to withdraw. One of the last to leave shouted toward Lt. 'Ferrens' command post, "Take a ten minute break, soldier. We'll be back!"

Lt. Ferrens responded, "And we'll be waiting for you, you son of a bitch."

In the meantime, the Troop C executive officer, 1st Lt. Aubrey Mills, had made it back through a hail of small arms fire into Kerwinkel in a half-track loaded with ammunition. As Ferrens had promised, the defenders were ready when the German paratroopers, wearing their white camouflage suits, made a second assault. Some got into the lower edge of the village, but that was all. At least 150 Germans died in the two assaults. In this battle, only two Americans were wounded and one killed. Lt. Aubrey was killed as he tried to bring up more ammo.

In the meantime, Capt. Reppa, in a defensive position above Manderfeld, ordered me to take the 1st platoon and do combat patrols to the north, east and south of Manderfeld to try to keep the roads open between Lt. 'Ferrens' troops and Manderfeld. This was a job! Germans were moving between the little villages, trying to cut them off from the rear. After some intense fire fights, we would stop one group only to have them break through somewhere else, but we did manage to keep the main road open.

Lt. Ferrens again was almost out of ammo, and as German troops were bypassing him on both flanks, he had to withdraw or be cut off from the rear. He was able to withdraw through Manderfeld, covered by guns of A troop. Capt Reppa ordered me back to A troop, where we were told that the German troops were passing to the southwest of our position in force and if we didn't leave at once, we would be cut off from the rear. Remaining in Manderfeld as the afternoon wore on, the situation around us worsened. Permission was given and we withdrew to the northwest. We were the last troops to leave Manderfeld.

As we left, German tanks were entering town from the east. In gathering darkness, artillery duels were taking place all along the line with 50 and 30 caliber tracers, buzz bombs and screaming meemies. This was lighting up the sky like the Fourth of July, only much more deadly. After several miles, we came to the village of Honsfeld where we set up defensive positions.

I set up my first platoon on the northwest edge of Honsfeld close to the road that led to Bullingen, which was about three miles away. In between these two towns were twin air strips for artillery observation aircraft. My location was good. We had a house, a barn and a machine shed all enclosed by a high, wide stone wall. I was able to get all my team and equipment inside, which later turned out to be a bad deal.

We got into Honsfeld a little after 2200 hours on December 16, 1944. We were told that we were miles behind the line of combat and that this was the 99 Division rest camp, so get a good night's sleep. I picked out a house and barn for my team, which consisted of an M8 armored car and two Jeeps. My men slept in the barn. There was a thick wall around the yard with an entrance wide enough to get my vehicles inside. The house was occupied by a family of five consisting of the mother and father and three children, one girl and two boys. They seemed very disturbed about what was happening, but I repeated what I had been told about this being a rest camp and that there was nothing to worry about.

Sadly, one more terrible deed remains to be mentioned about Honsfeld. Two nights later, the few civilians still living in Honsfeld had all settled for the night in one of the staunchest cellars in the village. Five SS troopers called down from the top of the stairs and wanted someone to show them the way to Bullingen. Although a young man offered to do it, the Germans spotted sixteen year-old Erna Collas, whom everyone said was the prettiest girl in the village. They insisted that she show them the way.

Erna went with the soldiers, but never returned. In the spring, after the snow melted, they found her body in a shallow grave alongside the road to Bullingen, shot seven times in the back. There was no way to tell if she had been raped. Sadly, this was the girl from the family we had stayed with earlier.

Because Capt. Reppa seemed concerned enough to put out a perimeter defense, I put a man in my M8 on the radio and got the other men bedded down. I took my blanket and went out and slept on the back of the M8 armored car. The vent from the radiator comes out on the top, and we had to keep the motor running for the radio, so I was pretty warm. The reason I was sleeping outside was that we had a new first lieutenant with no combat time and I wanted to make sure we were in close communication with HQ.

In the early hours of the morning, I woke up to the sound of the radio and heard the message that German tanks were in town. I tried to get HQ, which was near the center of town, but couldn't get an answer. Shortly after, Sgt. O'Brien (from Springfield, Illinois) came running up to tell us that our C.O., Capt. Reppa, and our C.P. had been captured.

I rousted everyone out with the first lieutenant and pointed out a place on the map for us to meet, and started out to see if there was any way of freeing our captured people (Reppa's group). By this time, there were a lot of flares, and by their light, I saw a heavy tank headed for our position. I ran back and grabbed an old captured panzerfaust (a heavy German anti-tank gun; I carried several of them as our bazookas would not stop the German Heavy tanks). With it, I was able to damage it, but it was not completely disabled and it came to a stop directly in front of the entrance to where my vehicles were parked. Unable to get our vehicles out, I headed on to the center of town on foot. As I got closer another flare went up and by its light, I could see two heavy German tanks and a lot of armored vehicles—half tracks, flack wagons and many German troops.

I realized that there was nothing I could do and saw why I had not been able to contact anyone by radio. Our HQ communication Jeep was crushed under the tread of a large German tank. At this point, I headed back to my unit. At one point on the way back, I saw Americans and Belgium civilians lined up against some walls. It looked like they were going to shoot them. (I understand that some were shot. I didn't find this out until later.)

I returned to where we were staying and my troops had already left. I checked my M8 and took the maps, daily radio code and code machine out of it and set a demolition charge. I decided to check the house again and make sure everyone was out. Everyone was out, including the family.

While I was checking the barn, several enemy troops entered the house, so I had to fight my way out. In a short time, I located the rest of my unit. A short distance north of Honsfeld, there were two air strips and I thought we might find some friendly forces there, but they were getting ready to pull out. There was a small group of combat engineers, I think from the 1st infantry division. They had been ordered to set up a road block between Bullingen and Honsfeld. They started to dig in at the edge of a patch of scrub brush on a hill overlooking Honsfeld. They had scant time to dig in when they heard tracked vehicles and German voices about six a.m.

We, along with this group, opened fire. In the darkness, we could make out German soldiers piling off a tank and six half-tracks. They were paratroopers that Peiper had sent ahead of his main force. We repulsed a first assault and what appeared to be two more, but shortly after seven a.m., as it was beginning to get light, twelve German tanks joined the attack. Lacking any defense against the tanks, the engineers fell back to the north toward Bullingen. They wanted us to go along, but that was heading out of our sector, so we headed west toward Moderscheid.

In Moderscheid, there was an aid station. It must have been temporary. There were two nurses and one doctor with one ambulance, a Jeep and some other vehicles. We informed them that they should get out fast as the point of Peiper's main force was only about three miles away.

Just on the east edge of town was a T road that went northeast to Bullingen. The way this was located, we had cover to get back through town. We had nothing to fight with, so we dug several holes like we were planting mines and tossed some brush over them, and as the point of Peiper's column came in sight, we fired a few rounds.

As we pulled back through town, we found an abandoned "tank recovery vehicle" that still had fuel, so we again had transportation and were able to keep ahead of Peiper's tanks. This was just luck, for I don't think we could have stayed ahead of them on foot. Anyway, we bought just enough time for the aid station to get out.

We left Modrscheid, headed for Baugnez. As we went through the town of Thirimont heading north, we noticed a side road leading west, so we took this road (hardly more than a trail). After about a mile, it hit the main road from Baugnez to Recht. As we hit this road, we stopped before turning north to Malmedy. We heard a lot of tanks, vehicles and shooting. The guns didn't sound like ours (the Germans had a high rate of fire). I dismounted and went into the woods at the top of the hill. From this point, I could see lots of German tanks and men. I couldn't see what they were shooting at. With the large number of German men and equipment, I figured we had better turn to the south, so we headed toward Recht.

What I had witnessed was the "Malmedy Massacre." This was Peiper's main attack group. If we had have turned north, we wouldn't have had a snowball's chance in hell. (For the uninformed: the Melmedy Massacre was the dastardly massacre of over seventy American POWs by the ruthless SS Panzer Division leader, Joachim Peiper, in his desperate counter drive to push the American forces back on his drive toward the sea).

As I said earlier, we hit this town, I think it was Recht, held by an American Infantry outfit, just as things were going all to hell all along the front. The commanding officer called us into the command post wanting to know what was happening up where we had come from and also the number of enemy troops, equipment and etc. We tried to tell him, but we were cold, tired, hungry and lacked sleep, so he gave us a couple of shots of Vat 69 Scotch to keep us going. After that, he sent us to the Mess for a hot meal and told us to then find a house and get a good night's sleep.

We found a house with a feather bed upstairs and sacked out. The next morning we awakened to the sound of gunfire. The American troops had pulled out (they must have forgotten about us). We had to go out the upstairs window and jump off the roof into an enormous manure pile. After things settled down, we were able to dispatch a couple German troopers to a better place and then make our way out of town.

It's a good thing that most of the houses had the barns attached. Although manure doesn't smell very good, it was warm and a good place to hide. It was very cold outside, especially after rolling out of those wonderful feather beds. We almost had trouble with the two German troopers. They smelled us almost before we got close enough to take them out.

As the Americans had already pulled out of the town, we were on foot again. We managed to find the road to Poteau, which we thought was only about 2 1/2 miles away. We just hoped we could make it there before the Germans.

We managed to make it. Although the Germans had captured the town we were in, they did not immediately march on to Poteau. If they had, they would have probably captured both of us and Poteau. We made our way on south to Poteau and joined the 18th Recon Squadron and some of the remaining 32nd Squadron Assault Gun Troops.

In Poteau, a small task force was created to attempt to retake Recht. The task force was composed of several light tanks and 75 mm assault gun tanks with supporting troops of the 32nd. In the darkness and fog, the task force had advanced only a short distance past the last house in Poteau when a rocket from a panzerfaust struck the assault gun, setting it on fire. German small arms fire erupted all along the road. The task force had run head-on into an attack on Poteau by troops of the 1st SS Panzer Division. Fighting a delaying action, the task forces' armored cars, half track, tanks and assault guns fell back on the road junction.

For the rest of the morning, these cavalry men held the road junction against a determined German infantry attack supported by self-propelled enemy tank destroyers. When a group of Germans set up a machine gun on a wooded hillock overlooking the road junction, a patrol of cavalry men swarmed up the hill from Poteau and we knocked it out. We turned back several attacks, but for all our valor, we were never-the-less engaged in a hopelessly uneven fight. The Germans were closing in when the colonel, soon after midday, ordered a withdrawal down the road toward Petit Thier. We had managed to hold the enemy up long enough to upset their timetable. It was small battles such as this that caused the Germans to lose the whole battle.

After the battle, my seven men and I were sent back to Petit-Thier to dig in on a hill above the town, as security for the 7th Armored Division artillery positions in the valley behind the hill. These were all self-propelled 155s and there were a lot of them. They were firing right over our heads continuously, twenty-four hours, day and night. At night you would see an enormous flash of light as all of these big guns fired, and then you would hear the sound, which was almost deafening. When you saw the light, you would put your hands over your ears and try to get lower in your hole. I can't remember how long we were there. It seemed like forever. I had lost track of what day and time it was, but we were there until all the units had been pulled out, along with the artillery, to Vielsalm.

We did no major fighting here, but we were still hungry. In checking out some of the houses, I found two hams hanging in the attic of one. It looked wonderful, BUT sometimes the Germans would poison things like this. There was a scroungy old dog hanging around, so we cut off meat from several different places and fed him. The next morning, he was still in good health, so my seven men and I had some good food for one meal. (This may sound cruel, but the old dog would have died of starvation without the bones and scraps.)

At some point while at this position, we had picked up a half track, so we again had transportation. There was no more fighting there except a few rounds of small arms' fire. We had orders to pull back into Vielsalm. On the way, at the last turn before the bridge, we ran into an enemy combat patrol, but we were able to fight our way through.

As we approached the bridge, the demolition team had finished setting charges and one of them was standing with his hand on the plunger, ready to blow the bridge. As we pulled up the hill into town, I looked back just as the bridge fell into the river.

This ended the Bulge Battle for me FOR A SHORT TIME.

We went on to Liege, where we got replacements of men and equipment and started back to the south around Andler. It is hard to put a time and location frame to this. While I was there, I received my Battlefield Commission for action in Luxemburg. I had not had time to pick it up previously because I had been moving too fast for it to catch up with me.

On the pull back, we crossed the Salm River into Vielsalm, and I thought, for a short time, that the Bulge was over for me.

Vielsalm was in our hands and there were still nurses and Red Cross girls in town. They helped cook, etc., so I thought we were safe. It was not long before I found out how very, very wrong I was. Several German tank divisions had crossed the Salm River several miles both above and below Vielsam and were attempting to encircle the town. Once again, we were caught between a rock and a hard place.

I still had my seven men and the same replacement first lieutenant and also my half-track. The job of the Americans in the town and surrounding area was to prevent the Germans from completing the circle. For the present, my group had not received any assignment. It just so happened, that sitting outside a nearby house, was a tank that no one seemed interested in. I said to my men, "Guys. I'm sick and tired of fighting tanks with carbines. I'm going to 'borrow' that tank." And with that, I told my driver to check it out. He wasted no time informing me that he didn't know how to drive a tank. Sgt. Pat O'Brian (from Springfield) was still with me, so I said, "Pat, you are the tank commander. Get a crew and I will drive."

I jumped in and told my driver to follow us in the half-track. I took off down the street, and not being used to the tank, I took off the steps of the houses on both sides of the street for a couple of blocks. I turned on the radio and received a call from an infantry unit that needed tank support, so off we went. I said, "Pat, have you got plenty of ammunition ready?" About this time, we came up to the rear of the American unit. They had some light German armor that was giving them problems, as they only had light weapons.

Immediately following my orders to Pat to fire when ready, I heard the angry response from Pat, "This damn @#*@ gun won't traverse. It will only go up and down!" I told him to put the gun on target and that I would move the tank to the right or left. On my execution of this maneuver, Pat said, "That's it. Hold it. Hot damn, that's right on. Now pull right. I'll make a sweep with my machine gun." Again came the exclamation, "Right on," and "Mad Dog, we had better get the hell out of here before we run into some heavy German armor."

We now knew why the tank had been sitting there and not being used. During this small battle, my half-track had cut loose with their 50 caliber gun and completely destroyed the whole enemy unit, so we came out smelling like a rose. We took the tank back and parked it where we found it. I'll bet the people living along that street still wonder what happened to their steps.

While we were playing with our tank, headquarters had started to evacuate all the non-military people like the Red Cross girls and nurses, along with non-combat troops. In the meantime, I managed to find an ammunition dump and replenished our ammo for our carbines and 50 caliber machine guns and also picked up a few grenades and 30 caliber light machine guns with ammunition. We also filled our canteens and were issued one K-ration per man.

Now we were attached to a tank unit as a security for their tanks. Again, as we pulled out, we ended up as rear guard to keep the enemy from hitting us in the rear. As far as I could tell, we got everyone out and were now headed for Liege, Belgium, where we hoped we would be able to get more replacements of men and equipment. I think Liege was about forty miles away, so were talking about possibly two travel days because of the fighting we would encounter along the way. One thing that did disturb me was that our back door would be left open because Montgomery (British) had pulled the 82nd Airborne back on a line to Vaux-Chavanne. I said it before and I will say it again, in my opinion, if they had sent the British Army home, the war would have ended six months sooner.

As we moved from Vielsalm on toward Liege, we moved through the 82nd Airborne's main line of defense and we were now pretty much on our own. As it was getting on toward evening, we began to look for a good place to spend the night. We pulled off into woods and found that it was already occupied with one of our tank outfits that had set up a defensive position.

I asked their commanding officer if we could spend the night and he said OK, but he could sure use some ground security as his tanks were in the woods and just across an open field with a small road running down the middle, was another patch of woods that was full of German tanks. He was concerned that after dark, some of the Germans would sneak in and destroy some of his tanks with their panzerfaust. He wanted me to take my men down to this road in the center of the field and set up a guard position against infiltration. We would have good cover getting to the road, so we didn't worry too much. The commander told us that he didn't expect the German tank force to attack until daylight and for us to get back to his group at first light.

The night was quiet with just a few rounds of artillery fire and a scattering of small arms fire. As dawn started to break, we headed back to our tank unit, but when they saw us, they began to fire at us. We had just found cover from their fire, when the Germans saw us from the other side and they started firing at us. Talk about being between a rock and a hard place! I didn't know what to do, so we just slung our guns (military jargon for placing the gun sling on our shoulder) and put our hands on top of our heads and started running toward our own lines and thank heaven, our people stopped firing. On the way back to our lines, we had to cross a barb wire fence and in crossing, I tore most of my clothes off. My point Jeep driver, Robert Ford from Novelty, Ohio, was running beside me (his nickname was "Bardouche").

After we reached our line, I said, "Bardouche, how did you get over that fence without tearing your clothes?" He gave me a quizzical look and said, "What fence?" That is just an illustration of how you can do almost anything when things go all to hell.

When we got settled down a little after reaching our lines, we discovered why we had come under friendly fire from our own troops. One of those few rounds that had been fired during the night had wounded the commanding officer, who had asked for our help, and he had been evacuated to the rear and no one else knew that we were out there. At that time, there were a lot of German soldiers dressing in American uniforms trying to sneak through our lines, so our men just considered us fresh meat. This illustrates how just one little mistake can get you killed.

I still don't know how Bardouche got over that fence. A little more about him. He lied about his age when he enlisted and he had his seventeenth birthday just shortly after we hit France. He was the best damn Jeep driver I ever saw. I would have to stand up in the Jeep so I could see better than he and he trusted me with any instructions I gave him. If I said, "Quick! Turn right!" he would do so without question, even though it might be over a fifty foot embankment.

After the friendly fire engagement, we left the tank unit and were very happy to do so, as they had become heavily engaged in battle with the opposing German tank force and our half-track had no defense against the tanks' big guns. I was afraid that some stray shell would destroy our only means of transportation and the rest of the troops and I had already had enough walking.

We went down the road and happily left the fighting behind for awhile. We were again heading for Liege, hopefully to get our replacements of men and equipment. We were also supposed to meet (in a small village just outside Liege) with any one of our unit who was lucky enough to have survived the horrible and one of the largest battles ever fought by the U.S. Army.

When we finally did reach this small village, I still had with me Sgt. Pat O'Brian, Bardouche, Hernandez, and the replacement first lieutenant (I don't think he could have made it on his own.) As for Hernandez, he was the best damn mortar gunner in the Army. I think he could have dropped one down a stove pipe if you gave him half a chance. This was a wonderful group!

On arriving at this small village, we were completely away from the combat zone. They were still sending over some of the old V-1 buzz bombs aimed at Liege, and since these were not very accurate, sometimes they would hit close to our village.

The first thing to do was to find a place to stay and a place for our mess sergeant to set up his kitchen. I really lucked out again. I ended up in the Burgomaster's (mayor's) house. He had a wife and a young daughter who was in her early twenties. The first thing the mother and daughter did was to cook us a good home-made meal. They raised cattle, hogs, a garden and fruit trees, so we had a wonderful meal of fresh food, even homemade pie. This could not have come at a more opportune time, because all of our kitchen equipment was lost during the Bulge and it would not be replaced and set up for another day. The rest of our guys had to settle for eating K-rations. Only the lieutenant and I ate at the Burgomaster's house!

That night, our commanding officer, who lived in another house (the command post) close to the Burgomaster's house, was invited to dinner. After dinner and a short meeting, we were able to take a bath and shave. The father loaned us some clothes to wear while the mother washed our filthy clothes. That night, we had the first good night's sleep in I don't know how long. We even had clean white sheets. This was as close heaven to as we were going to get. Being deprived of something can sure change one's outlook!

The next morning we had the luxury of sleeping in and awakened to the smell of frying bacon, eggs and the works. For a short time, we wondered where we were (thought maybe it was heaven), then they sent the daughter up and called us down to breakfast. After finishing that unbelievable meal, we started looking around to find friends who had been missing.

Outside of my own platoon, not too many made it out. I think one of the reasons was that when we went into Honsfelt, I placed my platoon on the northwest side of town and put a man on radio watch in each team so someone was awake to give us a chance to defend ourselves in event of an attack. Most of the others didn't have this chance, as the Germans hit the town from the southeast.

After another short meeting, we were assigned various duties and they included listing all the equipment we had lost in battle and explaining how and why we lost it. This proved to be a BIG job.

All the while, a few more of my friends began to turn up, but after all these years I can no longer recall their names. You cannot imagine the great feeling it is to see people you thought were dead

78

and then find them alive and well. Of course, there were many who had been wounded and had already been evacuated to hospitals in England and the U.S., and in this case, impossible to locate. Many others were killed in action, so the small remaining group of us was very lucky.

That night, after things had settled down, we (Pat O'Brian from Springfield and I from Lincoln) continued to look around for others that were missing. We noticed a 75 mm assault gun on a light tank, and since we had several in our group, we knocked on the door of the house that it sat in front of. A lieutenant came to the door and as he looked at me and I looked at him.

"Don't we know each other?" he exclaimed. After another careful look, I said, "I think so! I'm from Lincoln, Illinois. Your dad has the cab company there!" It was Lt. William Madigan from Lincoln! It really made me feel good to find someone from home this far away. We spent a lot of time together while we were at this location. The next day, we would continue on to Liege to start picking up our new equipment. Things were starting to shape up.

Upon arriving in Liege, instead of picking up equipment, I was ordered to report to the hospital. I had to have a physical and be discharged as an enlisted man and then re-enlisted as a commissioned officer. This sorta rearranged my day. The doctor finished his part of the examination and then the nurses had to take x-rays, blood test, blood pressure, etc. While they were performing their procedures, we received a V-1 buzz bomb alert, so we all had to make a run to the fallout shelter with me only in a hospital gown following this cute little nurse (Actually there was more than one cute little nurse).

I was afraid that being a healthy young man and not having seen a pretty girl in a long time, I might embarrass myself, but as an officer and a gentleman by an act of Congress, I used all my efforts to be proper. You don't realize how hard it was to be half dressed and have to follow a group of good looking nurses into a dimly lit fallout shelter. There should have been special training to cover situations such as this! I did survive, but it was hard and I got back to the hospital without making a complete fool out of myself.

One little nurse grinned at me and said, "You were having a hard time of it, weren't you?" I said, "Lieutenant, you don't know how hard." I asked her what she did when these alerts happened at night (their tent quarters were a long way from these fallout shelters). She said, "I just cover up my head and say a prayer. We only had one hit that wounded anyone and that was not serious, so I guess we've been lucky."

I sure hated to leave this sweet little thing. After getting all my papers signed, I headed back to our headquarters in our small village, although I would have much rather stayed there and protected the nurses.

When I got back, I was told to report to squadron headquarters. Major Krake told me that the news media wanted to do an article on me and to take some pictures in front of my armored car. This was fine with me. It was cold out and the snow was still halfway up to our asses. I thought we would get it over with real fast. He told me to report over to a park close to the center of the village in thirty minutes. I quickly shaved, and when I got there, the whole squadron was lined up in the deep snow. They stood with me in front of my armored car and Major Krake pinned my bars on while everyone stood at attention out in the cold with snow halfway up to their asses. I guess you know that this didn't make me many friends. They only took a picture of Krake and me in front of the armored car. The picture and article did make my hometown newspaper along with the Chicago and Springfield papers.

They dismissed the troops, and although people were happy for me, they were very unhappy about having to stand out in the snow for almost an hour. Remember, we had just come through the Bulge and had been sleeping out in these conditions for weeks, so although I had been leading my platoon for some time and I had only been an officer for a few minutes, they were already treating me like all the other officers and blaming me for making them stand out in the snow for an hour. I was beginning to think that maybe this being an officer was not going to be all that it was cracked up to be.

With the ceremony out of the way, the next day we started getting the replacements of men and the rest of our equipment. Now, as an officer, I received my first order from our commander. I was to take two half-tracks with twenty-four troopers and go to a supply depot on the edge of Liege and pick up twelve new M-8 armored cars with all the guns and ammunition that the "Table of Organization" called for. He also told me that any extra equipment we could pick up would be appreciated. I then asked him if I could pick the men to go with me. He replied that beside the drivers, I could use any men in the village that were not on duty.

With his permission, I called in Sgt. Pat O'Brien and told him to pick out any NCO that would be good at "Midnight Requisitioning." I told Pat to tell these guys to load anything they could get by with into our vehicles when we got to the depot. (During my examination, I found that I'd lost a little over fifty pounds in the two weeks we were cut off with no food. Sleeping out in twenty degrees below zero cold and snow, only food roots to eat, etc.)

We got on our way. I instructed Pat that when we got to the depot, if possible, I would get the officer in charge and he should get the NCOs and we would try to get them off to one side and then let our men see what they could do. When we arrived, we found that this was going to be much easier than we had anticipated. The Bulge was still in progress, and in the distance big guns sounded off. These people in the depot (all non-combat), officers and all, were anxious to know what was going on, so while Pat and I kept them busy, our boys were busy loading anything they could get their hands on. We let them think the enemy was much closer that they really were. When we pulled out of the depot, the M-8 armored cars were so full that no one but the drivers could get inside.

After we had loaded up and gone down the road a little way, I pulled over to the side of the road and stopped. I wanted to double check our map, since we had left town by a different route and wanted to make sure we didn't make a mistake and run into the Germans. The way we were loaded down, it would have been impossible for us to use our guns.

As Pat was looking at the map, he said, "Lindy, I have a brother in that infantry outfit down the road a short distance." I said, "Pat, let's go down there and see if he's there. We're not supposed to stop, but we have to rearrange this extra equipment so we can get some of these cars ready to fight. While I'm doing that, you can see if you can find your brother."

We proceeded down the road and stopped at the other outfit. We took stuff out of the cars and stacked it on the back of others, which we couldn't do back at the depot. As a result, we had four armored cars ready to fight. In the meantime, Pat found his brother right away and they had a good visit. It must have been great. I know it was not long enough, but we had to be on our way.

When we got back to our own outfit, I reported to our commanding officer. He came out to look at the equipment, and with an astonished look on his face, he exclaimed, "Fancher! Was there anything left in that depot?"

I replied, "Sir, if we had've had more room, there would have been even less."

He said, "We have to get this stuff under cover. If we have an inspection, we'll all be in the guard house!"

You must remember, we had just fought in the largest battle in US Army history, and if we only had the ammo and equipment the TO called for, we would've all been dead. We did not intend to be caught short again.

While we were gone, the commanding officer had sent another team to pick up twenty-four Jeeps, so we were getting back to fighting strength. I was able to put my armored car and two Jeeps in the barn where I was staying, so all we needed now was replacements of men, and the CO said they had been promised to him for the next day. He said we should make up a schedule so we could keep them busy, as we would not have much time until they would send us back to the line.

"I think," he said, "according to the last report I had, that we have the Germans in the Bulge stopped, so now, all we have to do is drive them back to where they came from. Tomorrow is another day and it should be interesting."

I had arrived late in the afternoon, and after I had reported to the CO and put our vehicles in the Burgomaster's barn and shed, I was called into the office for a short meeting, after which I started my equipment check. As I mentioned before, the Burgomaster had a rather pretty young daughter, probably in her early twenties. Every time that I would go into the barn, she would find some excuse to come in the barn also, but of course the mother or father would be close behind her. She followed me around like a love sick puppy and I didn't know what to do, as the mother and father watched her like a hawk. We really didn't want to make this Burgomaster unhappy, as he had really been wonderful to us. It was a little upsetting, as it became noticeable, even to the CO and all the other officers, who all teased me about not getting anything done.

Just to give you a little background, these people had been living under German occupation for almost four years. Although there had been very little fighting in that area, the Germans had taken all the young, able-bodied men and put them either in the German Army or work camps. This included her brothers, so the poor girl was starved for companionship. I tried to be nice to her but the way her folks watched her, it was pretty hard to have a one-on-one relationship.

This went on until one day the mother had to go to visit a sister. My C.O. said, "I think this girl (her name was Marie) has the hots for you. We' need to give her a chance to be with you or she's going to have a breakdown. Tonight we'll throw a big party in the Burgomaster's office and invite her and her father, and then we'll get her father drunk and give the girl a chance to do what she wants."

To be honest, I didn't much like the idea. Still, the party would be a lot of fun. They had the mess hall fix a lot of food, and as the evening wore on, bottles of fine French brandy were brought in. Everyone was having a wonderful time. They poured the father double and triple shots, and for me, maybe a half a shot. The old burger was going one-on-one with everyone. I was getting to where I was having trouble standing up, yet even the girl was going one-on-one with everyone. It was getting late. An old V-1 buzz bomb fell short and hit just outside the village. This put a damper on the party.

That was about all I remember, except the next morning I woke up undressed in bed in the Burgomaster's house, with a terrible hangover. The Burgomaster came in and told me that Marie had gone to the barn to get fresh eggs and would be fixing breakfast soon. I asked him, "How did I get home?"

"Marie helped us both get here, and I was pretty drunk so I went on to bed," he said. "I think Marie undressed you and helped you into bed."

I don't remember any of it, so I guess the best laid plans of men and mice often don't work. As for me, I don't know if she had her way with me or not. If she did, I don't remember a thing. She did bring me up a cup of coffee and set it by the bed and smiled at me. "Breakfast!" she said. "Get dressed and come on down."

To this day, I don't know what happened that night. I do know that I had one of the worst hangovers of my life. Drunk as I was, I don't think anything could have happened, but she sure seemed happy the rest of the time we were there. Maybe the girl just needed some male companionship. She must've had some experience, because I know how hard it is to get someone in my condition undressed. When I woke up, I was bare as a baby's butt and my clothes were neatly folded on the chair and looked like they had been pressed. All I really knew was that it was going to be a long day with all those new replacements arriving.

The replacement men were supposed to start arriving around 10:00 a.m., so until that time, we busied ourselves checking our equipment and deciding how we would use some of the extra equipment we had picked up, like the twin 50 caliber machine gun. It would fit right on the ring mounts of our armored cars. This would double our small arms firepower, and with the AP incendiary ammunition, would give us something with which to respond to the German fire from the multiple barrel 20mm flack wagons. A round from one of these would blow an arm or a leg off even if it just nicked you. They were supposed to be used against aircraft, but against ground personnel, they were horribly deadly. At least, now we had a weapon to respond with. This was just one of the many problems we tried to take care of.

Shortly after 10:00 a.m., our replacements began to arrive and it turned out to be pretty sad. They consisted of non-combat day room orderlies, cooks' helpers, typists and almost anything else you can think of. None of these people had any combat training and some were not even qualified with their individual weapons, so we really had our work cut out for us. One nice thing did happen as more people began to show up. Two men from my old troop showed up, Sgt. Charlie Wall from New York and Corporal Frank Ehrig from Chicago. Both were good men.

As these new men started arriving, we realized that we were going to have to move from this village to a place where we would have more room. We also needed a building big enough for a class room. After meeting with our officers, our CO called Squadron and they informed him that they had already found a place, as well as an old German SS range where we could target in our weapons.

I immediately took a detail and went to this new town to find quarters for our men. Being early, we would have our choice of some of the better places before they were all taken. This done, I sent Sgt. Wall and Corp Ehrig to take a 6 x 6 truck and get the replacements settled in.

By this time, it was getting close to evening and Sgt. O'Brian and I had to find drivers to move all our equipment early the next morning. I hated to leave where we were. The Burgomaster and his family were great and I usually had a home-cooked breakfast and a bed to sleep in. At the new place, it would be bags and floor.

We finally had everything ready to go for the next morning. We had to be on our way at daybreak because we had a short time to get these new men ready for combat. I don't think they should have sent any men overseas without proper training. Hopefully, we would have a few who would make drivers and gunners, as we were a highly mechanized unit. We had to get it across to them quickly that they were not going to stay alive very long unless they learned fast.

I wish that I could remember the names of all these small towns, but I've lost so many of my records in the move down here to Atlanta that I don't have much to go by. It really doesn't matter that much, as they are all pretty much alike.

I wanted to get a good night's sleep because I knew I was going to have "hell" for the next few days. I would probably earn my nickname "Mad Dog." Thank Heaven, I had Sgt. O'Brian, Sgt. Wall, Corp. Ehrig and also a PFC driver (can't remember his name) that I could depend on. Tomorrow was going to be the big day. I had been looking forward to being able to go back to the front and kicking some ass, but with this fresh group, I was worried.

The next morning, we departed from Liege. I rolled out of bed just before daybreak and called Sgt. O'Brian and said, "Get these guys out of their bunks." Outside, it was raining and cold.

"When you get them mounted up, let me know, and if you have any trouble, have Wall, Ehrig or Bardouche help you. Don't take any crap off the new guys. They have to learn fast. When you get done, send Bardouche back to me, as I want him for my Jeep driver. Corp. Ehrig knows PFC Franklin and knows he is a good driver."

Soon, Corp. Bardouche reported to me they were formed up and ready to go. We pulled around in front of this convoy and took off for our new location and arrived there wet and cold. We got the new guys into their assigned house and I reported to our CO. He said to have O'Brian get all the new guys into the gym with their individual weapons, and make sure they were all cleared.

After this, we had a short officers' meeting to update us on conditions and problems. The CO said, "I want you to have everyone possible paired with an old experienced soldier or NCO by the end of the day. I want everyone to be able to field strip their weapon as fast as they could get the clothes off a good looking girl, and of course they will also have to reassemble it in working order."

When I got back to the gym, I found a bunch of "smart alecks" who were not paying attention to their instructors. There was a small stage at one end of the gym and I climbed up there along with Sgt. O'Brian. Some stupid asshole accidentally shot a hole in the ceiling.

My answer to the shooter was, "I'm going to give you a break this time because you lack training, but if it happens again, I will court-martial you and send you to the stockade."

One guy smarted off at this. Sgt. O'Brian said, "That's enough!" The smart mouth was a big guy and O'Brian was small, so this guy said to O'Brian, "What are you going to do about it?"

I said, "That's enough. We will have no more of this. I don't like standing up here trying to teach you how to stay alive when I would much rather be double-checking our equipment to help keep us all alive."

There was some grumbling, and at that point, my Jeep driver, Bardouche, jumped up on the stage beside me, raised his Thompson submachine gun to fire about three feet over their heads and triggered off about 20 rounds, shoved in another clip, and in the deafening quiet said, "I want to introduce you to 'Lt. Mad Dog' If you were not so damn dumb, you would realize he's trying to teach you how to stay alive."

He went on to say, "I've been with him since we hit Europe and he was my sergeant, my platoon sergeant, and now my friend and platoon leader, so if you're going to screw up and get us all killed, I might just as well lower my gun and take care of you now. Also, for your information, we just came out of battle where we were outnumbered as high as 50 to 1, and if you open your eyes, you can see we are still here. If you endanger anyone here again, outside of that first accident, I'm not sure what he might do. Now, we are going to try again. I'm going to stand here beside 'Lt. Mad Dog.' I want to be sure he has your attention because down the road, what he says will probably save my life as well as yours."

I guess you know that after that, I had very little trouble. Every time I or any other NCO had a class, Bardouche stood beside us.

It was getting on toward evening, so we had to start checking to make sure all of our weapons were in working order, even though we were supposed to be in a safe location. If you remember, we were supposedly in a safe location when the Bulge started. Tomorrow would be another day and I sure hoped it would go better than this one. I also wished that these troopers were in better physical shape. It would be tough to choose enough men to go on an emergency combat foot patrol.

I called Sgt. O'Brian and told him to get the men out and call the roll and get them fed. After that we would start checking their records and qualifications. We needed Jeep drivers, and after much searching, I found one who qualified and told Sgt. Wall to bring him to my HQ.

The young trooper reported in and I said, "I understand that you are qualified as a Jeep driver."

"Yes, sir," he replied.

I then asked him to take the captain's Jeep down to the motor pool, which was only about a half mile away. A very short time later, he came back into HQ.

"You can't have already been to the motor pool!" I said.

His reply was, "No, sir, Lieutenant. That Jeep just quit and won't even move."

I called Corporal Ford (Bardouche) to pick me up and we went to the stalled Jeep. To make a long story short, he had driven almost to the motor pool with the emergency brake on and it had burned out and locked up. After only one small task, we already had a vehicle out of service, as the parts would have to be ordered. The only thing that could be done was to have Corp. Bardouche take him to the mess hall and put him on KP for a couple of days.

When I reported to the captain and told him what had happened, he said, "This is exactly what I expected. We need to get these troopers qualified with their individual weapons as soon as possible." I said, "Captain, it really scares the hell out of me. We'll probably have more casualties than we would in combat."

Much to my relief, he replied, "I just got off the phone with Squadron, and the major said they would have a training instructor sent." I once again had lucked out.

I had just breathed a big sigh of relief as he finished, when he added, "You are to take the troopers to the other range for heavy weapons, anti tank, grenade, bazooka, heavy machine gun and mortar training. When I checked with the range officer, they informed me that they had an opening at 2:30 p.m."

In the meantime, I explained to the troops some of the safety features of the 50 caliber machine gun. After this, we went on over to the mortar range to start training.

I had three mortar gunners that were all qualified, one being my old gunner, Hernandez, who had been with me since my former gunner had been killed on Stromberg Hill in Luxemburg. If you asked him to, Hernandez could put a mortar round in a stove pipe over a half mile away.

As for this range, it was the craziest set up I had ever seen. About a half mile away, they had three wooden sheds about 10 X 15 feet square, set up in plain sight. The whole thing with mortar fire is that you don't see your target from your mortar's location. You depend on your observer to target your objective, which in most cases, would be over a hill or behind buildings.

Be that as it may, we were behind the firing line, laughing and having a good time. Hernandez saw an old friend that he thought had been missing since the early part of the Bulge. They were having a good reunion when this smart aleck 2nd lieutenant instructor came over and chewed his butt out and told him he should be paying closer attention.

I didn't say a thing because I knew what was coming. The crew that he was instructing finished up and this range officer walked back over to Hernandez and said, "OK, mister smart aleck. Let's see what you can do."

At this point, I interrupted and said, "No, Lieutenant, I want him to go last, because if he goes first, there won't be anything for my other gunners to shoot at."

Hernandez said, "Lieutenant, that's right."

Each of the previous teams and its officer had fired three rounds each at these targets all day long and had not damaged one of them. My first crew fired and damaged the first target. My second crew fired and destroyed the rest of the first target. After this, I said, "OK, Hernandez."

He stepped up, set up his gun, held his hand up to shade his eyes, looked at the targets, aimed and dropped the first shell in. The second target disappeared completely. Again shading his eyes, he looked at the targets, aimed and dropped in his second shell and the third target disappeared. Looking out again, he turned to the smart aleck lieutenant and said, "Sir, would you like to see the first target hit in the middle?" He dropped his third shell and it dropped right in the middle of the first target. This was great for me.

Having finished our mortar practice, my next job was to assign crews to the Jeeps and armored cars. We had to transfer some of the replacements out, as they just couldn't grasp the training to use the equipment. With the troops we received as their replacements, we got some people who had been trained for mechanized cavalry reconnaissance, so this made my job much easier. Some of our wounded also ended up back at this time, along with a few more troopers who had been missing since the Bulge. Things were beginning to shape up for me now, and I had drivers for all our vehicles and most of them were qualified with their individual weapons. All they lacked now was a little practice, which they would receive on the way to the front.

I took all my armored car drivers and anti-tank gunners out to the range to shoot at some old, knocked-out enemy tanks so that they could see the difference between the armor on the light and heavy German tanks. I think this, more than anything else, showed them that our 37 mm anti-tank gun would not stop a heavy German tank and would only serve to make them "mad." This was a lesson that I learned the hard way when I first got over here. Even after making four direct hits on an enemy tank, he was able to return fire. Thank heaven, he used AP instead of HE, and I only had a couple of holes instead of being completely destroyed.

What I had to teach them was to use a captured German panzerfaust, as it would stop anything they had. Now we were ready to move up again. All the time, we were getting closer to where the fighting was going on.

There is one thing I want to mention before we leave this location. Several of these men had no training with grenades. A grenade training range has a four feet by six feet pit about five feet deep with targets set up about twenty feet in front of it. You hold the grenade with the spoon in the palm of your hand and then pull the pin. The grenade doesn't arm itself until it leaves your hand, releasing the spoon. After that, you have a four and one half second delay before it goes off. This is one of the most dangerous times for the instructor.

It is impossible to tell you how scared some of the troopers get when they first start grenade training, and when people get scared, no telling what might happen. This happened to me here for the third time. The trooper dropped the grenade when his arm hit the side of the pit, and in his excitement, he tried to climb out of the pit. Never enough time! I tried to grab the grenade, and all the time, he was in my way. I did succeed and threw the grenade out of the pit or I would not be writing this book. Again, thank heaven for that four and a half second delay.

I was watching for a mistake, so I was prepared! When I told him to stand still, you could have heard me all the way back to the good old USA. I think all the troopers learned one thing that day, ya gotta keep cool, but this was too close, as he was blocking my way. This might not be of great interest but it just goes to show, that you don't have to be in a combat situation to die.

90

Things were starting to come together. We would be moving out the next day. The day was about over and we went back in to chow down and settle down for the night. I didn't know what the next day might bring.

I had to report to the commanding officer on the day's progress, and in doing so, I got my rear chewed out. He said, "Fancher, you're an officer now. That instruction should have been done by a sergeant"

"The only sergeant we had available at that time didn't have grenade experience," I replied. We were still short two men at that time and as you know, good men are hard to come by. With that, he pulled out a bottle of Vat 69 and said, "I think you need a drink to relax. Tomorrow is going to be a rough day." That night, I said a prayer and tried to get some sleep.

The next morning after roll call, the men had breakfast in the mess hall and then went back to quarters to get all their personal effects together. We got "A" troop formed up and ready to go. We had several of our old men back and the new replacements were doing much better. We moved out, heading down to the area in the vicinity of St. Vith, Malmedy, Andler and all the other places where we had gotten the hell kicked out of us.

We had no more than got started when we got a radio call to hold up. It seems that they had some trouble back in "B" troop. One of the new replacements accidentally stepped on the floor trigger of his 37 mm anti tank gun and shot the head off the trooper in the car ahead of him. The poor guy's head was blown completely off. The safety should have been on because we had been ordered to load all our guns as our route would take us close along the line where the fighting was going on.

Things like this were the reason I was so tough and raised so much hell with my replacements. After the accident, we moved on down the road. I never did know what happened to that trooper. Probably someone got the book thrown at him over the incident (as they should have).

About an hour later, we ran into a German combat patrol of about fifteen or twenty men. I buttoned up our armored cars and we opened up with our 37 mm using HE (high explosive) and our 50 caliber, as well as our 30 caliber machine guns. The entire German patrol was wiped out. Thank heaven they did not have any panzerfaust, although I think we kept them far enough away that they could not have used them. Our only damage was some bullet marks in the paint of our new armored cars. In a way, this incident was a good thing as it gave our new men a feeling of what it was like to be shot at. A lot of the credit for us coming out of the incident unscathed was due to the vigilance of Bardouche, my point Jeep driver. He spotted the ambush before we got close enough for them to do us much damage. I think he must have had a sixth sense.

After this brief skirmish, we reformed and moved on down the road. All the new men were more alert now than they had been just a brief period before. I hoped we wouldn't have any more trouble as I had seen several mistakes that needed to be corrected. As a whole, though, I was not unhappy with the way they had performed.

I hoped we would get into this little village not far from St. Vith, before dark so I would have a chance to look everything over and make sure the town had been properly cleared. Then I'd need to find the best places for my men to sleep before all the choice places were taken. A lot of the signs with the village names on them had been knocked down, and unless you had an enlarged map, the names were not on the maps.

We did make it into the town before dark and it looked pretty good. I checked things out and started to get all settled in. The men were assigned to houses and I picked out one for my CP and then had Sgt. Wall post sentries while I checked out my CP. It seemed OK, although about all that was left was the basement. As I descended the basement steps, I was confronted with a horrible odor that I thought was probably from rotten potatoes, as the basement was piled all the way to the top with them. As I continued down the stairs, I heard a noise or movement of some kind that alerted me to take the safety off my gun. I said, "I think you had better come out and show yourself!"

Out from behind the potatoes crawled a little girl about nine to eleven years old and she was a terrible mess. She had gone to the toilet all over herself. She did speak English, but she was scared to death. I took her to the aid station where we got her cleaned up.

After getting her cleaned up, we tried to feed her, but it had been so long since she had eaten that all we could do was get a little water down her. I think that the only water she'd had while she was down there was what little seepage there had been in the basement. I don't know how long she had been down there, but she definitely needed water. Thank heaven, she could speak English. After getting a little water down her, she was able to tell us her name was "Anna." I can no longer remember her last name. We still needed to get food of some kind in her.

In our K rations, we had some beef bullion cubes. I put several of these and water in a canteen cup and set it over a quarter pound block of TNT to heat it up, as this was the fastest way I knew. Again, we could only feed this to her very slowly, just a spoonful at a time. To keep her warm and from going into shock, we wrapped her in an Army wool blanket, which is very scratchy next to the skin. I sent a detail out to try to find some kind of clothes we could put on the poor little thing. She kept saying, "Upstairs," and I realized that she meant in this house. This was the house she had lived in but by the time the men had found the clothes, she was fast asleep. She slept only for a short time, and then we were able to feed her some more, this time with a few crackers, but she was still very weak.

When she was finally strong enough, we found out what had happened. When the Germans had come through the town, her parents told her to go hide, which she did. She ran upstairs and hid in a very small closet under some old bed clothes. The soldiers found parts of American uniforms in the girl's house, so they shot her mother and father. Anna heard the shots, so she remained hidden there for a long time. When she finally heard the Germans leave, she came back downstairs and found both her parents dead. She thought she heard the Germans returning so she ran to the basement and hid behind the potatoes. She must have been there for a week or more. I think this was the same group of Germans who had murdered people in Honsfeld and Malmedy, including many captured American soldiers in many other small villages.

After all this exertion, Anna finally went back to sleep. She seemed to be sleeping soundly, so I figured I might as well try to get some sleep too. I brought my sleeping bag in and put it on the floor beside the cot where Anna was sleeping, then I decided to the check the area and the sentries we had out before I turned in. Everything checked out OK. Even though we were not in a combat zone, it was better to be safe than sorry. I'd seen too many people get caught with their pants down the past few days.

I wanted to be up early the next morning to see if I could locate some relatives of the little girl and I also wanted to scrounge up some extra equipment before we hit any heavy engagements. It's better to have too much than not have enough, and after being out of ammo in the early part of the Bulge, I didn't intend for it to happen again.

My "A" troop was in good shape, but in some of the other troops in the squadron, they still needed a few more men. While they were filling these gaps, I would have a chance to "fine tune" some of the few problems I had and would hopefully be able to find someone to take care of the little girl. I crawled into my sleeping bag and settled down for a good night's sleep. I was thankful that I was able to spend another night inside, as it was still pretty cold outside. We were supposed to have our Mess kitchen set up for the next day, so that would mean hot food to start out with, and also I hoped to get some solid food in the little girl. No one can realize how wonderful it was to see the appreciation in the eyes of this little girl for the kindness we had shown her in the middle of all this horrible carnage she had been through.

The next morning, still in the town where we had found the little girl, I was up early and not sure how long we would be there. I knew that we just couldn't leave Anna there alone, but I still had a platoon to take care of. I touched her gently to awaken her and told her that I was going to the mess hall to get her some food. Our mess sergeant found some dehydrated orange juice and some milk, and then made her some bacon, toast and jelly. I took this all back to Anna, who was wide awake and alert by now. I wish you could have seen that little girl's eyes light up when she saw that food. It made all the suffering and misery we had been through worthwhile. I had a very hard time trying to keep her from eating too fast, but she was keeping the food down and seemed to be gaining strength by the minute.

I told her that I was going to have to leave but that I had called my friend, Bardouche, to stay with her until I returned and had instructed him not to let anyone bother her. I had also told him to get as much water down her as possible but to do it slowly. With Bardouche caring for her, she would be as safe as if she had been in her mother's arms.

I then went to the commanding officer to see if there was anyway we could find some of her relatives. He said he was aware of the problem and would help as much as he could. We started checking all the villages around the area, some by our phone network and some by Jeep. This went on for a couple days and we finally found an aunt whose child had been killed while the Bulge was going on. This turned out to be a joy for two people.

I headed back to our unit, and when I told Anna the wonderful news, she exclaimed, "I don't want to go with her! I want to stay with you and your friends!" I explained to her that we were going to have to leave soon and wouldn't be able to take her because we would be fighting. She cried for awhile but finally said she did like her aunt and would go with her. I really think Bardouche had spoiled her while he was staying with her.

I informed the captain of the plans, to which he replied, "That is good! I have just received orders that we will be leaving day after tomorrow, so we had better get her transferred sometime tomorrow."

I sent a Jeep to pick up the aunt and bring her to us as I wanted her to see if she could find some clothes for Anna in the house.

The aunt arrived the next day about mid morning and checked out the house for clothes. She found several of the mother's clothes that she could make over for Anna. To make things even better, we took them both down to our officers' mess so they could eat lunch with us. To see them sit there and eat was really great. I don't know who enjoyed it more, our officers or Anna and her aunt. I don't think the aunt had been able to find much to eat for some time. Things were really rough for these people. The weather had been colder during this time than any time in the last fifty years.

After eating, I told Anna and her aunt goodbye and sent some food with them. Although the little girl cried some when she left, she was sitting on her aunt's lap, holding onto her very tightly. I think they were happy that they had found each other. It was sad to see these two people go, but wonderful that they had been united and I was sure that the fighting was over in this sector.

It is too bad that all Americans could not see some of the horror that these people had endured. It would make you pray that there would never be such a war as this in the United States.

My next job was to get things together as the next day we would move out and I didn't think things would be too peaceful. These stops did help get all the replacements more training and used to working as a team with the experienced troopers.

The next day, we were on our way again. I didn't know where we were headed, but I was hoping we would get back in the 3rd Army, but it appeared that we would remain attached to the 1st Army, and none of our troopers looked forward to this. The 1st didn't seem to know how to use a mechanized reconnaissance unit, but I guess that's life in the Army. No one seems to know where we were heading, but rumors had it that we were going up to the Roer River in Germany and that our route would take us through several villages that were still in enemy hands.

As we approached this one small village, I sent a recon patrol to check it out and they reported back that it was held by a small German force. We found a trail through the woods and by-passed the village with a combat team, thus subjecting the enemy to crossfire. We opened fire and in a very short time, inflicted heavy losses on the German force. They fought back for a short time, but we had killed or wounded about half their force. The rest surrendered and we sent them and the wounded back to Headquarters to be transported to prison camp.

As this village was in Germany, we had expected a cool reception, but evidently these German troopers had taken the civilians' food and molested some of the young girls, so they seemed glad to see us. We did a house to house search but found no enemy or equipment. As there was another small village just a short distance up the road, I sent a recon patrol to check it out. While we were waiting, we decided to eat. We were eating K rations, and there was always candy in them. The little boys and girls looked so hungry, we started giving them our candy. These were little kids, probably between five and ten years old. They seemed very happy to get the candy!

I then moved the platoon on through to the edge of the village and our recon patrol returned to report that there was no enemy in the next village. I told them that they might as well eat before we proceeded on. While we were eating, a little boy came alongside of our armored cars and the armored car behind me gave him some candy. He was probably eight or nine years old and seemed very happy to get the candy. I looked both back and forward checking the road and had just raised my hand to give the signal to pull out, when he jumped into the ditch at the side of the road and came up with a German panzerfaust and fired at the armored car.

In his haste, he almost missed, but the flying metal wounded two men slightly. That would have been the end of it, but he pulled another panzerfaust out of a culvert and was aiming again, so we had to shoot him, since a direct hit would have completely destroyed the car and killed all the men in it.

This is the horror of war. To this day, I can still see that little boy. We were just lucky. The civilians in town said he had been with the German soldiers and that he was one of the "Hitler Youth Gang." These children would shoot their own family members if told to do so or turn them in to be thrown in prison work camps or worse. I think that this was one of the most disturbing things that happened to me during the whole war. I have no idea who shot the poor misguided boy. We all just reacted when everyone saw the panzerfaust. I don't think anyone realized how young he was until after it was all over. I know it disturbed my sleep for weeks. This only goes to show you, WAR IS HELL.

We moved on out of this village on our way to more of the same. All these villages and towns were now in Germany and from the looks of it, we were heading for the Roer River Dams above Bonn, Germany. I think all the remaining towns and villages ahead had already been cleared.

I received orders that the 1st platoon of "A" troop would be going to the town of Berstein, Germany, which was on the Roer River above the dams. Again, the First Army had stuck it to us. We were taken out of our armored cars and unable to fight the kind of war we had been trained for. (Oh to be back in the 3rd Army where they knew how to use their personnel.) We were put into bunkers above these dams to try to keep the Germans from blowing the dams and flooding the Roer Valley across which the First Army was to attack. If the Germans succeeded in destroying the dam, it would turn the valley into one huge swamp.

We pulled into this town, again I no longer remember the name, but it was about five or ten miles from Berstein. There they set up Troop Headquarters, and there I had to leave all my armored cars, Jeeps and heavy weapons. We were only allowed to take our individual weapons, grenades, and two light machine guns. Thank heaven, they didn't put a limit on how much ammunition we could have.

I got a chance to go up and look at the town of Berstein, and then I realized why we couldn't take our own vehicles. The unpaved roads had thawed out and the mud was knee deep. As we looked over the town, it was at least sixty percent destroyed, but at least there was some cover from the enemy and some places for the 2nd platoon of "A" troop to be protected from the rain, which was coming down hard. The second platoon was our backup and relief, so after a week, we would exchange places.

We started back (we had gone up in a Jeep with chains on all four wheels), but I still didn't think we were going to make it as it was raining hard again. We did make it back and had a late hot lunch.

They then provided us with two 6X6 trucks and a Jeep with drivers, and then at about fourteen hours, we started out. We had only gone three miles when this stupid Jeep driver got stuck. If I'd had my driver Bardouche, this would not have happened. This turned out to be a big problem as we were in artillery range of the Germans across the river, and with all the noise he was making, they started to bracket our position.

I was riding in the first 6X6 truck and crawled out in mud up to my knees. I went up to the lieutenant in the Jeep who was in charge of the convoy. I asked him what he was going to do, to which he replied, "We're stuck!"

I said, "I can see that, and you also have two truck loads of men back there that are going to be dead if we don't get moving."

It was like talking to a rock, so I just reached in and grabbed the driver by the collar and gave him a pull and he landed face down in the mud. I got in the Jeep and in thirty seconds, I had the Jeep moving and gave the signal for the rest of the trucks to follow.

The Jeep driver whined, "What about me?"

I said, "Walk! Because you sure can't drive a Jeep."

We made it on into Berstein and I got the men and equipment unloaded quickly and told the lieutenant to get his damn trucks out of there, as they were only attracting artillery fire. He said, "I can't. My driver isn't here." I replied, "Then you had better drive it yourself or I will hook a cable onto the 6X6 and they can drag it out."

I could never understand why they would put people in jobs that they were not qualified for. He could have caused a lot of people to be killed. When you are under artillery fire, you have to keep moving.

After getting them out of the way, all we had to do was wait for dark. We would have to move across one of the worst mine fields I had ever seen, all the while with the enemy looking down our throats ready with rockets, 88 mm, artillery, machine guns and hard telling what else.

Berstein, Germany, the town that we were in, had been over half destroyed in the fighting. I don't think there were over two buildings left standing that had a roof or even part of a roof left on them. We still had at least three hours before it would be dark enough to start out. The unit that we were replacing had set up their headquarters in the one building that was pretty much intact.

I was called in by our commanding officer and we went over the locations of the bunkers that we were to occupy—which were located in a heavy forest across a big mine field that we would have to cross in order to reach them to set up our positions. They were on the steep forward slope leading down to Roer River and just above the Roer Dam. Our job was to keep the Germans from blowing the dam and flooding the Roer Valley, across which our American troops were attacking.

There was only one path cleared through the mine field, so we would have to wait for a guide to take us through after dark. Across the river, sloping up to two or three times as high as our side, was the enemy positions, some fortified with concrete emplacements with

88 mm rockets, machine guns, mortars, artillery and God knows what else.

After the bunker orientation, it was still raining and there was still no room in any of the shelters for my men. Finishing in HQ, I went back outside and we all lay down on the ground (in the rain) and put our steel helmets over our faces to keep from drowning, and then tried to get a little rest before we had to start across the damn minefield into the unknown. I hoped those bunkers were well built, because from where we were, we could see that they were being shelled every few minutes with enemy artillery. I understood that my command bunker was right in the center of these units and that there was room for only four troopers (that is if they were friendly), and that it was not high enough to stand up in. You could sit up without hitting your head on the top.

All the other bunkers were down the slope closer to the river than my command bunker, and they were only large enough for three troopers. I also heard that you couldn't leave the bunkers in the day time without drawing enemy artillery fire. I guess we got screwed again, as we were not trained or equipped to fight this kind of a war, but that's the way it goes in the Army. If the people at the top had to get down to action level, things would probably be different. As it was, all we had to do was wait for dark and our guide to start our new adventure. I think the waiting was one of the hardest parts of the whole war. When things start happening, you don't have time to think or worry, all you have time to do is die.

The following action resulted in my receiving the Silver Star.

As darkness started settling in, I headed back down to our CP to see if our guide had arrived to guide us through the mine field. I had just walked in and started to talk to our commanding officer when a trooper walked in to see the CO. He said he was to guide our men across the mine field.

Our CO said, "Lt. Fancher, get your men ready."

"Sir," I replied, "they are ready and we have been waiting out in the rain for over three hours."

With this, I went back outside and told my men to fall in and to make sure that everyone was there. I again went over the bunker positions where each team leader was supposed to place his men and made sure they all understood. Everyone seemed to know where they were to go after they got across the mine field and into the woods.

By this time, it was completely dark, so I asked our guide to explain how he wanted us to proceed. He told me to hold on to his back pack and have each trooper behind hold on to the pack of the man in front of him and step in the same place he did. As we started out, everything seemed to be going fine. When we were about two thirds of the way across, someone sneezed and the alerted enemy sent up a flare lighting the place up like midday. The guide froze in position and I looked back to check my men, who were each still holding on to the man in front of him as he'd been told to do. I turned back to the guide to tell him to get the hell moving, but found the no-good bastard had taken off, leaving us stranded in the middle of the mine field.

While this was happening, the Germans cut loose with everything they had—machine guns, mortars, everything. The German weapons took their toll. My platoon sergeant was killed and four men wounded, but the men stayed in position, thank heaven. To have moved off the path would have meant sure death by the mines. The flare soon burned out and again, thank heaven, the Germans did not send up another.

I whispered to the man behind me to stay in position and to pass it back that I was going to try to get them out. I got down on my stomach and started working my way back down the column. As I started back, I didn't know if I even had room to get turned around, so I started feeling with my fingers. I was able to identify the mines as the German S-mine, or as everyone called them, "Bouncing Betsys." This was a very dangerous mine. It had a propelling charge that would send it up in the air about three or four feet, then it would explode, usually taking out the groin area and stomach of its victim. This mine had a pressure type detonator which wasn't quite as sensitive as the spike detonator.

I started back down the column, giving first aid to the wounded men and marking the locations of the mines that I found, all the time whispering to the men to remain quiet. I was also very concerned about giving first aid to the wounded men after digging in the dirt

101

with my fingers, but I had no choice. Most of the men were not wounded too badly except for Sgt. Pat O'Brien, and I had to have someone carry him out. When I had taken care of these problems, I started to work my way back to the front of the column accompanied by a friend carrying Sgt. O'Brien.

I finally made it back to the head of the column, still on my stomach with my arms outstretched in front of me and feeling with my fingers. I instructed the man behind me to hold on to my feet and to pass it on back for each man to do the same and I would get them out. This proved to be much easier that I had thought it would be, because I could feel the foot prints in the dirt where people had crossed before. Anyway, I got my men out of the mine field and got them into their assigned positions in the bunkers. I was very upset at having one of my men killed and four others wounded, but all in all, we were very fortunate not to have lost more.

If that guide had moved faster and hadn't left us stranded, we probably would have had no casualties at all. I don't know what happened to the guide as I never saw him again, which was probably a good thing. Had I run across him, I don't think he would be alive today after deserting us in that terrible mine field.

I was very thankful for the time we spent in Normandy near the Cherbourg Peninsula, where I studied and disarmed at least two dozen of the S-Mine types. I found out that you had almost an eighth of an inch to play with on this pressure type detonator before it would go off. With the spiked detonator, all it took was one touch and it was too late.

On a lighter note, on working with mines and explosives, I found that I had a very sensitive touch. I attributed this to the specialized training that I received before I was even in the Army, like trying to get a pretty girl's panties and brassiere off in the back seat of a Model T Ford. I really think that this helped make my fingers sensitive, although I don't think the girls would have exploded like these mines if I'd made a mistake. I think you can see that one can never tell what kind of civilian experience will help you in fighting a war. It's much better to think of something like this instead of getting yourself blown up by a mine. Just as a footnote, I had more luck disarming mines than I did in the back seat of the Model T Ford, but now, at my age all I can do is dream.

Now back to the hell that is war. As I said, these bunkers are not high enough to stand up in, and with only room to sit up without bumping your head. In my command bunker, there was only room for four troopers at one time and someone also had to be awake all the time. As lieutenant in charge, I had to be able to leave and check the other bunkers, but I had no idea what all these positions were like, because only being able to move about in the dark, one could see nothing. Although it was not very cold, it was still uncomfortable. But with four men crowded into the small space, enough body heat was created to make the temperature half way tolerable. Now all we had to do was wait.

It was almost daybreak and I hadn't had any sleep, as I had been busy getting the wounded men out of the horrible mine field and to the aid station before daylight. When that was done, I had trouble sleeping so I took the three to six watch to get a better feel of the situation since it started to get light.

Although these bunkers were not large enough to stand up in, they were very well built. They were pits dug down in the ground and lined with logs on two sides and running back into the hill. They had logs across the front, leaving a firing slot about sixteen inches high all the way across the front. These logs were about six inches in diameter. Across the top, logs about eight inches in diameter were piled with dirt on top, then more logs across the other way, then more dirt and then more logs and then more dirt on top. The entrance was through the side. It was almost like a cave.

In my CP, we had telephones and one radio. We had light machine guns in the lower bunkers along with our individual weapons. A bunker with a mortar pit was what we needed up by my position, as our main objective was to keep the enemy from destroying the Roer Dam. I checked in with all my teams in the bunkers by telephone. These locations were down the slope closer to the river than my location. I could see the rear of all these bunkers through the trees from time to time. We would receive some artillery or mortar fire occasionally, but I think it would take a direct hit to do much damage to these bunkers.

Lincoln Officers in 32nd Cavalry that Held up Nazi Drive

LINCOLN COURIER, JAN. 30, 1945

Lt. William Madigan Jr. and Lt. Frank L. Fancher of Lincoln are members of the 32nd Cavalry squadron of the 14th Cavalry group that held a 9,000 yard sector on the left flank of the ill-fated 106th Infantry division at the point of the von Runsted counter offensive in Belgium Dec. 16 and held up the German drive for two days in a valiant stand that cost the cavalrymen heavily.

Both Lincoln officers came through the Battle of the Bulge safely although their mechanized group lost half of its vehicles and suffered severely in killed and wounded. Lt. Fancher, previously a Staff Sergeant, had been commissioned in the field prior to the battle in Belgium for bravery in action in Luxembourg while the squadron was attached to the Third Army.

When the German breakthrough came near St. Vith the 32nd Cavalry was in reserve with the First Army in Belgium, reorganizing after hard fighting with Patton in Luxembourg. The small cavalry group held a section of front that would ordinarily have been assigned to two divisions and stayed and fought off German tanks until ordered back to St. Vith the night of Dec. 17 for reorganization of its shattered ranks.

Press release on local men (including the Author) that held up three German Divisions that attacked through a 9,000 yard gap during the Battle of the Bulge. This gap was defended by only seven or eight hundred US soldiers.

104

Lt. F. L. Fancher Wins Silver Star

Fancher, 309 Pekin st., has been awarded the Silver Star Medal for gallantry in action against the enemy Feb. 9 in Germany. Lt. Fancher was previously commissioned in the field from the grade of staff sergeant for leadership of his platoon in securing and holding an important hill in Luxembourg last January.

The citation accompanying the award reads: "Lt. Fancher, a platoon leader, was leading his platoon at night through a heavily-mined field when the enemy sent up flares and then laid down a barrage of artillery, mortar and rocket fire on the platoon. He instantly deployed his men and then, in the face of enemy fire, courageously administered first aid to four of his wounded men and assisted in their evacuation. Lt. Fancher's outstanding leadership and gallant action further enabled his platoon to reorganize and successfully accomplish its mission."

Lt. Fancher, son of Mr. and Mrs. Ben Fancher of Mason City, is a member of the 32nd mechanized cavalry reconnaissance squadron.

Public Relations Office press release on Author being awarded the Silver Star for Gallantry in Action Against the Enemy.

Picture of Author receiving his Battlefield Commission. The picture was taken just outside of Liege Belgium in January, 1945

Picture taken of Author receiving the Silver Star award for Gallantry in Action Against the Enemy. Paris, 1945.

As the morning wore on, things stayed about the same. Several times, the enemy tried to reach the dam with explosives, but my lower bunker teams would take them out before they got very far. If we would've had mortar, I think we could have blown up their explosives long before they even got close.

As you have probably guessed, the trees were all bare. With no cover, if nature called and you had to go to the bathroom during daylight hours, you had to do your job in an empty K ration box, which is quite a feat (it is only about as big as an old Cracker Jack box), then close the box and throw it as far as you could through the firing opening. To get your pants down and hit this small box in such a cramped place where you could not even stand up straight poised quite a problem. Where else could you have this kind of fun and togetherness?

This is where we should've had a co-op Army with women. I think it would have been interesting to see how they would have handled this situation. Most people never realize how difficult and sometimes almost impossible everyday situations can become under battle conditions, but we did cope and managed to survive. I have often thought that if a man and a woman had to live under these conditions for a short time, there would either never be a marriage or it would be a marriage that would last forever.

Back to the action, I got on the phone and checked on my troops. Sgt. Charlie Wall had seemed a little upset about being in such a closed space as small as these bunkers. When he answered the phone, he seemed very happy. His team had wiped out an enemy demolition team before they even got close to the river, let alone the dam.

It was still very upsetting to be in this kind of a position where the enemy is just across the river, twice as high as we were and looking right down our throat from above. So far things were going good, so we ate our lunch and kept the empty K rations boxes for our toilet.

As I have already mentioned, things had been pretty quiet with the exception of a few rounds of enemy artillery that hadn't done much damage. One of these light barrages had just finished and we had started to eat our lunch, when all hell broke loose.

It was one of the heaviest artillery barrages that I had seen since we were in this location. It was even starting to rip the logs off the top of our bunkers. On closer examination, I discovered that it was our own artillery.

I immediately grabbed the phone and called command. Just as they answered, the artillery took out our phone lines. I immediately set my radio up outside the entrance so that I could raise the antenna, and just as I pulled the mike down inside the bunker, another round hit close and put a hole though my radio that you could have put your fist through.

This was not the first time that I'd had problems with friendly fire, although it was the first time in a fixed position and I was mad as hell. I had no communication with command at all after my radio was destroyed. In order to contact HQ, I would have to leave my bunker and go through the timber and make my way across the ungodly mine field in broad daylight. As the commanding officer, I could have sent one of my men, but since none of them had crossed the field without a guide, it fell on me to do it myself. I told them that I would go and for them to keep their heads down.

When there was a slight lull in the barrage, I took off running and when I hit the mine field, I didn't even slow down as I had already made three trips across it in the dark. (I was so damn mad that I really didn't care!) For some reason, the Germans didn't use rockets and artillery on me, just machine gun fire, but I kept on going. I even shook my fist at them. At one time, they were walking this machine gun fire along a path toward me, and again, as I saw the strikes advance right toward me, I didn't even slow up. I just jumped as high and as far as I could and it must have missed me because I still have both feet. It kept going right on down the path just behind me. By this time, I was across the mine field and had gained the cover of buildings at the edge of town.

I don't know how fast I had been running, but I'll bet I broke some speed records. From there on, I had cover and made it to HQ and got the artillery stopped. Then I found out what had happened. Another unit to our left had seen a German demolition team headed for the dam and had called in artillery fire to stop them. In the meantime, my unit had already taken them out, but the unit to the left had lost track of them due to the slope of the hill and their barrage was falling short and on our positions.

Even though I got the artillery barrage stopped, my problems were not over. I still had to repair the telephone lines to the command posts. Thankfully, most of the breaks were in the timber with only one being in the mine field, but the repairs would have to wait until dark. I still had to get back to my men across the mine field, so I took a radio with me to depend on for our communication until dark. The telephone wire would have to be repaired in the dark by feel only. Here again, you can see why it is important to have sensitive fingers in war time. Do you realize that if those girls in the old Model T had been easy and I had not developed this "delicate sneaky touch," that I might not be alive today to relate this story. Honestly, when you are in terrible situations such as this, you must think about happier times now and then.

To get back to the real world, I believe someone had to be looking out for us. Although one of our bunkers had one layer of logs ripped off, we had no one wounded or killed, just a lot of men, VERY SHOOK UP. At this point, I would like to add, that being under our own artillery fire was much worse that that of the enemy. Being back with my men and knowing that more trips would have to be made across that damn mine field, we ate more K-rations and saved the containers for our "K-ration toilets." Hopefully, they would last till night.

I finished my lunch and it looked like I was going to have to take one more trip across that damn mine field. The break in the phone line was in the mine field and it had to be located before I could make the repair after dark. Off I went again, only this time no one was shooting at me for a change (they must have been asleep). I found the break and after examining it, I thought that I could just twist the wires together before they started shooting. As I was already two thirds of the way across, I decided to go ahead and give it a try.

I got the splice made and made it on across to the cover of the first building and couldn't believe my luck. I went on down to HQ and we checked out the phone lines and found that they were OK down to my bunker. They told me to be careful on my way back because they had been receiving some sniper fire from the partly destroyed church tower next to the river.

I made my way back to the edge of town and was leaning against the thick outside wall of a brick building where I would have some cover. I was getting up my nerve to make the return trip across the mine field. All of a sudden, I heard an ungodly screaming coming in. It was a German "Nebelwerfer," or, as most of us called them, a "screaming meemie," which was a five barrel rocket.

That was the last thing I remembered until I came to inside the building. There was no wall left where I had been standing just a few minutes before. I didn't seem to hurt anywhere, but my nose was bleeding and I couldn't hear anything. Slowly my hearing returned but I was still dizzy and didn't seem to have all my senses about me. There was only a pile of rubble where most of the building had been standing a short time before. It must have been one hell of an explosion.

As I was trying to pull myself back together, I looked up, and coming toward me was a German with his hands clasped over his head. He must have been the sniper in the church tower. As I started toward him, I realized that I didn't have my gun. When I was blown through the wall, it must have ended up somewhere inside the building. I really wasn't too worried as he seemed to want to surrender.

I started to climb up that pile of rubble. He dipped down behind it, and as I came over the top, he picked up a machine pistol with the barrel pointed straight at my chest. I jumped for him and knocked his arm with the gun up just as he pulled the trigger. One or two slugs hit my left arm as it went past the barrel. As I was jumping, I pulled the only weapon I had, an old German bayonet that I used to probe for mines (I kept it razor sharp). I started a wild swing while I still in mid air and connected with his throat, almost beheading him. It was probably the most coordinated move I had ever made in my life, and if it hadn't have been, I probably wouldn't be writing this story now. I think some greater power was looking out for me.

I had no pain in my arm at that time; it just felt numb. I managed to get my first aid pack open and dumped the wound full of sulfa powder and put on a bandage to stop the bleeding, then headed to the

CP and the first aid medic. I thought it was just a flesh wound, but when the medic checked it, he found that one or more bullets had hit and shattered the bone just above my hand. I wanted to go on back to my men but the commanding officer said, "No, we're sending you to a field hospital."

This started a trip on a stretcher by Jeep, then by ambulance, and finally by train to a hospital outside Paris, and from there, on a plane to England. The strange thing was, that through all this, there was no major pain, just a dull ache. I don't believe that I ever received any pain medication at all.

I guess I was still pretty shook up while I was at the forward aid station. They looked over my wounded arm and said that it seemed to have a little infection in it and they started giving me a shot of penicillin every two hours. It was there that they put me in an ambulance and, I guess, started me to the train station. The next thing I knew, I was on a hospital train, starting what I thought would be a short trip of only about 250 to 300 miles.

By the time they got the train loaded, it was already dark. The bunks (I should say stretchers) were stacked so close together that you could hardly turn over without hitting the one above you. I had just got settled down, and here came a cute little nurse who told me it was time for my shot. They had been instructed to give the shots to me in my left shoulder as I still didn't have much feeling there and it didn't bother me much.

The train lurched and we started to move but at least it was smooth, not like the ambulance (that had to be the roughest riding vehicle in the world). It seemed that we had hardly got under way when we stopped again. It seemed that the German planes had bombed the track and we had to wait for it to be repaired. Lying there helpless was like being a sitting duck. The only answer to this dilemma was to try to get some sleep and hope that they had parked the damn train in a tunnel, but from the movement I saw through the window, I knew that it wasn't true.

I had just dropped off to sleep when here came that cute little nurse again to give me another shot. This went on for twenty-four hours, day and night. The bad part of this was that with all the stops and track repairs, a trip that should have taken twelve hours took us four days. One consolation was that in the daytime and no faster than the train was moving, I could get a good look out the train window.

I had been through most of this country before, and I could hardly believe the destruction that had taken place. As the hours wore on, my left shoulder began to look like a pin cushion and there was probably a bulge in the side of the train where I kept trying to get away from that needle. I don't know why I was flinching so much because it didn't seem to be hurting me.

As we got closer to Paris, the train picked up speed and at the end of the fourth day, just as it was getting dark, we pulled into Paris, the city of light. There they loaded us into another ambulance and took us to a hospital that was close to the airport. At this hospital, we were able to actually sleep in a hospital bed but were told that we would be there at least two days, as the weather had closed down England and no planes could land for at least twenty-four hours.

I was still receiving my shots, but now they were four hours apart, and with the nurse's help, I could have a bath and hot food. Hopefully, while I was there, I anticipated getting a little rest. They had stabilized my arm in some kind of a cast so now I was able to walk and go to the bathroom by myself. Man, you don't know what a relief that was! Speaking of that, I needed to use the john and when I asked where it was, the nurse pointed out in the courtyard. I went out there and there were a bunch of stalls with no fronts on them. The toilet was a print of two shoe soles, raised up about six inches high on each side of a hole about three inches high and six inches in diameter between them. Talk about being exposed. With no doors on the stalls and the doctors and nurses walking back and forth all the time, it was sure hard getting everything started. Just to keep my mind occupied, I tried to imagine how the nurses would use these. Surely there must be some other way, but you know the French.

I was still in the hospital outside of the Paris airport when one day, after being loaded and unloaded on this C-47 hospital plane three times in eight hours, we were loaded one last time and were on our way to England. I told you about it being crowded between the stretchers on the train, but on this plane, it was even worse. You couldn't even turn over, but thank heaven, we were only on board the plane just a little over an hour when we arrived in southern England and were again loaded in an ambulance and taken to a hospital. It seemed like it was a long trip, but any distance in one of those rough riding "meat wagons" seemed long.

We arrived at the hospital, and for the life of me, I can't remember the name of either the town or the hospital. I don't think I was drugged but I still didn't have any major pain. After a long wait, I finally got to see the doctor. He told me that they would have to remove the cast and open up my arm to try to remove all the small bone particles. He said he probably could bind the larger pieces together and be able to save my hand. This surprised me, as no more pain than I'd had, I assumed that the wound wasn't too serious. He went on to explain to me that the bone was shattered for a little over an inch. The reason that I had no pain was that for some reason, I had no feeling in my left side, arm, shoulder and on down to my waist.

This was all I could remember as they put me back to sleep and started to work on the arm. I thought that nerve damage was done when I got blown through the brick wall just before I got shot.

When I came to, I don't know how much later, my whole left side and arm were in a cast, and as I said before, I had no pain. I was just groggy. I was in a hospital bed with clean white sheets and believe me, it felt like heaven. I went back to sleep and when I woke up, I was really hungry and had no idea what time it was, but I could see outside that it was daylight. They brought me some food and it was hot and good.

The doctor came in a little while later and to my relief, said that the operation had gone well and that he had been able to find enough larger pieces of bone to hold everything together and that he was sure that I wouldn't loose my hand. He told me that he might have to open it up again but he didn't think so.

I had lost all track of time and I had no idea of how long I had been there or how long I would have to remain. I could walk OK so he said that in about a week, I could have a pass to go to town but to do no heavy drinking. This I was really looking forward to.

I did finally get to go to town and drink a few beers or as the British call it, ale. I also had fish and chips which I was not too crazy about. There were a lot of movie and entertainment people there also. One group was the Glenn Miller band so I spent a lot of time with them. They were a great bunch of guys although they were a little sad at that time as Glenn had disappeared over the channel in a small plane on his way to France.

Things went along like this for what seemed forever. I finally got my body cast off and just had a cast from my elbow to my hand, so I could wear my jacket. I was beginning to feel almost like a human being again. I didn't think it would be too long before I would be released to go back to France—just as soon as I could get this last cast off. Now it was just a matter of time. I ate my meals at the hospital but the rest of the time I spent out running around. I still had no feeling on my left side and the doctor said it could be anywhere from a few weeks to as long as a year for it to return, but return it would.

After spending a few more days in the hospital, I was doing a little better. I seemed to be getting a little feeling down around my waist on my left side. They took my cast off and started giving me a little therapy because it had been so long since I had used that arm and hand. Much to my surprise, I was able to bend my wrist and move all of my fingers. The doctor said I would be released the next morning and that I would be sent back to Paris, France and be assigned to "Detachment of Patients at Large." There I would have to report to the hospital for a check up and therapy once a week. I didn't know what all this meant, but I was happy to still have a hand and have everything working. For a long time, I was very scared that I might lose my hand, and when you are thousands of miles away from home and away from all your friends, that is a very sobering and lonely thought.

All that remained to be done now was to get together what few belongings I had left. You must remember that everything that I had was in Germany except for my Colt 45. How I had managed to keep it, I'll never know. Anyway, I went to sleep that night wondering what was in store for me next.

The next morning, I got orders to report to Portsmouth, England, where I was to board a British Hospital ship headed for LaHarve, France. I went by train to Portsmouth and boarded my ship for what should have been a six hour trip to LaHarve. I don't know what happened, but I heard that the ship's captain received a German submarine alert so he turned around and ran. After forty-eight hours and six of the worst meals I've ever had in my life, we finally got to LaHarve. There I boarded a train for Paris, France, and after a short fast ride, I arrived at the Paris train station where I was met by an ambulance and was then taken to some Headquarters.

I was ordered to report to a WAC captain, who took my orders and told me that I was assigned to "Detachment of Patients at Large" and that she had found me officer's quarters at "Boys Town." This turned out to be girls' dormitory at a university close to the edge of Paris, but of course, there were no girls there (no such luck). She supplied me with a map of the Metro (a subway) and told me that I was supposed to report to a colonel at Place de la Concorde at eight o'clock the next morning. I would be sitting on a "Court Martial Board" several days a week (this was like jury duty).

Having never been on a metro or subway and not being able to speak or understand any French, I knew I had my work cut out for me because I lived clear out on the edge of Paris. After a lot of misgiving, I went down in the Metro and found that with the maps they had posted in the cars, it was very easy to find my way. I only had to make two changes.

When I got to my officers' quarters (they were only a block and a half from the Metro station) I found that they were not too bad. They had a single bed, bath, hot plate and telephone. I unpacked the few belongings I had and thanked heaven that I had been able to hang on to my 45. It made me feel very secure, as it is pretty scary to be thousands of miles away from home and know no one. If I had only had a radio it would have made things more tolerable, but there probably would not have been any stations in English. Being alone and lonely, I decided to get a little sleep, then go over my orders so I would be able to find my way easily in the morning. I had a little trouble, but sleep finally came.

I had no idea how long it would take me to get there, so I set my alarm for 6:30 a.m. My orders said to report with a clean shave and in a class A uniform. The only transportation was the Metro, and "Boys Town" was miles from "Place de la Concorde," which was located near the center of town.

I started out and had no trouble at all getting down town. I arrived and still had about 45 minutes before I had to report, so I stopped and got a roll and coffee at a sidewalk cafe. As soon as I finished, I reported to a Colonel Jones at eight a.m. and he gave me my schedule for the week. I was to report at ten o'clock for my first sitting. A French girl accused a soldier of getting her pregnant. It didn't take us long to discover that it was a Frenchman who got her pregnant and all that she was looking for was money. Needless to say, the charges against the soldier were dropped.

I had been given a food voucher for my meals at an officers' mess at Place St. Augustine, so I had to find my way there. This meant another ride on the Metro, but again, with the maps posted in the Metro cars, it posed no problem. When I arrived at the location, it proved to be a beautiful three story restaurant with very good food. I had a good lunch, but didn't eat too much as I was not feeling very well.

After lunch, I went to a store and bought a chain and lock so that I could lock up the only cabinet in my room. I had drawn my back pay in England and it was in English pound notes, each worth four dollars. I had so many that I could not even fold my billfold, so I had to have some place to lock up my money and my gun.

After taking care of this, I was feeling pretty bad so I went to see the doctor. He said that I had the flu and sent me to the hospital. After several tests, they said I not only had the flu, but also had "Glandular Fever" and would have to stay in bed for at least two weeks, so back to the hospital again. I was beginning to think that if I had any luck at all, it would be bad luck. Anyway, I got settled in and they started me on penicillin again, but the nurses were real nice. Most of the patients were field grade officers, colonels, majors, and captains, all "rear echelon" or what we called non-combat troops.

I really was not sick-sick. I just had to be quiet. I didn't know what Glandular Fever was, but they said that if I did not remain quiet, the consequences would be serious. I didn't mind this though, since the beds were comfortable, the food was good, and the nurses were pretty. Aside from one other lieutenant and me, these other officers bitched about everything. The food wasn't good, the beds were too hard, and it was either too hot or too cold and anything else they could think of. The nurses hated them all, so it was not long before the other lieutenant and I became the favorites of the doctors and the nurses. After what we had been through only a short time before, we were very happy to be in out of the weather and have a warm place to sleep.

It wasn't long before we were getting almost anything we wanted from the doctors and the nurses, they just let these "rear echelon" guys go and took care to the other lieutenant and me first. We always had two or three of the nurses hanging around our beds and getting anything we wanted, books, papers, etc. They were spoiling us rotten but we loved it and I for one was in no hurry to leave. Some of the nurses even came back when they got off duty, to talk to us. A few of them had husbands or brothers who were in combat outfits in the same locations that we had been just a short time before, so we had a lot to talk about. It sure helped ease the loneliness for both them and us.

Another morning rolled around with breakfast in bed with good food. I knew this couldn't go on forever, but it got even better. After breakfast, I got a bath and a rub down from one of the nurses. We were being pampered and we loved it. After the shift change, some of the off-duty nurses came back in to talk to us again. No one can believe how wonderful it was just to talk to these young ladies.

At noon, we had lunch in bed again and the nurse came around to give me my penicillin shot. I didn't hurt much, but I was sure getting tired of them. After giving me my shot, one of the nurses said, "I know that you must be getting bored. We get off shift at 4:00 p.m. After we have dinner and you have yours, we will borrow a couple of the doctors' white coats for you guys and sneak you out the back door to the sidewalk cafe for a drink. You'll have to promise you will have only one and that you will sit quietly because you are not supposed to move around."

Believe me, we nursed that one drink and behaved ourselves. It was a wonderful break for us and we did it several times during our stay.

During one of our conversations, I noticed that a couple of the girls had nice sun tans. I said, "How in the world did you get that tan?"

One of the girls replied, "The nurses' quarters are in a house just beyond that big tree outside the window by your bed. We sun bathe on the second floor deck behind the tree. We use that because we don't have any swim suits, so we just wear our panties and bras."

"Aren't you afraid someone will see you?"

She smiled. "Tomorrow, I'll show you."

The next day, she looked out my window and said, "See how well we are protected?"

And sure enough, with the naked eye, you could see nothing. I still had my spotting scope in my bag. Like a fool, I took it out. "What about this?"

She took the scope and looking through it. "You can even see the design on the panties!" She dropped my scope in her pocket. "I'll be keeping this."

She thanked me and told me that she was going to check all the belongings of all the old grouches in the rear echelon department.

I didn't get my scope back until I left the hospital.

I can only say that this was the most enjoyable hospital stay that I ever had, and for me, it was going much too fast. We had a lot of fun and I don't think anyone ever got hurt. Even after the scope incident, we were all still good friends and the nurses thought it was funny. Before long, the other lieutenant was gone, leaving me the only one to be pampered.

One day, a couple of the nurses came in and brought a doctor's white coat and pants and a stethoscope to hang around my neck. They took me to the adjoining building, which was a women's hospital for WACs, Red Cross girls and nurses. We were to give them their physical examinations, which the nurses thought would be great fun. I will have to say that I enjoyed it very much and would have enjoyed it even more if I had not been so shy, but I did learn that boys are different from girls. I worried about getting caught, but we managed to get back to our section of the buildings without any problems. Those nurses really had a ball, but the next morning, some of the patients in the women's hospital asked what happened to the new doctor that made the rounds the day before. This led the nurses to decide that we shouldn't try it again.

119

It appeared that I might be released that day or the next morning. Although this had been one of the most pleasant stays for me since I had been over there, I knew all good things have to come to an end sometime.

After a few more good nights' sleep, I was released back to duty. This was one hospital I hated to leave. I could have spent the rest of the war there, for the beds were good, the rooms were warm and the nurses were pretty and friendly. I actually think that they hated to see me and the other lieutenant leave, because after our departure, all they had to look forward to was putting up with all those grouchy old field grade officers.

I reported back to my WAC captain. Her name was Ruth Morgan and she seemed happy to see me. She told me I was supposed to report to some colonel down at Place de la Concorde at three p.m. When I reported in, he assigned me to another Court Martial Board that would start at nine a.m. the next morning.

I caught the Metro to "*Place St. Augustine*," had lunch and headed back to my room at "Boys Town," where I needed to find some way to press my class A uniform. I finally managed to borrow an iron and ironing board from one of the other officers there. If you showed up for board duty with a dirty or wrinkled uniform, it was entered on your service record. Appearing neat every day was difficult for me because I only had one class A uniform. Just as soon as I could get to the Quarter Master supply, I intended to buy another uniform. (Being that I was now an officer, I had to buy my own Class A clothes, as they were no longer furnished by the Army.)

While I was getting these little chores done, I noticed that I had an itching down around my groin area. I thought it was because I had only had sponge baths while I was in the hospital, so I got my towels and went to take a shower. When I undressed and examined myself, I found that I had the most wicked looking angry bumps and breaking out all around my crotch area that I had ever seen. The itching was getting worse by the minute, so I finished my shower and called my WAC captain and asked where I could find the nearest Army doctor. She gave me an address and I immediately headed there. Another ride on the Metro, but by this time, I was getting used to it.

I walked into the office and I didn't have to wait long. The doctor asked what my problem was and when I told him, he told me to drop my pants. He looked me over and asked if I had been messing around with any of these French girls. I said, "No, I've been in the hospital in England, and after arriving here, I had to go to the hospital for the flu and glandular fever and I just got out today."

He said, "You got the scabies," to which I answered, "Can you get them from bedclothes?" His answer was that the only way you could get them was through belly to belly contact. When he told me this, I lost my cool and told him that he was full of crap clear up to his neck. He didn't like that very well, so I told him to call my commanding officer, and when he did, she told him the same thing. After that, he admitted that he didn't know what it was.

I asked him to give me something for the itching and he gave me a salve that did help the itching, and it all cleared up in about ten days. I found out later that the problem was that being wounded and then having a high fever, I had received so much penicillin in my two hospital stays, that I had developed an allergy to penicillin. Later, back in the States, I was told that had they given me the same large shots that I had received before, it would have probably killed me. After what I had been through the preceding month, that would have been a hell of a way to go. I guess my pure heart and soul must have saved me again.

Back sitting on the Court Martial board, I was not getting along very well with my WAC captain (I'll go into that later). I was beginning to get more feeling in my left side down around my waist but not in my shoulder, arm and hand, although they worked just fine and I wanted to get back to my outfit and friends. A funny thing was, when the nurse in France took my temperature and held my hand, I couldn't even feel it.

The feeling was slowly coming back to my left side. If a girl pinched me in the ribs, I could now feel it. I started back sitting on the Court Martial Boards and it was probably the most boring thing that I had ever done in my life. I even had a hard time keeping myself awake, and they sure didn't like it if you fell asleep. Most of the trials were French girls trying to rope some poor GI into marrying her so she could get into the United States, or some poor soldier running

121

over a cow, pig or chicken with a tank and being sued—anything to get some money out of the Americans.

Once in awhile, we would get a black market case, which would always prove to be more interesting. We had one case where a French girl was trying to make a GI continue to pay for her apartment and food because he had been living with her. He had left her and she couldn't find him, but she wanted the government to keep on paying. She lost. We finished this case around three p.m.—too late to start another trial.

Some of the other officers on the board and I were sitting around shooting the breeze, and I asked if there was a place where one could get a mixed drink and just sit around and enjoy himself. One said there was a club in the Bouy LaFayette Hotel called the Bouy LaFayette Club. They served the usual cognac, wine, and champagne, and one special mixed drink called the "Bouy LaFayette Special." This place sounded good to me, so I took the Metro back out to "Boys Town," showered, shaved, and then got my billfold and went by Metro to the officers' mess at St. Augustine. After having a good meal, I headed for the club, which was within walking distance of our officers' mess. I knew it wasn't very far.

It was located on the corner of LaFayette and another street that I assume was Bouy. I walked into the door of the hotel on LaFayette Street, and it turned out to be a WAC barracks. They told me that the club was located around the corner on Bouy. I went around there, and this was a transit officers' hotel. The club was located in the Bouy on the first floor. The two hotels were located in the same building, but had two separate entrances.

I entered the club and found it to be very unusual. As you probably know, in the service, there are separate clubs for the officers and the enlisted men. In this one, everyone was welcome—officers, enlisted men, WACs, Red Cross girls and nurses. There was no rank. When you walked in the door, you were just another person.

I had all my back pay in English pound notes, and I found that these bought three times as much as you could get if you went to the regular exchange and exchanged them for French francs. I was looking forward to a great evening when I ordered my first drink, a "Bouy LaFayette Special." I had better explain what this drink contained. It was served in a water glass and consisted of: 2 shots of Cognac, 1 shot of gin, 1 shot of Benedictine, and the rest of the glass was filled with champagne.

I had never heard of anything like this before but not caring for wine or champagne very much, I thought here goes nothing (believe it or not, it tasted real good).

That was the first mixed drink that I'd had in months so it didn't take me long to finish it off and order another. I was sitting at a table with a WAC sergeant, a PFC, a Major, a WAC private and a Nurse. No one said anything except the WAC sergeant who said, "Lieutenant, those are very potent!" I thanked her and replied, "Forget the lieutenant stuff. Just call me Lindy."

I thought to myself that this was going to be a great evening. I had all that back pay so I could really have a ball with everyone around the table being friendly, so I ordered my third "Bouy LaFayette Special." Believe me, I was still just as sober as I am now some sixty years later. I got up to go to the john, and it felt like someone was swinging me around their head by my feet and then lights went out.

The next thing I knew, I woke up in a strange hotel room and it was morning. I had been sick during the night and had thrown up all over my bed and had no idea where I was. As I slowly forced my eyes open, I realized that someone had undressed me and hung my uniform up (thank heaven, as I only had one dress jacket and only a couple of shirts and I was going to have to report for duty again at one o'clock that afternoon). Slowly, I began to recall the night before at the club. I jumped out of bed when it dawned on me that my billfold with my ID and all my money was in my uniform. I checked my pockets and found nothing. I had all my back pay in the billfold, so I was beginning to feel mighty low. I couldn't draw my pay or even get into the mess hall to eat without my ID.

I thought I might as well get cleaned up and then see if I could get this mess straightened out. I was half way to the shower when the phone rang. I picked it up, wondering who it could be, when a female voice said, "You don't remember me. My name is Eleanor. I'm the WAC sergeant you were sitting with last night. When you got up to go to the john, I think you bounced off every wall in the place. I noticed that your billfold was hanging half out of your pocket. I waited until you came out, then took your billfold and helped you out to the front desk, rented you a room, and then took you up and put you to bed. I hope you didn't mind my taking enough money out of your billfold to pay for the room."

I breathed a sigh of relief.

"If you're going to be there, I will bring your billfold right over."

I happily answered, "I'll go open the door for you."

"No need. Just open your window."

I pulled on my pants and opened my window. She was on the balcony, which ran all the way along the side of the two hotels. She stepped through my window and handed me my billfold. I tried to pay her for all she had done but she would take nothing. She told me that her room was next to mine on the balcony. I again tried to pay her and she still refused, telling me that I had already done her a favor, as she had gone out of my window into hers last night. She said that I could do her another favor if I would. Let her, along with some of her friends, into my room after bed check so that they could go down to the club without having to check out at the front desk. To this, of course, I agreed.

After she left, I finished cleaning up and went down to the desk and rented this room for thirty days until I could get my voucher transferred from "Boys Town" to Bouy Hotel. This was much handier and closer to the mess hall and also to where I had to sit on the Court Martial Board. Once again, I had lucked out. It just goes to show that there are still a lot of good people in this world, and as far as I was concerned, that little WAC could do no wrong. She was my friend and the only reason she held my billfold was that she was afraid that I would get mugged.

The next morning, when I rented the room in the Bouy Hotel, I found that it would not be available for ten days, but being that I wanted that particular room, I would just have to wait. I guess I shouldn't have complained. I had come through my first night on the town with my money and my honor intact.

I called HQ and checked in with Capt. Ruth Morgan, my C.O., and she told me that I was supposed to report to the hospital to get my wound checked at nine a.m. They checked me all over and everything seemed OK. I was improving and getting more feeling back in my left side each time they checked me.

I called Capt. Morgan and made an appointment to see her at 10:30. I wanted to talk to her about getting back to my outfit. She was waiting for me when I got there and said that she was sure glad that I was there. She said that she had just got a call from SHEAF Headquarters and that I had received a Silver Star award. I told her that I already knew that, but she said that this would be a formal presentation for the Stars and Stripes and the Chicago and Springfield papers, and also the St. Louis Post Dispatch. I was to meet a Colonel E. F. Berendt at the Hotel Rivoli, just off Place de la Concorde at 12:00 to have lunch and have pictures taken.

"As long as I'm here, do you have a little time to talk to me?" I asked. "I want to get back to my unit."

"I won't even talk to you about that," she replied. "You have had enough. I'm not going to send you back into combat."

"OK, then. I'll just go over your head."

"You can't do that."

"Just watch me! I said.

"If you do, I will court martial you."

"Well, at least I will be back with my friends." That ended our discussion and she told me that she would escort me to the hotel and introduce me to Col. Berendt.

Being that the hotel was within walking distance of her office, we took a leisurely walk down to the hotel. During this walk, she became friendlier, and by the time we reported in, I was glad she was with me. There was nothing but big brass there—generals, colonels, majors, captains—leaving me the lowest ranking officer there. I think the only reason that most of them were there was that they just wanted to get their pictures and names in the papers.

We had our meal and then the presentation. I would like to add, that as nervous as I was around all this brass, I believe I handled myself well. The only people that had to have their pictures taken and say anything was Col. Berendt, a captain whose name I no longer remember, and myself (the captain also received a Silver Star). Anyway, I was glad when it was all over. I was ready to get back to my quarters and relax.

After my normal Metro ride, I made it back to "Boys Town." It was sure too bad that they still didn't have girls in this old dorm. I decided to stay in that night and maybe do a little reading and write a few letters.

Next day, I had to sit on the darn Court Martial Board again, all the while wishing that I was back with my old outfit. That darn WAC Captain wouldn't even talk to me about going back, since I had received my Silver Star. She just said that I had already had enough. I talked to an MP friend of mine and he told me that there was an opening in the "Criminal Investigation Division" and that with my background, I would easily qualify for the position. I decided to give it a try. If I got that job and got into my new room at the Bouy Hotel, things would not be at all bad.

I went back to my room, cleaned up and went back downtown to eat. Some of the guys were talking about a great stage show that was going to be at the Leado Club. Called "The Follies," it was supposed to be one of the most famous shows in the world. It did come to the States after the war and played in Las Vegas Nevada for several years.

I finished my dinner and the guys and I walked from there to the Club Leado to take in the show. We had a few drinks at the bar while we were waiting for the show to start.

Since I was from a small town, I had never had the opportunity to see a real stage show before and it was everything that people said it would be. The girls were beautiful, the costumes fantastic (some were very brief), and the dancing and acting were unbelievable. One thing stuck out in my mind though. Although this was a French show with hundreds of girls, only a few of them were French.

I was having such a good time that I decided to stay and take in the second show. When I came out, much to my dismay, I discovered that the Metro had quit running at 11 o'clock and I was over four miles from home and I wasn't even sure that I knew the way.

I decided to simplify things and just take a taxi. When I finally found a taxi and told the driver where I wanted to go, he informed me that it would be 3000 francs (at that time, a 1000 francs was about $20.00). I had to tell him that I didn't have that much money.

I resigned myself to the fact that I was in for a long walk, so I got out my little map and started down Champs Elyees to Place de la Concorde, where I would have to cross the River Seine. From there, I was not too sure which street to take. The lower part of the Champs was bordered by a beautiful park and usually there were a lot of people sitting on the benches. I figured I could ask one of them for direction, but just my luck, that night it was almost empty.

When I was almost to Place de la Concorde, I finally saw a girl sitting on one of the benches close to the sidewalk. My luck was finally changing. This girl wore a business suit and was very attractive. When I spoke to her, she spoke English even better than I did. I showed her my map and the place where I lived.

She said, "That's a long way and you look awfully tired."

"I know, but I have to get home," I said.

"Just sit down and rest for a little while."

Tired as I was, I thought that it would be a good idea so I sat down. No sooner had I settled down, she began telling me about her life under the German Occupation.

As we sat there and talked, she told me how bad the German occupation had been and how she had started medical school to become a doctor. This all came to an end with the occupation. Now they were having a hard time just getting enough food to eat and trying to keep warm. We talked for some time and I finally told her that I was going to have to get started home. "I have an apartment about two blocks away," she said, "and I would be happy to let you stay with me for the night."

I could hardly believe this. Here was this beautiful and attractive girl who had been studying to be a doctor and she was asking me to spend the night with her!

We started walking, and after a few blocks, we came to the apartment. As we started in, she said, "As I told you, we have been having a hard time getting by so I will need 1000 francs (about $20.00)."

Right then, a light should have gone on, but I had that much money and I thought, "What the hell, it's better than walking." I gave her the money and we went on upstairs to this one room apartment.

127

It had an electric hot plate and the usual for French rooms, including a bidet or douche bowl (like a toilet except it sprayed water up on your private parts), a toilet and sink. I sat down on the double bed and had started to take my clothes off when I glanced around at her. She had taken off her clothes, wig, false breasts and false teeth. Her private parts and head had been shaved. She stood with one foot on the floor and the other in the douche bowl washing her foot. I don't think I have ever seen a woman in such an ugly position. Talk about a turn off!

I knew immediately that it was just a big line of bull that she had been feeding me. The French had taken these girls who had fraternized and slept with the Germans, stripped them down and shaved their heads and private parts and then marched them down the streets naked so all the people could see their shame. I had learned another valuable lesson, and besides, after she had removed her clothes, she didn't look clean.

I figured it was worth $20.00 to learn this lesson, so I put my clothes back on and started for the door. She said, "I'm not going to give you your money back!" I said, "That's fine. All I want to do is get out of here."

I started my long walk home, and before long I thought that maybe I should have spent the night with her because it was a long way home. But I don't think anyone could have paid me enough money to stay. One thing I do know was that old single bed in "Boys Town" sure looked good when I finally got there.

For only $20.00, I had learned a valuable lesson. So called good-looking girls sitting on a park bench at midnight wearing expensive clothes are not always what they appear to be, but what could you expect from a shy rural boy like me from a small town in center of Illinois? I should have realized when she spoke better English than I that something was wrong. Live and learn.

The next day started with the same old grind—ride the metro from the edge of Paris to the downtown mess hall for breakfast, then go to the court for the rest of the day and sit there listening to the French try to "screw" the Americans out of some money or try some soldier for desertion or going AWOL. This went on day after day with no end in sight and it sure was getting old. I wanted to get the war over so I could go home. I was gaining strength every day and was getting most of the feeling back in my left side, but I couldn't see that I was doing anything to help bring the darn war to an end.

All the time, I am trying to figure out some way to get out from under the control of this WAC captain I decided the job the MP lieutenant friend of mine told me about in the Criminal Investigation Division would be my next endeavor.

I finished for the day and went back to "Boys Town," got cleaned up, and then went downtown to eat and see when I could get into my new room at the Bouy La Fayette. I had also managed to get another uniform. I walked down to the Metro Station and jumped aboard for the trip to the mess hall. As I boarded, I noticed three Red Cross girls looking intently at a Metro map. It appeared that they had just come from the airport and were having trouble finding their way. By this time, I knew my way around pretty well, and as always, I was ready to help a damsel in distress, so I asked them if I could be of any assistance. With a sigh of relief, they told me that they were to report to this certain hotel. I told them that they were in luck as that was the location where I would be getting off and I would be going right past the hotel and would be happy to show them where it was. They were delighted.

One of the girls looked at my uniform with my crossed saber and told me that she had a brother in the cavalry. When I inquired if she knew what unit, she said it was the 32nd. I told her that I had been with the 32nd before I received my Battlefield Commission and that I had been the platoon sergeant of the 1st platoon of A Troop.

Amazed, she said, "You must be Lindy!"

It turned out that she was Gloria Clark, the sister of Lt. Clark, my first platoon leader on Stromberg Hill. If you remember, he was wounded so badly in that action that he had to be evacuated to the States. For us, this was just like old home week. I had no idea what had become of him since he left the field.

I went into the hotel to wait for them while they checked in so I could take them to eat and catch up on the stateside news.

While I was waiting for the girls, I noticed a major in a Red Cross uniform. We kept exchanging glances until I finally walked over to him and asked him where he was from. His reply was, "Lincoln,

Illinois," to which I happily answered, "So am I." It is amazing that one could travel half way around the world and then meet two different people from different locations within a half hour that have something in common with you. Gloria was from Philadelphia, Pennsylvania and Bill Redis was from Lincoln, Illinois.

I continued to talk to Bill while I waited for the girls. It turned out that we both were acquainted with a lot of the same people. I explained to Bill that I knew Gloria through her brother and that I was going to take all the girls out to eat and catch up on the news. I invited him to come along with us to eat, but he had to decline as he had to wait for more girls to check in.

When Gloria and the girls came back down, I asked them if they would like to go with me to eat at the officer's mess, as I hadn't had time to make reservations at any of the better restaurants. They said that would be fine so we went down to Place St. Augustine. This was a three story high restaurant and was very fancy. It was loaded with young officers from every branch of the service. I thought for a while that I was going to lose the girls, but they seemed content to stay with me. I didn't know whether to feel good or bad when Gloria started calling me "Pappy." She said that her brother had told her that was one of the better names that some of my men called me.

We had a wonderful meal and shared a bottle of wine. (Wine was cheaper than a fifth of water.) In our conversation, I was very happy to find that Lt. Clark was gong to make a complete recovery and be able to lead a normal life, although he would have to spend a lot of time in the hospital and in therapy before his release. This was good news to me, as he and Lt. Striker were two of the best officers in our unit. There were so many things to talk about that I don't remember a lot of what was said. The two other girls had lost their husbands in the war and this Red Cross work was their way of doing something to help the war effort. For me, being able to talk to three normal girls fresh from the USA was a most wonderful thing. I was fed up with my situation here in Paris with no end in sight and just talking with these girls relieved much of the tension.

We had tied up the table for an awfully long time, so I asked the girls if they would like to walk back to their hotel and enjoy some of the sights along the way. I told them that if we grew tired, we could stop along the way at a sidewalk cafe and enjoy some wine or coffee while we rested. We walked up to the Arc de Triumphe and then down the Avenue Champs Elysees to Place de la Concorde. We stopped at one cafe and talked some more as we enjoyed our coffee and "people watched."

Time flew by all too fast and before I knew it, it was time that I was going to have to head back for home because the Metro stopped running at 11 o'clock. When I explained this to the girls, they were ready too because they had just flown in from the States that day and had no time to rest up. I took them on back to their hotel where they thanked me for the good time they'd had and said that they would be there several more days. I gave Gloria my phone number and she promised to call me the next day.

I went back to my room at Boys Town after that wonderful evening with Gloria and her friends. I had a message that my room was ready at the Bouy La Fayette Hotel and also another from the Criminal Investigation Division notifying me that I could report to work there just as soon as I could get released from my duty at the Detachment of Patients. Things were finally beginning to look up! I had already talked to Captain Morgan and she said she would release me so I could take this new job. With this in mind, I thought I might as well get up early the next morning and move my few belongings down to the Bouy Hotel. I had also found out the name of the WAC sergeant who had saved my rear end and money was Eleanor Stein.

I got my "stuff" together, then called Gloria to give her my new phone number because I didn't want to miss a chance of getting together with the girls again. Things were beginning to look a whole lot brighter, and at last I felt that I would be doing something to help bring the war to an end.

The next morning, I moved my stuff down to my new room and found that it was close enough that I could walk to breakfast and then on down to where I worked. I had already called Gloria and given her my new phone and room number, and asked if she and her friends would like to go for breakfast. She had to decline, but said maybe they could make it for lunch. I called the WAC sergeant and gave her the good news and told her that I would have an extra key made so that she and her friends could use my room as a way to slip out for a drink after bed check.

I walked on down to officers' mess and had breakfast, then headed for what I hoped would be my last day sitting on the Court Martial Board. When I arrived back at my room, I had a call from Gloria letting me know that she and the other girls would like to have lunch with me. I told her this sounded fine and that I would pick them up in their hotel lobby.

The lobby was only a short walk away and once again, we had a very enjoyable meal with wonderful company. While we were eating, the conversation ranged through several topics, but mostly it was about how things were back home in the States. The conversation made me feel good, almost as good as actually being home.

The girls told me that they were probably going to be there for two or three weeks. On hearing this, I told them that if they had not already exchanged their money, I would exchange it for them. If they exchanged it at the bank, they would only get 1000 francs for $20.00, and I could get 3000 francs for the same $20.00. That would give them a lot of extra money. I guess you know that I had made three girls very happy.

I had to get back to work and the girls had some afternoon classes, so we parted all too soon, but having lunch with them sure made my day go much faster. Before we parted, we made a date to go out to eat at a fancy French restaurant and then take in the first show at the "Follies." It looked like it was going to be another interesting evening. It was sure great to be downtown where I wouldn't have to depend on the Metro to get home.

When I left the girls, I stopped at Capt. Ruth L. Morgan's office on the way to the Court Martial Board. She informed me that I would be released from the Detachment of Patients at Large that afternoon a 4:00 p.m. I was supposed to report to Capt. Seidel at Pont de Neuilly, which was clear out on the other edge of Paris, even farther away than Boys Town. It looked like I would be riding the Metro again, but I was finishing up my last day on the "board" and that made me very happy.

I returned to my room at the Bouy, took a bath and cleaned up, then called Gloria to tell her that the first show would start at Club

Leado at nine o'clock, so this would give us plenty of time to eat first. She happily told me that this would be great. I told her that I would pick up her and the other girls at their hotel in twenty minutes. I walked on over and picked them up, and from there we proceeded to the restaurant. Though it was one of the better ones in Paris, I can no longer remember the name. We had a wonderful meal and the girls insisted on paying for mine because I had exchanged their money for so much more than they could have. I had a nice steak and the girls tried some of the fancy French food. There was a live band playing for entertainment and dancing, but I didn't know how to dance. This did not deter the girls. Each one of them took turns trying to teach me a few steps. I didn't learn much, but it sure was fun trying.

We finished off our meal with a bottle of French wine and started for the Club Leado. By this time, it was dark, but evening with all of the lights of Paris was beautiful. As we strolled by the sidewalk cafes, people smiled and nodded their greetings as we passed by. Passing other cafes, music flowed out to the sidewalk, making for a very pleasant walk.

We arrived at Club Leado a few minutes early, so we went on into the bar for a drink. Again, the girls would not even let me pay for a drink. (These were my kind of women.) We finished our drinks and then went to find our seats before they were all filled up. As I mentioned earlier, though this was a live French show with hundreds of girls, very few of them were French. As it was the first time I saw the show, the girls were beautiful, the costumes fantastic and the acting and dancing were almost unbelievable. Gloria, having lived in Philadelphia, had spent a lot of time in the great entertainment city of Atlantic City, but she said she had never seen anything like this show. We all had a great time and the evening ended all too soon.

I started walking the girls back to their hotel and on the way we stopped off at one of the sidewalk cafes for coffee. We sat watching the people and the bicycles on the streets go by. Even back then, the girls wore loose skirts which would blow up around their hips when caught by the wind. After awhile Gloria said, "Pappy, I don't think those girls are wearing any panties!" I answered with, "Honey, you haven't seen anything yet."

We finished our coffee at the sidewalk cafe and I walked the girls on back to their hotel and told them goodnight. I told them that I didn't know what I would be doing the next day as I had to report to Captain Seidel at the office of Criminal Investigation Division for assignment. I promised Gloria that I would let her know as soon as I found out anything.

It sure was a pleasure to walk the few blocks to my room at the Bouy La Fayette and not have to depend on the Metro. Even though it was late, the Bouy La Fayette Club was still going strong so I walked in for one more drink. As I walked in, the WAC sergeant (Eleanor Stein) saw me and called me over to her table and wanted to buy me a drink. I told her that I was starting a new job the next day with the CID so I would have only one beer. As we sat and talked, I told her about running into Gloria Clark, the sister of my old platoon leader, and related some of the recent news she had passed on to me about home.

Eleanor was a very nice girl and it was wonderful to see her again. As I had promised her, I gave her a key to my room so that she and her friends could get in and out after bed check. That was not very much after she had saved my rear as well as my money on our previous meeting. As always seemed to be the case when I was having a good time, it was getting late and I would have to be up early, since I didn't know how long it would take me to reach my new office half way across Paris. It was located at Pont de Neuilly at the very end of the Metro line.

Rising early the next morning, I had breakfast and then caught the Metro to Pont de Neuilly and reported to Captain Seidel. After filling out more paper work and signing more papers, he showed me around the office and to my desk, which he informed me I would spend very little time at except to complete my paper work. He also showed me the detention area or jail where the troops were held until we turned them over to the prosecutor when our investigations were finished. He also explained that there were no regular hours, but that when you were given a case, you had to finish the case within two weeks. If the case took you out of the country, you would have extra time. I had a number two priority for air travel, which meant that very few people could get ahead of me. Sometimes, if I requested it, I could even have a Jeep with a driver or even take a cab. Now, here comes the catch! If I didn't complete the case in the allotted time and couldn't explain why, it was a court martial offense, and that meant I could possibly end up in jail!

My first case was that of a Mess sergeant in Paris, and it looked like this was going to be an interesting case. Army regulations said that you could not send home an amount of money more than your Army pay. As the sergeant was sending home hundreds and sometimes more than a thousand dollars a month, it really perked up my interest, but that's another story.

I finished up my first day at CID and caught the Metro back to my room at the Bouy. As it was only about four p.m., I called Gloria and asked if she and the other girls would like to catch a floor show and a meal at a very unusual private club. The answer was yes.

When I picked Gloria and the girls up at their hotel, I asked them if they would like to walk, as it was only about ten blocks and there were a lot of interesting things to see. They were only too eager to take in more of the interesting sights of Paris. This route took us through a district with a lot of houses of prostitution, so I informed the girls to stay close to me because the prostitutes would probably try to pick me up. At this, the girls only laughed and informed me that these girls on the street did not look like prostitutes. I said, "OK, then. I'll just walk a little ahead of you and we will just see what happens."

We hadn't gone a quarter of a block when it happened. I heard one of the girls scream and they all came running up beside me. One of the girls told me that a Frenchman had tried to proposition her. The girls were learning one of the lessons of the big city, but with me to take care of them, they were still enjoying themselves.

Gloria said, "Pappy, without you, we wouldn't be able to see and do any of these things!" I told her to just wait until she saw this private club.

"It really isn't all that unusual is it?" she said.

I replied, "It sure is!"

I should explain here that this club, The Victoire--Club Prive, was located at Seven Place Pigalle. The show was really just a high class strip show and the show girls were above average and could really dance. It was amazing to Gloria and her friends because they had never seen a strip show before. When it was time to eat and the waitress came for our order, the girls were thrown for a loop. The waitresses didn't wear any clothes, just a transparent apron with a red heart over the crotch area and a pair of very, very high heels. Girls dressed in costumes such as these have to be built perfectly and move very gracefully. Even Gloria and her friends said they looked good, but that they could never do anything like that. I told them that if they had gone through what these girls had gone through, who knows what they'd do.

We finished our meal and were enjoying an after dinner drink while discussing the evening. We all agreed that the food was great, the waitresses beautiful and the show girls could really dance. We all thought that with our servers dressed as they were it might upset our eating, but the lights were dim and we all agreed that it was a great experience.

We again decided to walk back to our respective hotels, and on the way decided to have a coffee at another of the sidewalk cafes. Across the street from this particular cafe, was a partition about fifteen feet long on metal posts with one end closed and an L shaped shield around the other end. It was painted a dark green and covered one from the knees to the shoulders. Men would walk in, turn and face the wall for a few minutes, than walk back out. I watched the girls intently watching this procedure for several minutes so I just waited for the question.

Soon Gloria said, "Say, Pappy, what is that over there, a telephone?"

I smiled and said, "No. That's a toilet when it is painted green like that."

She exclaimed, "You mean right out on the street like that?"

I replied, "Yes! And I have also seen women use them. They will even nod and speak to you when you walk close by. Things are sure different here in France. Most of the restrooms are used by both men and women."

I went on to tell Gloria that at one club, I had been standing using the urinal when one of the doors to a stall opened and suddenly I got a whiff of perfume, which caught my attention. A young lady had come up and was washing her hands at the lavatory almost at my elbow. She nodded her head and said, "Good evening." That first time it was very embarrassing for me, but after a few more of the same kind of experiences, I became used to it. All the French girls seemed to be that uninhibited.

We finished our coffee and proceeded on to the girls' hotel where I dropped them off. I walked on back to my room at the Bouy, and before getting some shut eye, went over a few notes pertaining to the case I would be working on the next day.

Getting up early the next morning, I had breakfast and then went to the mess hall where the sergeant that I would be investigating worked. I arrived and found that he was not there. He was at the quartermaster picking up supplies and wouldn't be back until late. I talked to the people who worked with him and to a man, they all seemed to like and respect him. No one thought he would do anything dishonest. I made an appointment to have him meet me the next morning after breakfast at nine o'clock and left word that he should be there without fail or that he would be arrested.

After completing this task, I still had time on my hands, so I called Gloria. She said, "I am sure glad you called! We are being moved out of the hotel and into a house not too far away. The Red Cross has rented several here in Paris as they seem to think that because we are going to be here a while, we would be happier in a house (this was sorta like a sorority house), so I wanted to give you our new address and phone number. I think it's going to be great. It has a high stone fence around the back yard, giving us privacy if we want to sunbathe. We each have our own room and there is a kitchen for those who want to use it."

With all these "goodies," I asked, "Do you think that I could get a room there too? It sure does sound wonderful for a poor shy boy like me."

"I know you're just kidding!" she said.

I then told her that when they got settled in, to give me a call because I would be in my room until I went to dinner.

I went back to my room and started making out a list of the things I needed to talk to the mess sergeant about. I also made arrangements for the next day to pick up my special identification and my priority for air travel. All in all, I'd had a pretty busy day.

Gloria called just as I was getting ready to leave for the officers' mess. She said that they had just finished moving into their new quarters and that everything was just great, but that they had not had time to make arrangements for food "Pappy," she said, "if you will take us out to eat, we will buy."

I thought to myself that I might just have the best of two worlds and wondered how long it would last. "Why don't we just go to the officers' mess until we can make arrangements to go to a better place?" I said. All agreed and we had a great meal and a couple bottles of wine, then went home early. We all had a busy day planned for the next day.

Rising early the next morning, instead of going to the officer's mess, I went to the mess hall of Sgt. Keeley, the sergeant that I needed to see. I sat at the officers' table and explained to the mess officer the reason I had to investigate his sergeant He told me that he thought the sergeant was doing a good job. I finished my breakfast while waiting until Sgt. Keeley got his kitchen help organized. I then asked him if there was some place we could talk privately. He said that he had a small office just off the kitchen.

I asked Sgt. Keeley if he knew what this was all about and he answered that he didn't have a clue. I said, "According to the censor officer, you have been sending home large amounts of money, hundreds of dollars a month and even a thousand dollars one time. Do you realize that you are not allowed to send home more money than the amount of your salary?"

He said he didn't know that.

"You should have! You are a noncommissioned officer, but now that is beside the point. I have to find out where you got the money. As you know, being a mess sergeant and drawing your supplies from the quartermaster, they seem to think you have been selling Army food and supplies on the black-market. If I can't find that you got this money honestly, you could end up in the stockade. I have already checked your order forms from the quartermaster and your output

138

of food and can find nothing wrong, so you're just going to have to tell me where the money came from."

A very nervous sergeant replied, "OK." (This is where the story gets interesting.) "Some time back, I caught a French man going through my garbage can trying to pick out and separate the used coffee grounds. In the conversation that followed, he told me that the used coffee grounds still made better coffee than any of the stuff that they could buy at that time. From then on, I started to save and dry out my used coffee grounds and sell them to this man. It wasn't long before he wanted more, so I started going around to the other mess halls and had them save their used grounds for me. Before long, I had a great sideline going. I had no idea that I was doing anything wrong by selling something that we were just throwing away."

I had to agree with him and that it was just good, enterprising American know-how.

When I turned in my report, I thought that I was done with this case, then some smart #+|%# officer decided that the garbage was still government property and that he should still be prosecuted. It took me several more reports and a letter from his mess officer before I finally got him cleared. I think he finally worked out a deal with the garbage man and the Frenchman where he sold the grounds and took a cut of this and sent the money home. It was still an interesting case and well worth mentioning. I believe that the officer that wanted him prosecuted was just jealous because he hadn't thought of it.

I reported to the CID office the next day and the CO gave me my new case. It was not quite as interesting, but not dull either. This case was a French girl who was accusing a GI of getting her pregnant and she was trying to force him to marry her (a ticket to the USA) or to give her a large sum of money.

I talked to the GI and he informed me that he had not even been in France when she was supposed to have gotten pregnant. I talked to the French girl and then took her to the doctor, who examined her to determine when she became pregnant. He found that the GI was on leave in England at the time it happened and this girl was living with a Frenchman in Paris at the time. I guess she enticed the GI to have sex with her when she was two or three months pregnant in the hope that she would get money from either the GI or our government.

Of course this simple case ended in a dismissal, but it was too bad that we couldn't have thrown both the Frenchman and the girl in jail. There was a lot of this type of scam going on.

After completing this case, I decided to hold off turning in my paper work for a short time so that I could take a few days off. I had found out from a letter from home that an old friend of mine, Manual Plokin from Lincoln, was stationed at air strip number two near Paris. He was a pilot flying C46s and C47s. Manual and I had been buddies in Lincoln and had run around together for a long time before the war, so I decided to go see him. His mother Anna and his father Ben were wonderful people and had treated me like one of the family. With my connections within the intelligence department, I found that this base was located at Villacoubuay, a village just a short distance from the edge of Paris. By checking my Metro map, I found that I could ride the Metro to the edge of Paris and from there take a bus the short distance to the airfield, so off I went.

Arriving at the field, I went to the administration building and showed them my identification and said that I would like to see Manual Plokin. They informed me that he was on a flight delivering gas up to Patton at the front. They of course wanted to know if he had done anything wrong and I told them that I was just an old friend from home. Somewhat relieved at this, they informed me that he would be arriving soon and would park in the number three revetment and that I could wait for him there.

Taking care to stay out of the way, I walked on over there. I had no more arrived when I saw his plane taxiing up and turning into the revetment. It had so many holes in it that I was surprised that it could even fly. Some of them were big enough that you could throw a chair through. These planes had no guns and were used to haul gas and supplies up to Patton at the front, which was a sure way to get shot at.

The exit from these planes was at the back and had no door, as they had to shove out the supplies almost on the run. The bottom of the exit was just about even with my shoulders and I was standing there the moment Manual spotted me.

In his excitement, he jumped from the plane threw both his arms and legs around me. "I thought that I would never see anyone from home again! They were shooting at me with everything they had and all I had was this 45!" Going on in the same breath, he asked, "What are you doing here?"

I told him that I was with the CID stationed in Paris and had found out where he was located and had come to see him.

With a very excited reply, he said, "I'm sure glad you did. Just as soon as I close my flight plan and we have our debriefing, I will be off for twenty-four hours." He pointed out the officers club and told me to go on over and order anything I wanted and have them put it on his tab. "You can't even begin to believe how glad I am to see you. I'll join you shortly!"

I went on over to the club and I didn't even have time to finish my drink before he showed up. He ordered his drink and we took them over to a table and he again told me how thrilled he was to see me.

"It is just as wonderful for me," I said. "It's the next best thing to being home!"

With this, we began updating each other on what we knew was happening at home. Neither one of us could stop talking long enough to drink our drinks. He couldn't believe that I had come through the Battle of the Bulge safely and had received a Battlefield Commission and Silver Star before being shot and evacuated to England and was now back in Paris with the CID. He told me that in all the flights he had made, he had never been wounded and that most of the flights were not too bad.

I told him that judging from the number and size of the holes in the plane that he had just brought in, he was a very lucky guy. No one can believe how wonderful it was to sit there, hundreds of miles from home and talk with a friend and buddy that I had spent so much time with at home.

We talked and talked and finally he asked me if I was hungry. I said, "Yes, I could stand something to eat," and asked if they had a good officers mess there.

Manual answered, "Yes, but I live off base. I have an apartment in a Chateau in town and I'm living with a French girl. She is a good cook and does my washing and takes real good care of me. I'll call her and tell her to chill some wine because I will be bringing company home for dinner."

I don't know how he had managed it, but he had a Jeep to drive and we took off for town. He had a nice apartment. When we arrived there, he introduced me to his girl friend, who was very nice and just a pretty girl.

We had a very good dinner with wine, pleasant company and loads of conversation. I told him about meeting Gloria Clark, the sister of my platoon leader who had been wounded and evacuated to the States, and also meeting Bill Redis, the Red Cross Major who was also from Lincoln. Manual said that he also knew Bill. It's a small world.

While Manual's girlfriend was clearing off the table, we sat there and continued our conversation. All of a sudden, Manual exclaimed, "My God, Lindy, whatever you do, don't write anything to anyone back home where it will get back to my folks that I'm living with a French girl. You know what a strict Jewish family my folks are. I'd probably never be able to go back home again."

I was sure glad he told me this, because I probably would have mentioned it without thinking. We talked a long time and it was getting late, so he told me that he had a couch that I could sleep on. We exchanged phone numbers and addresses so we could get together again. He wanted me to show him around Paris. I think his French girl kept him too busy to do much sightseeing.

When Manual's girl friend finished in the kitchen, she came back into the living room and we all sat around and drank a little wine, talked and spent a wonderful evening. She spoke English as well as Manual and I, and was very interesting to talk to. I believe she worked in one of the nearby small towns. As usual, the time flew by in a hurry and it was almost midnight before we hit the sack.

The next morning, I went on back to the base with Manual and we had breakfast together and more reminiscing. He had to check out the repairs on his plane, so I headed on back to Paris. By this time, it was almost noon, so I had lunch and headed on to the CID headquarters. I reported to Captain Seidel and turned in my report on the pregnant French girl. He seemed happy with that report and assigned me another case.

This new case dealt with the black-market in Paris and the surrounding area. To give you a little perspective on this, in the four years of Nazis occupation, the French had a great black-market organization going because they thought stealing from the Germans was the patriotic thing to do. When they were liberated by the Americans, that easy money was just too hard to let go. They were making thousands of dollars because people need everything. Also, at this time in Paris, there were between 25,000 and 30,000 American soldiers either AWOL (absent without leave) or deserters. After being AWOL for 90 days, you were considered a deserter, and after being classified a deserter, you could be shot if convicted. It did not take long for these men to run out of money, and seeing the thousands of dollars of easy money the French were making, they would decide to get in on a little of it.

To mention a few of the top items that they stole, one was the rotor caps for Jeeps. They brought $40.00. (When you left your Jeep parked, you removed the rotor cap and took it with you so no one could steal the Jeep). Another of the top items was cigarettes, which would bring anywhere from $50.00 to $150.00 a carton. Gasoline brought $4.00 to $5.00 a gallon. There were many other things that were easy to move like food, clothes, shoes, soap and almost anything else that they could get their hands on.

After being handed this case and Paris being such a large city, I had absolutely no idea of where to start. I began by looking around and hanging out in some of the lower class dives in the city trying to pick up information. I checked passes and IDs but was getting nowhere fast. Taking a short cut through a back alley, I saw a 6X6 parked in an out-of-the-way place where it shouldn't have been. On checking the cab for a trip ticket, I found none. Neither did I find a requisition form, which should have been with the trip ticket. I went on to check the back cargo area and found it was loaded with gas cans, all of them full. This load of gas was worth thousands of dollars.

As this seemed to be a very dangerous neighborhood, I thought that I had better call for some back up. This proved to be more of a chore than I thought it would be. I had to go halfway across Paris to find a phone. After finally locating a phone, I called Captain Seidel at CID headquarters and asked for at least four men, armed and with radios and a Jeep. They were to pick me up at the location of the phone that I was calling from.

When they picked me up, we proceeded on to the alley where the truck was parked, but by the time we got there, it was gone. We had lost not only a truck loaded with thousands of dollars worth of gasoline on the black market, but more importantly, several good leads to the whole gang. With much disappointment, I left a sergeant and two men and made my way back to headquarters.

Meeting with Captain Seidel, I asked for a Jeep with a radio and two more men, all of us to be supplied with hand held radios. He gave me these and also gave me another MP officer. This officer happened to be another officer that I knew and he had also received a Battlefield Commission.

Before headed back to the area where I had found the truck, I went by my room and picked up my 45 automatic along with several spare clips to use instead of my off duty Browning 7.65 automatic, which was about as effective as a BB gun.

Arriving back at the alley where we had left the men on watch, they informed us that they had observed a small hotel nearby that seemed to have an awful lot of unusual activity going on. People were constantly going in and out, and although they were dressed in civilian clothes, they walked like military soldiers. We decided to check it out after we had checked the area for Army vehicles that seemed to be out of place. One of the men did find a 6X6 truck inside a deteriorating building and the back end was filled with full gas cans and several cases of hand grenades. We put a guard on this truck and put a guard on both the front and rear of the hotel. Taking the lieutenant with me, we began to check out the rooms and the passes and IDs of their occupants. Things were moving along smoothly (for awhile).

The hallways were laid out in the form of an "H." The MP lieutenant had just turned down the far end of the connecting hall and I was at the other end facing him. All of a sudden, a door opened about half way down the hall. A man stepped out and turned in my direction. I was carrying a submachine gun and he started to shoot at me with a Luger in one hand and a P38 in the other. This put me between a rock and a hard place, because I couldn't return fire with the lieutenant directly behind him. I shouted for him to hit the deck and I opened up with the machine gun. The man was still shooting and I was shooting also. I could see that I was hitting him but he wouldn't go down. Finally he did. I think I had put at least eight to ten 45 slugs in him before he fell. I don't know how he missed hitting me. He was only thirty-five or forty feet away from me in this hallway that was only about five foot wide and he had emptied both clips at me before he died.

The MP lieutenant said, "Lindy, you have to be the luckiest guy living in this world!"

I was still pretty badly shook up and replied, "Thank heaven you hit the floor when you did. If you hadn't, I wouldn't have stood a chance."

We later found that this man that I shot was the ring leader of the largest black market operation going on in Paris. He had started out as an American sergeant in charge of a detail of truck drivers hauling gas from the supply dump to the units needing gas. I don't know just what had happened, but his route led through Paris where they often stopped to party. My guess was that they ran out of money, and having these trucks loaded down with gas, they decided to sell them. He went AWOL and sold the whole truck load on the black market. Having had a taste of this easy money, his AWOL soon ran into desertion and he began to recruit other deserters into a gang whose sole purpose was to steal trucks, gas and other supplies and sell them on the black market. At this, he was very successful and he went on to get false passes, false IDs, false trip tickets, false requisition forms, and even forms for drawing rations from the quartermaster so he could feed his men. He didn't stop there. He bought an interest in this hotel and he had his own mess hall, food, clothing, and everything else they needed to carry on a successful operation. It was not long before he bought a house of prostitution a short distance away. Now he had everything to keep his men happy, including money.

When we discovered that first truck, his gang started to collapse. After the shooting of the leader and the raid on the hotel, we arrested most of the gang and about two or three were killed. When the

Finance Department checked the leaders' papers, they found that he had a bank account containing thousands of francs. Now we had to turn much of the paperwork over to the French Police. There were a lot of French involved in the operation of the gang and although we could arrest the French, it was standard operating procedure to let the French police do it themselves, since they would have to be tried in a French court.

This investigation was winding down and I had reported back to Captain Seidel at Headquarters. He went over all the paperwork with me to make sure we had covered everything before it was turned over to the prosecutor. I also had to fill out a form because I had shot the guy in the hallway. I don't remember much about the form but I do know that I had to pay for the ammunition that I used. They even wanted to know why I had shot him so many times. I told them that the only way that they could know that was to put themselves in the same situations.

The only thing that I could say for sure was that I was glad that this case was over. It had been a very dangerous case and I had learned a lot. I would never start another case without my 45. Had I been carrying my off duty weapon instead of my 45, I would not be telling this story. I think it would have been safer back on the front because at least there you knew that someone would be shooting at you. All I wanted now was to get back to my room for a shower, clean clothes and a good meal.

With this case completed (where I had the shoot out in the hallway), I turned it over to my CO and he told me to take a few days off, which pleased me to no end. Leaving the CO, I went on back to my room, cleaned up, then called Gloria to see if she would like to go to the officers' mess with me and then later take in a show at some club. She said that she would love to go.

Just as I was leaving my room to meet her, the phone rang. It was Manual Polkin, who informed me that he was free that night and would like to come into Paris to have me show him around a little. I told him this would be great because I was just leaving to have dinner with Gloria at the officers' mess and he could meet us there. He happily agreed to meet us there but he told me that his French girl friend was tied up that night and he wondered if it would still be all right. I told him it certainly would be, but if he wanted me to inquire, I would see if Gloria had a friend who was free for the evening.

To this, he happily said that it would be great. I called Gloria back and explained the situation and she told me that Pat Easley wasn't doing anything that night (This was the girl whose husband had been shot down and killed). Gloria thought that it would be good for her to get out a little because she had been having a pretty hard time coping.

With this settled, I picked up the two girls and we met Manual at the officers mess. We had just been seated when in walked MP Lt. Roger Bassett (he was in the shoot out with me). He asked if he could sit at the table with us (it seated six). I asked if anyone minded and of course, no one did. He said that he wished that he had a date because he felt that he was going to stick out like a sore thumb. At this, Gloria, God bless her, said that she had another friend and that she would probably enjoy getting out, not as a date, but just to fill out our party. She had also lost her husband a few months ago. Gloria called her and she showed up about twenty minutes later. What had been a dinner for two was now a party.

We finished our dinner and left to go to another club where they had dancers and other entertainment. This club had a stage and a bar with a balcony on three sides. We found two tables on the balcony that would seat all of us, and ordered drinks while we were waiting for the show to start. Everyone was having a great time and Roger was telling everyone about the shoot-out in the hallway. He told them that with all the bullets flying, that I, Lindy, had to be the luckiest guy in the world. We were all having a great time with champagne corks popping, people laughing, and best of all, Gloria's two friends seeming to relax and enjoying themselves. It was wonderful to see two people who had lost so much being able to enjoy themselves for one evening.

By the time everyone had started to relax, the show started and as they turned up the stage lights, Roger looked over the balcony. Seated almost right on the stage was this old bald-headed colonel who was the Provost Marshal. (A Provost Marshal is the head of the MPs.) If he had been any closer, his nose would have been up the rear end of one of the dancers. He was a real butt hole and I'd had a run in with him earlier while I was on a case. I was purposely out of uniform to try to fit in with the people I was investigating. He started chewing me out for being out of uniform and saying that my conduct was unbecoming an officer.

When he'd had his say, I replied, "I'm not an officer, I am just an enlisted man with bars!" I showed him my ID and added, "You are interrupting an investigation and if you don't stop, I will arrest you!"

I thought that he was going to explode, but after seeing my ID and realizing that I could arrest him, he settled down and left. That made my day. I think this was one of the highlights of the time I spent with the Criminal Investigation Division. I think Roger hated this colonel almost as much as I had hated detached patients at large, but like I had been, he was stuck with him.

Our seeing the Provost Marshal sorta threw a little damper on our party, but we decided not to let it bother us and to go ahead and enjoy the show, which turned out to be very good. We were laughing and having a good time when suddenly someone popped a champagne cork. Would you believe it, it hit the old Provost Marshal right on his bald head. At this point, the red-headed MP Rogers' eyes lit up like a pinball machine. He was immediately down on the floor gathering up champagne corks. He was soon joined by everyone in our party. From then on, every time someone popped a cork, Roger would let fly at the old butt hole's bald head and he seldom missed.

The old guy's head got redder and redder every time a cork connected. Seeing the old bird in such discomfort put the joy back in our evening. Even the girls were laughing and enjoying the show. Having enjoyed a few drinks helped matters along immensely.

This was not a strip show, but the dancers' costumes were very skimpy and they were good dancers and all were attractive. When the show ended and the dancers came back on stage to take their bows, we were amazed to find that all of them were men. The girls couldn't believe it and it was even hard for me to comprehend.

As usual, the evening ended all too soon and we took the girls home. The girls thanked us for a wonderful evening, but it was dampened somewhat when the girls informed us that they would be receiving their assignments within the next few days and would be leaving Paris. I certainly hated to see the girls go, but knew that they, like everyone else, had jobs to do.

Manual and Roger expressed their joy at having had such a wonderful time and commented that we would have to repeat it as often as possible, so we exchanged telephone numbers and promised to try to get together again soon. I wished that I could have had Roger transferred to the CID, but I knew that the MPs would not release him.

The next morning after our night out with the girls and my friends, I woke up feeling great with all my nerves back in my body and no one in my room shooting at me. I received a call from CID headquarters that I was to report the next morning for my new assignment. This meant that I had another day free. How lucky could I be!

I got a call from Sgt. O'Brian and he told me that he and some of the old group were in Paris on a pass. They were going to be at the Red Cross unit at Rainbow Corners for about an hour getting cleaned up and having their uniforms pressed and wanted me to meet them there. I went over to meet them, and while I was waiting for Pat, in walked Gloria to pick up some equipment. I asked her to wait so that she could meet Pat because he was a good friend of her brother, Lt. Clark. When Pat came out, I introduced Gloria to him and his friends, and again, it was just like old home week. She gave Pat the telephone number of a Red Cross girl who was the head of "Rainbow Corners" and that he should contact this girl if he needed any help as she, Gloria, would be leaving on assignment soon.

I took Pat and the guys to a sidewalk cafe where the food was good and the prices reasonable. We ordered our food and Pat started to bring me up-to-date on my old outfit and the progress of the war on the front. He told me that it appeared to him that the war in Europe would be ending soon. He said that even some of the crack German troops were beginning to give up by the hundreds. It would be none too soon for these guys.

He said that they were in Paris to have a good time, but they would be limited because they had very little money. I informed them that I could let them have some, and at that, some of his friends added that they had brought back some souvenir items that they had "liberated" that they might be able to sell. They had eight cameras, six pairs of field glasses, three spotting scopes, and some guns. With my connections, I told them that I would have no trouble selling all of these items except the guns and they would take just a little longer. I told them that if they could get by until that night, I could get rid of everything except the guns and the money from them I could set aside for them to pick up when they came back. I told them that I could probably get 12,000 francs for each of the cameras and 5,000 francs for each pair of field glasses and 3,000 francs for the spotting scopes. "That's 120,000 francs or $2,000.00 that I can have for you by tonight, and I will meet you at the Bouy LaFayette Club and give it to you."

I told them how to get there and that I would meet them at four that afternoon. Pat looked at me with an expression of gratitude and said, "Mad Dog, I just can't believe this!"

"This is all legal loot—except the guns—and you guys sure deserve it."

While Pat and the guys were taking in some of the sights in Paris, I was busy getting rid of the loot. Even though it was legal, I was still very careful. When I had sold it all (except the guns) and got the cash, I met the guys at the club.

We sat there drinking a little wine while I explained what had happened to me the first night there. I would have enjoyed taking them to the officers' mess to eat, but no enlisted men were allowed there, so I ended up taking them to the special Club Prive where the beautiful waitresses wore nothing but a transparent apron with a red heart over the crotch area. Aside from the food also being good, I imagine that this pleased the guys even more than going to an officers club.

After enjoying the food and entertainment at the Club Prive, I took them to where the Follies Show was. We had a drink at the Follies Bar but didn't stay for the show. I next took them up to Place Pigalle where all the strip shows were and where all the prostitutes hung out.

After seeing these sights, we found a good sidewalk cafe and just sat and enjoyed our drinks while watching people go by. As we were sitting there relaxing, Pat told me that we had lost very few of the old guys from our old unit. He said that Captain Striker, after getting out of the hospital in England, rejoined them as they continued to advance across Germany. He expressed what a relief it was to have an officer who knew what he was doing to lead them.

Again, the evening was ending too soon. I told Pat that I would have to leave soon as I had to work the next morning and still had a little paper work to do before I turned in. I did sit there a little longer just to see how long it would take before some French gal would try to pick up one of the guys. It was not long, about ten minutes, when a good looking girl stopped and spoke to Pat and asked if he would buy her a drink. I told him that I had to leave and would see him before he left Paris. Letting nature take its course, I left for home.

Arriving at home, I began thinking about what Pat had said concerning the ending of the war there in Europe before long. This worried me because the war with Japan in the Pacific seemed to be going much slower. I was sure that with all the special training and experience that our old recon unit had, they would be one of the first units sent to the Pacific. I wanted to rejoin them because I didn't think I could handle trying to break in a bunch of new green troops after what I had been through in the "Bulge."

By this time, I had been completely released from the hospital. My left shoulder arm and hand were fine. It was very upsetting to me trying to figure out how I could get transferred back to my old outfit. I made up my mind to talk to my commanding officer at the first opportunity to see if I could get this done. The only nice thing about this job with the CID was that it allowed me to send all the money that was allowed home to my family. This was considerable because my cigarette rations were as much as my salary as an officer and I could send all that money home since I was not a smoker. (15,000 francs at regular exchange or 30,000 francs otherwise.) Another thing was that after all this soft living, I would probably get myself killed my first day in combat, though I was in better shape than most.

With all these things running through my mind, I decided to hit the sack and see if things looked brighter the next morning. Just then, my telephone rang and it was the WAC sergeant, Eleanor Stein. She told me that she hadn't seen me for some time and that she was still using my key and window to get in and out after hours and wondered if it was still OK. She wanted me to come down and have a drink with her and the girls. She said that they would even buy. It sounded like a good idea to me and as it was still early, I went on down to join them. After a couple of drinks with pleasant company, I went back upstairs and slept like a baby.

The next morning, I awoke to another day of reality in life in the city of Paris. It was hard for me to realize that only a short distance a way, the war was still going on and men were dying.

I dressed, then caught the Metro to the headquarters of the CID and reported to the Commanding Officer, Captain Seidle. We sat down and went over the cases on the docket. Most were only minor. I was assigned to one case concerning the theft of a Jeep and to another concerning an officer who wouldn't pay his apartment rent to his French landlord. Both of these, I considered minor.

After receiving my assignments, I asked him if he had a few minutes to spare. He said, "Yes." I proceeded to tell him of my concern about the war in Europe soon being over and that with my qualifications, my being sent to the Pacific and Japan. I told him that I didn't want to start out with green troops in another all-out war and that I would like to get transferred back to my old recon outfit. He said, "Lieutenant, I will not approve a transfer. In my opinion, you are needed more right here and if you do write a request for a transfer, I will not approve it."

It looked as if I was stuck again.

After I had collected all the information that I could find on the stolen Jeep, it was easy to run down. It appeared that some GI just needed a ride so he "borrowed" it and left it beside the road when he was through with it and then disappeared himself. I picked up the Jeep and returned it to unit it belonged to. There was little use in trying to find the GI, as he was long gone.

I decided to hold the apartment case over for a day and just go over the paper work. On arriving back at my room, I had a message waiting from Manual Plokin. He wanted to bring his girl friend into Paris to take in the "Follies." I immediately called him back and told him that it sounded great and that I would meet them downstairs at the club. I called Gloria and asked if she would like to join us and see the show again and she said that she would love to. She added that she was sure glad that I had called because she had just received her assignment and would be leaving the next day. Her two friends had already left that day and all three of them were to be scattered over France and Germany.

After dressing, I went downstairs to the club and soon Manual and his girl friend arrived and we went by and picked up Gloria. We all then proceeded to the officers' mess where we had dinner.

After dinner and a few drinks, we headed for the Follies. I think it was even better this second time. Manual's girl friend really enjoyed it. It was hard for me to believe that she had lived just outside Paris all these years and had never seen this famous show. (I sure wish I could remember her name.)

When the show was over, we stopped at one of the sidewalk cafes and had coffee. Manual had to fly early the next morning and didn't want to be out too late, so they headed home early.

I wanted to spend a little time with Gloria, being as she was leaving the next day. I told her that I was going to miss her an awful lot. She said, "Let's spend the rest of the evening together. We have a lot to say to each other before I leave."

We tried to figure out a place where we could go to just sit and talk to each other. I don't think anyone can understand the relationship between Gloria and me. She was more like family to me because she was Lt. Clark's sister. The most we had ever done was a good night hug and kiss. It is seldom that you can find a girl you can be friends with instead of getting involved in a romantic situation. Had times been different, and had I not been married, our relationship might have developed into a romantic, sexual thing.

I finally suggested that we pick up a bottle of wine and go to my room. I told her that I didn't want her to think that I was going to try to get into her pants. She reassured me that would be the last thing that she would have thought of. She added, "There is so much I want to say to you. I want to thank you for all the things you have done for me and my friends. I really wanted to do something for the war effort, but when I ended up half way around the world in a strange country, I was scared to death and all I wanted was to go back home. You took me under your wing, and suddenly all that fear was gone. My two friends whose husbands had been killed in the war were in

153

the same situation and they wanted me to tell you how much they both appreciated your kindness and how much you had helped them. They, as well as I, got to see a side of Paris that we would have never seen had we had to see it by ourselves. Another thing was that we could just be ourselves and we didn't have to worry about you taking advantage of us. It was almost like having our family around."

"Gloria, you have done just as much and maybe even more for me," I said. "You will never know how much you have really done. To get together with you and your friends was as close to having family near. I certainly hate to see you leave because I will be very lonely just knowing that you are gone and we will not be able to see each other. Our friendship is a very rare thing. Friendships such as ours, between a man and a woman, are very unusual. It has been one of the high points in my life. Shortly before you came over here, I had a very rough time. First was the battle of Stromberg Hill, where your brother was wounded. Then there was the Battle of the Bulge where we lost over half of our men, and then up in Berstein, Germany, where I was wounded. Of course, during my stay in the hospital in England, I was worried about losing my left hand and part of my arm. After my arm had healed and my recovery looked bright, I was stuck here in Paris with the Detached Patients at Large, which I hated with a passion. You made me feel that life was worth living again. So you see, you have done a lot for me too."

We sat there in my room enjoying each others' company (probably for the last time), drinking our wine and talking until almost three in the morning. It was wonderful therapy for both of us. Gloria promised to keep in touch with me and let me know where she was located. With my priority for air travel, I hoped I would be able to see her again. I walked her back to her home in the wee hours of the morning, and we parted with a tearful good bye. She said, "I'll write."

After spending that lovely evening with Gloria, it was a sad and hard job to get up and get going the next morning. Not knowing when or if I would ever see her again left me with a very empty feeling, but life had to go on.

I called the Frenchman about the case of the lieutenant and the apartment rent. To my relief, he told me that the lieutenant had come in and paid the rent, so that case was closed. All I had to do was complete the paper work, and that I would do the next day.

That decision settled in my mind, I decided to have a late breakfast at the officers' mess. While waiting for my food to be served, another lieutenant asked if he could join me at my table, and I told him that I would appreciate the company. I inquired why he too was having such a late breakfast. He answered, "I'm with the transportation division and we got a call earlier from the 32nd Cavalry Squadron up in Germany. They are in need of ammunition and supplies, so I am having a meal while our trucks are being loaded."

I excitedly answered, "I was in the 32nd until I was wounded and sent back to an English hospital! Do you think that I could ride up there with you?"

"I'm not supposed to let anyone ride with us."

When I showed him my ID and my transportation priority, he said, "That makes a difference. Come on along. I'll be happy to have the company. We have four trucks going up and you can ride in the second truck."

I could hardly believe my luck. This was going to be a big boost to my morale, which I really needed after Gloria left.

When we arrived at the 32nd's squadron headquarters, which was located somewhere in a woods well into Germany, the first person that I saw was my old friend, Captain Sam Woods. When he saw me, he threw his arms around me and I thought that he was going to hug me to death. I had known Sam since my first service days in Camp Livingston, Louisiana and my days in Panama. He took me to the HQ tent, and the first officer I saluted was Major Krake, the commanding officer and the same guy who pinned on my lieutenant bars when I was in Belgium.

Major Krake suggested that we go to the mess tent and have some coffee, which sounded like a good idea to me after that long ride. We had not been seated very long when in walked Captain Reed, who was from Springfield, Illinois and who had been a former CO of A Troop. Captain Striker showed up shortly after that and the mess tent was becoming almost like a homecoming reunion. Besides seeing all these old friends, it was also great to hear first hand just how the war was going. All of them seemed to think that the war was in its last stages.

As I had heard before, they said that a lot of the crack German troops were beginning to surrender by the hundreds. Their concern was the same as mine. They felt, that because of our special training, we would be some of the first to be sent to Japan, and taking the main Japanese Island would be a long, drawn out process.

Again, as usual, the time went all too fast. The transportation lieutenant came in and told me that we would have to get on the way soon. Major Krake said, "Lieutenant, send your men to the mess tent for lunch." This would give me a little more time to visit, but I felt badly that I would not have time to see any of my NCO friends at the front. They were so far ahead that HQ would have to be moved forward the next day. Thankful for the time that I did have with my old friends, but still a little disappointed that I didn't get to see more, I joined the lieutenant and we headed back to Paris.

On arriving back in Paris, the lieutenant dropped me off at the officers' mess at Place St. Augustine. Having spent a lot of time with friends over the last several days and weeks, it was rather lonely to sit down and eat all by myself. I was still on a high after seeing so many officers and men from my old unit, but I still couldn't get my mind off their comments about the war soon being over in Europe and the likelihood of the unit being sent on to the Pacific and Japan. Before that happened, I was going to have to figure out some way of being reassigned to my old unit.

I finished my dinner and walked back to my hotel, and then decided to stop and have a drink at the Bouy LaFayette Club. I had been there only a short time when someone tapped me on the shoulder and asked if I would mind if she joined me at my table. Looking around, I found that it was Eleanor Stein, the WAC sergeant who had the room next to mine.

"It is sure good to see you again," she said. "It's been a long time." She turned and pointed to the two WACs with her and said, "These are my friends, and since you let us use your room to get in and out, we have a lot more freedom to come and go as we please."

We sat there in the club for a long time and just talked. They bought me another drink, which I couldn't very well turn down. Anyway, being a little lonesome, I was happy with the company.

Eleanor worked in HQ and she had also heard rumors about the war in Europe soon being over. She wanted to know what I had heard. I told her that I had just returned from a visit with my old unit up in Germany and they were all of the same opinion that it would soon be over.

It had been good to have someone to talk to for awhile, but soon she and her friends had some soldiers that they knew join them. I was tired after my long trip and said, "I think that I'll go up and hit the sack. It's been a long day." She said that I was welcome to stay, but I declined, telling her that I was going to call it a day.

I went on up to my room and went to bed wondering, until sleep finally came, what was going to happen in the next few days or weeks. The girls must have been awfully quiet when they came through my room when they returned from the club, because I didn't even wake up. (I didn't even find any of the girls in bed with me the next morning. Sometimes one doesn't have any luck at all, although I was so shy, I wouldn't have known what to do if I did get lucky. I sure hoped that I would get over this shyness one of these days.)

The next morning, I went to the CID office to find out what kind of a problem that I would have to take care of that day. It looked like things were going to be quiet for awhile. When I arrived at the headquarters and reported to the commanding officer, he said that he didn't have any investigations that he didn't have people assigned to. He went on to say, "Why don't you take a couple or three days and hit all the trouble spots that you know of. Try to dress to fit into the crowd to see what you can pick up. In three days, bring me a written report of anything that you feel needs to be investigated." This sounded like a good deal to me.

I even had an expense account for food and drink. This was almost heaven for me! I started off by making all the trouble spots that I could think of. I didn't want to get too much done that first day and shorten the assignment, so I just played a little and found just enough to make it look like I was working. Paris is a big town and it was not hard to find a few things that should be investigated.

157

I was near the HQ of Detached Patients at Large so I decided to pay a visit to the CO, Captain Ruth Morgan. This was the same WAC captain that I had fought with over my transfer from the DOP AL back to my old unit.

She seemed happy to see me and wanted to know how I was doing. I told her, "Fine," then proceeded to tell her about the shoot out in the hotel hallway. She seemed very concerned and said that she would like to hear more about it. I told her that I had plenty of time right now, but she said that she had an appointment in ten minutes but maybe we could meet for a drink after it was over. I asked her if she knew where Bouy LaFayette Club was and she said, "Yes," so we arranged to meet there when she had finished her appointment.

We met at the club, and over drinks, I described the shoot-out to her and when I finished, she said, "You are lucky to be alive!" I then reminded her of her not being willing to approve my transfer back to my old unit after I received the Silver Star. "You said that I had seen enough combat, but as you can see, I don't think that there is any place that is really safe. I could just as easily get killed right here."

After seeing her again, I realized that she was much more attractive now than she had been when she was my CO and we were fighting. It might have been that I was looking at her differently now that she was no longer my CO. To make a long story short, we left there and had a lovely dinner and evening together, after which she said, "This was fun. We'll have to do it again soon."

When I offered to take her home, she suggested that we walk. I told her that sounded fine because it was a beautiful evening. On the way, we stopped at a sidewalk cafe and had another drink. We talked about the war here and of the war in the Pacific and what would happen when the European war was over. Everyone seemed to think that most of the soldiers here would be sent on to the Pacific. To me, this was very upsetting, for it seemed that I was never going to get home. This thought made me very lonely and just having someone to talk to made me sorta feel better.

After walking Ruth home, I headed back home myself, but I stopped at the "Bouy" to say hello to several people I knew and then went on up to bed. Tomorrow was another day.

I rolled out of bed the next morning, had breakfast and reported to CID headquarters to see if any new cases had come up. Captain Seidel told me that he'd had a call from a French girl who said she was living in a beautiful apartment with a major from the quartermaster (supplies) department. He was paying all the bills for everything, but she had found out that he had another French girl in another apartment with whom he was spending a lot of time and was neglecting her. She felt that the major had to be selling Army supplies to be able to support this other girl.

Captain Seidel gave me the first girl's address and told me to go see her and find out everything that I could. We sat discussing the case and he said, "This sounds like a real bag of worms. I want you to take all the time you need. I don't care it takes a month or even six weeks. I think this guy has been selling everything but the kitchen sink. We want this guy."

I took the address and went there to talk to the French girl. She was a real knock out and spoke English better than I did. She was really p---ed off about the major's other girl. I looked around the apartment, and at first glance, saw dozens of items that should not have been there. I told her that she should tell no one about me contacting her and went on to explain that if she did, she would be arrested and sent to jail. She said that she would not say anything and all that she wanted was to see that bastard get what he had coming to him. She went on to say that she had been true to him and had not been screwing around with anyone else.

I think, at this point, she would have probably given me some of the wildest sex of my life just to get back at this major. I decided to get out of there. She was wearing a pink French negligee and I think you could have read a newspaper through it. I am only human and my willpower was growing weaker by the moment. If I had been weaker, there could have been some good "fringe benefits" to this job.

Anyway, I got out of there with my honor and integrity intact. People just don't realize how many temptations there are out there for a shy, innocent small town American boy. What I didn't tell the girl, was that if we did arrest the major, she would also lose her golden nest.

I went on back to the officers' mess at Place St. Augustine where MP Lt. Rogers, the one who was with me during the hotel shoot-out, joined me. We brought each other up on the activities going on in our respective departments. When I told him about the French girl and how hard it was to turn down the implied offer, he said, "Lindy, you have all the luck!"

I replied, "Yes, and if I had taken that luck, you would have probably had me in your jail by now and wouldn't that a--hole Provost Marshall loved that!"

"He is still an a--hole, maybe worse." Rogers went on to ask how Manual was, and I told him that I had not seen him for some time but that we were going to have to get together again soon. It would not be the same with Gloria and her friends gone, but we could still have fun.

While we sat there finishing our meal, we talked about how the war in the ETO (European Theater of Operations) was going. We both thought it would be only a short time before it was over, but the war with Japan was moving along much slower. If it came to the point that the Americans had to invade the homeland of Japan, the American casualties would be 3,000,000 and the Japanese 12,000,000. The way it looked to us was that all trained and experienced combat men would be sent right on over to the Pacific, especially reconnaissance and intelligence units. This was a very sobering thought that made me sad. Remember, I was married and my wife had given birth to a little girl that I had never seen, not even a picture.

We finished our meal and I left to continue work on the case of the major and the two French girls. I got the address of the second girl and proceeded to that address to interview her.

She was also living in a beautiful apartment with all the bills paid by the major. When I started talking to her, I discovered that she had found out about the first girl and that the major was paying all of her bills. This second girl was also a very striking individual, but unlike the first one, she was more mature and smarter. She was even dressed in a business suit.

Again, looking around her apartment, I discovered several items of contraband that should not have been there. I went through the process of explaining to her in no uncertain terms, that she was to tell no one about me contacting her and that if she should do so, she would be arrested and jailed. She went on to explain to me that the major had bought a department store in her name and that she was running it for him. She said that she would do anything I wanted if I would help her.

I told her that I would do what I could if she would testify in court against the major when the case came to trial. She promised she would and added that she had a bank account in her name, but the major gave her the money to deposit in it. She, in turn, would give him cash when he asked for it.

It looked like this was going to be an endless bag of worms! I decided to dig around a little more to see what else I could dig up. Trying to find out how he was getting rid of this stuff without a loss showing on the inventory was a part of the investigation that would be fully checked into after he had been arrested. Having gone this far with the investigation, I decided to call it a day. If I could pull all of this together, this major will be either shot or never see daylight again. (Most of the military prisons over there were pretty dark.)

In the meantime, I had heard rumors that the German prisons were releasing some of the American POWs. They said the war was lost so it sounded as if the end was close in Europe. I decided that I would eat at Place St. Augustine that night and then head on over to the Bouy LaFayette Club and check out the latest rumors.

When I arrived at the Club, I called Eleanor (the WAC sergeant), and she said that she would be right down. Within just a few minutes, she showed up. It had been some time since I had seen her, so I inquired how she was doing. She confirmed that rumors were flying that the European war would be over soon, and to add credence to the rumor, she said that much of the paperwork coming through her HQ concerned troop movement. That meant that combat troops were being pulled off the front lines to clean up isolated pockets of resistance that had been passed up in the drive to take Germany. Since she worked in HQ, she should know.

Talk like this always made me a little sad and upset. I was still doing everything that I could think of to get transferred back to my old unit but my commanding officer, Seidel, still would not give me a transfer. I could hardly face the idea of going to fight the Japanese in the Pacific with a bunch of green troops. Seeing my concern, Eleanor suggested that we change the subject to something a little more pleasant, so I started telling her about some of the cases that I had been working on. We both got a good laugh over some of them. We sat around and shot the bull and had a few more drinks. We were joined by several people we both knew that happened to drop in and sat with us at the table. It turned out to be a very enjoyable evening.

It was starting to get a little late so Eleanor and I ordered a couple of drinks to go and took them up to my room, where we sat and talked for a long time. We were only good friends. She again thanked me for letting her use my room so she wouldn't have to check in and out. Remember, although the two hotels were separate, her room was next to mine and she could go along the balcony from her window to my window. I think if I'd had any idea of the problems I was to have with my marriage when I got home, we could have had an affair with plenty of sex and all the trimmings. She was a very attractive young lady. As it was, we kept it on a friendship only relationship, more like a brother and sister. Good friends of the opposite sex are hard to find. She told me which girls were bitches and I told her the same was true with many of the guys and when she would inquire about a guy, I always told her the truth. Of course, if sex was what you were interested in, it was available in any way, shape or form.

While we finished our drinks, we sat there and talked about home and family and what we would do after the war. Both decided it was time to hit the sack, so she headed out my window to return to her room. This would have been a great location for an affair but, as you will see later, she would be able to do me a great favor at the headquarters where she worked. If we had been involved in a serious affair, she might have not wanted to do it for me.

After Eleanor had left by the window, I reviewed what I had on the major and the two French girls. With the evidence that I had, I thought to myself, "I'm going to do OK on this case."

The next morning, I went down to the mess hall for early breakfast and when I finished, I started walking across the street from Place St. Augustine using a short cut that I often used. This was on a circle with about five streets taking off like the spokes of a wheel. I would cut straight across the center, as this was the shortest way to get to the Metro and my office.

I had reached almost the center of the circle when I looked up. Approaching me were two of the scroungiest looking men that I had ever seen. They were clothed in beat up parts of military uniforms and part civilian clothes. When they had approached to within about twenty feet of me, they both broke into a dead run straight for me with a wild look in their eyes. I was so shocked that I just stood there.

The first guy grabbed me like a long lost brother and shouted, "Mad Dog! I thought you were dead!" It was only then that I realized that it was Lt. Reppa who was captured on December 17th at Honsfeld during the Battle of the Bulge.

I looked him over. "Reppa, I thought you were dead! The last time I saw you, they had you lined up along the wall ready to shoot you along with a lot of civilians."

We just stood there looking each other over. When I looked at the other guy, I realized it was Lt. Sharp. Here were two guys that I had lived and slept with for over four years, and after being prisoners of war for only five months, I hardly recognized them. They were just skin and bones and I didn't even know who they were until I heard Reppa's voice.

"What are you doing here?" I asked.

He replied that the German prison camp released them, saying that the war was over. (This was three days before V.E. Day.) Almost in the same breath, he said, "Let's go get something to eat. We're starved."

I turned around and we went back to the mess hall.

We went in and sat down, and man, you should've seen those guys eat. Reppa said that he had lost forty pounds the first week and had lost a pound a day for days after that. He said that they got a ride into Paris after they were released and they were supposed to catch a plane back to the States the next day. He thought that most of the enlisted men had been released, but he wasn't sure. The officers and enlisted men were kept separated.

I got a bottle of wine for our table and then Reppa wanted to know what had happened to me. I gave him a rundown on the 32nd's finish of the Bulge and of our replacements of men and equipment and how we ended up in Berstein, Germany and what had happened to me there (being wounded and ending up in a hospital in England and then being returned to Paris).

After bringing them up to date on my activities, I said, "Let me take you to the quartermaster and get you some new clothes. Then you can come to my place, take a shower, shave and get cleaned up. After that, we will celebrate and I will show you around Paris."

When I got them outfitted with new clothes, I dropped them off at my apartment. I went on back to the office for a meeting with my commanding officer. I told him about Reppa and Sharp being released and said, "Everyone in Paris will be going wild for the next ten or twelve days, the Americans and the French alike. I think we should try to get the two French girls out of town for a few days to keep them away from Major Morton. He will probably want to celebrate with one or the other of them and I don't want to take the chance of him finding out that we are on to him. I understand that both girls have relatives in Southern France. I'll see if I can convince them to go visit their relatives for a short time."

Seidel agreed.

I went to see the first girl, Toni, and on this day, she was dressed in spiked heels and a very beautiful tight red dress that left very little to the imagination. All I can say is that she was built like a sex machine with everything in the right place. I think that she would do anything for money and I was sure the major had plenty.

I told her that I would like for her to go visit her aunt in Southern France and to have no contact with the major. Pouting, she asked if I was going to go with her. I told her no, but that she had no choice. It was either visit her aunt or go to jail. Again, I got out with my honor intact.

I went to see the second girl, Aletta, at her department store. I asked her if she had a place where we could talk privately and she said that we could use her office. When we sat down, she inquired if I would like a drink, which, of course, I had to refuse. But I did add that I could use a cup of coffee, so she asked one of her girls to bring it in. At this point, I would like to comment on what Aletta was wearing. She was very striking, wearing a light gray business suit with a low cut white blouse underneath, high heeled shoes, and silk stockings on long, long legs. She too had all the equipment in the right places, but wasn't advertising it.

I told her why I was there and went on to ask her if she could get one of her employees to manage the store for ten or twelve days and for her to have no contact with the major. She said yes to all of this.

I then asked her to go visit her uncle in Southern France for those ten to twelve days. I explained to her that it was either that or spend that time in jail. She said that she would be only too glad to go to visit her uncle, as she would be glad to get away from the major. She said that he was a bald-headed, middle aged man that was going to pot and couldn't satisfy a woman if he tried and that he didn't try. He thought only of himself. When he hired her, she didn't realize that she was going to have to sleep with him, but since good jobs were scarce, she complied.

I enjoyed very much talking to her and went on to ask if she would testify against him in court. Of course the answer was yes. I thought that she had been getting a raw deal, so I asked her to have her girls get rid of anything in the store that even remotely had any resemblance to government property. I informed her that I would see her when she returned. At this point, she said, "The beaches are warm in Southern France and the women are beautiful."

Another temptation, but I told her goodbye and went on back to my friends, Reppa and Sharp. We had some celebrating to do.

When I arrived back at my place, both of them had shaved, showered and dressed. They looked 100% better, even though I don't think either of them weighed a hundred pounds. They informed me that I could not even begin to know how good that shower felt. I told them that I knew that it had not been long since they ate, but would they like to go down to the officers mess for lunch? They both gave a resounding "Yes."

As we were walking to the mess hall, Paris was beginning to respond to the rumors that the Germans had quit fighting and that the war would be over in two or three days. The French were running around on the streets yelling and shouting, "We whipped the Huns (as they called the Nazi Germans)."

Slightly irritated, I thought to myself, "If they whipped them, why in the hell were all these American boys over here fighting and dying?" Oh well. Anyway, the streets were getting wild.

Reppa, Sharp and I found a table and ordered a bottle of good wine (a bottle of good water cost more than a bottle of wine). While we were waiting, Reppa wanted to know what had happened after they were captured in Honsfeld. I went over what had happened and how we had fought our way out of first one town and then another, and that by that time Patton was in the south going like hell. I went on to explain how they had placed us in the First Army, where they'd stuck it to us again. Continuing on, I gave him a rundown on the action in Berstein, Germany, the minefields, the bunkers, and my being awarded the Silver Star. I went on to tell him about being wounded and evacuated to England, then being sent back to Paris to work while completing my recovery, first being assigned to Detachment of Patients at Large and then finally my assignment to the Criminal Investigation Division and the shoot out in the hotel hallway.

"Now, I want to know what happened to you," I said.

Reppa told me that after they were captured in Honsfeld, they were lined up against a wall and orders were given to shoot them. They had already shot several of the soldiers and civilians when a German Infantry Colonel arrived and took over and started them on a march back to a German prisoner of war camp. He said as they were marched back, the Germans would try to run over them with their tanks, hit them with their gun butts, and sometimes even shoot at them. He told me that the first thing the Germans did after the capture was to take all their heavy winter clothing, and that often, the temperature would drop down to fifteen to twenty degrees below zero. Sometimes, they would be allowed to sleep in barns, and that was the only thing that kept more of them from freezing to death. After they reached the POW camp, their treatment improved a little, but there was still very little food. Of course, the Germans had little food either.

"That's enough of that bad stuff," he said. "Now let's go have some fun!"

I agreed with Reppa and Sharp and we set out to have some fun. I asked, "What do you guys want to do?"

They both replied that they wanted to see the sights, but not the museums, as they both thought they were pretty boring. They did want to see the Notre Dame Cathedral. I had told them it was close by so we went.

In only a short time we arrived, and I cannot even begin to describe this enormous church, which I understand was built in 1100 AD or, at least, started at that time. Although Reppa and Sharp both enjoyed it very much, I think that they wanted to see it so they could tell their families about it.

What they really wanted to see was the wild side of Paris, so we started out by hitting some of the bars in the wilder parts of Paris where all the prostitutes hung out and that had all the wild strip shows, etc. The first one we went to was a bar with a large window from which we could see the street and watch the action. I had brought along my "ditty bag" containing a fifth of Vat-69. We would have a drink of Scotch and buy a beer for a wash.

Reppa said, "We're drinking your scotch so I'm buying the beer." With this he placed a thousand franc note on the bar for the three beers that cost 100 francs each.

As we were sitting there drinking, Reppa remarked, "That guy didn't give me any change!"

I told him to go ahead and ask for his change. When he asked the bartender for his change, the bartender replied, "No understand English."

I said in no uncertain terms, "Give the man his change!"

With this, he gave me the same old song and dance. I pulled my 45 out of my shoulder holster and laid it heavily on the bar with my hand resting firmly on top of it. I looked at the bartender and patting my 45 said, "This doesn't understand French."

"Mad Dog, don't." Reppa said. "We are going home tomorrow and we don't want to end up in jail today!"

As I pulled out my ID, I smiled at Reppa and said, "Don't worry. I'm not going to shoot him. If anyone goes to jail, it will be this bartender."

I guess you know, that bartender learned English real fast, and not only did Reppa get his change, we all got a free drink also. The bartenders tried to pull this ruse on a lot of the soldiers who were on leave. What I did was a kind of sting operation that all of us in the CID would pull when it got too bad.

A bartender like this takes all the fun out of things, so we finished our drinks and got out of there and took in a strip show that wasn't very good. We left the show and had a drink at a sidewalk cafe while we watched the prostitutes ply their trade. We were not far from the Eiffel Tower, so we walked on over there and went to the restaurant on the second level for a couple more drinks.

From there we watched the excursion boats on the River Seine. Leaving the tower, we took the Metro to the Arc de Triumphe. By this time, the boys exclaimed that they had seen enough sights for awhile and that they were tired and would like to rest for a little while. I told them about my favorite restaurant and floor show and the Follies.

They said that they sounded great, so I said, "Get some rest. I'll pick you up in about two hours and we will head for 'The Victoire' (the private club). We can eat and catch the first show and still make it to the Follies."

I made a few phone calls and took care of a couple small problems, and after a couple hours, picked up Reppa and Sharp and we headed for the Victoire Club Prive. This was the private club where the waitresses wore nothing but a small transparent apron with a red heart over the crotch area and very, very high heels. These girls were not prostitutes and they were all beautiful. The service was superb and the food was excellent. Reppa and Sharp were impressed. I know they didn't believe me when I first told them about this place, but anyway, we sat there and ate and enjoyed a great floor show. The girls could really dance, even though they wore more clothes than the waitresses.

The boys finished up a great meal while discussing going home and seeing their families. This again made me feel rather sad as I could see no way, in the near future, that I would be able to get home and see my new baby girl "Linda." Of course, I was very happy for the guys after all they had been through. We had a few drinks and I told them that we had better get started for the Club Ledo to get good seats to see "the Follies" show. Off we went and we did arrive before the crowd grew too large and we did get good seats.

While waiting for the show to start, the discussion again turned to the war in the Pacific with Japan. Both of the guys agreed with me that it was going to be long and drawn out. They, of course, having been prisoners of war, would never be sent back into a combat zone. Also, as ex-POWs, they would be promoted one grade higher in rank.

The discussion ended when the show started, and as I have already mentioned, this was a world-famous show. The girls were beautiful and the costumes were fabulous with some of the most superb acting I had ever seen.

As they sat there watching the show, the boys asked, "Where did they get all of these beautiful girls?" I explained to them that although this was a French show, most of the girls were not French. Almost ninety percent of them were from some other country.

This show, like all good things, came to an end all too soon. We left the show and stopped at a sidewalk cafe for a coffee and talked about all the crazy times (both good and bad) we had experienced over the years past. I repeat again, you can never, unless you experience it for yourself, know how wonderful it is to again be talking with friends that you thought were dead and who, in turn, thought that you had also met your maker.

The boys had to catch an early flight to the good old USA in the morning, so once again we parted not knowing when or if we would ever meet again. My future was uncertain as the prospects of being sent to the war in the Pacific looked certain. Very sad, but one of the heartaches of war. There was little consolation in the fact that I was not alone.

As I headed back to my hotel, I felt my world was coming to an end. Here I was again alone in Paris, the "City of Light." It didn't help any that I didn't get many letters from home. I got more from my family than I did from my wife. With all these sad thoughts running through my mind, I hoped that I could sleep and at least maybe dream of home. Tomorrow would be another day.

No such luck. I went to bed and lay there awake for hours. I could see no end to my problems. I still wanted to get back to my old unit as I was sure that they would be going home as soon as this war in Europe was over and would at least have some time at home before being sent to the Pacific and the war with Japan. By the same token, I was sure that my CO at CID would not approve my transfer. Again, I was between a rock and a hard place and the only thing I could do was to keep trying. I finally did fall into a restless sleep, but no dreams of home, only nightmares.

After breakfast the next morning, I went into the Criminal Investigation Office and talked to the CO about our upcoming investigations. We decided we had better put a hold on everything due to the extensive rumors about the war coming to an end almost anytime now and with people going crazy celebrating (especially the French). As for the case of the Major and the French girls, we would have to talk to a lot more French people.

I not only thought that this was a good idea, but with the mood I was in (feeling lower than a snake's belly), I didn't feel much like working. It really seemed unfair to me that my men and I, who had fought our hearts out winning the Battle of the Bulge, would not be going home without going through more combat. The ones who gave up and surrendered would be going straight home when they were released. Such is war.

With all these negative thoughts running through my mind, I decided to celebrate, come hell or high water and to hell with everything—home, marriage, family and all. I was going to live for me and today and not worry about tomorrow. I was going to do anything and everything that I wanted and felt like doing and God have mercy on anyone or anything that got in my way. Paris, girls, nurses, WACs, Red Cross girls and all others, LOOK OUT. The shy small town boy from the central USA was going to celebrate the same way he fought his combat battles, all out. The "Mad Dog" was on the loose again.

The first thing on my agenda was to go to my room and pick up all my liquor rations, which, being a good boy, I hadn't used. Next I headed down to the Red Cross at Rainbow Corner to try to find Gloria Clark's friend to find out if any of my buddies from the 32nd were in town. I was in luck. There were several in town, including Bardouche, who was my point Jeep driver and who also happened to be one of my favorite people. I asked Gloria's friend for Gloria's phone number and address, but she only had the address, no phone number.

By this time, it was almost noon so I decided to have lunch. I sure didn't want to start out on an empty stomach. I went by the officers' mess, hoping to see some officers from A Troop, but no such luck. I then started my search for Bardouche by heading for all the trouble spots, and sure enough, it was not long before I spotted him. The MPs already had him, but thank heaven, my MP friend Roger was in charge. I had lucked out again. He turned over Bardouche to me and said that maybe we could get together later, but I told him that I wasn't sure, but that I would call him and then thanked him for taking care of my friend.

As we were leaving, I asked Bardouche what he had done this time. He said, "I just got in a little fight. Some GI insulted a waitress and tried to pull her skirt up, so I told him to apologize. He said, 'Make me!' so I did."

I said, "Let's get back to my room and get you cleaned up. You've got to stay out of trouble. With the war this close to being over, you don't won't to end up in the stockade and not able to return home with the rest of your unit."

"I guess you're right," he said.

After cleaning up at my place, we took a double deck bus to a place that I knew served good food. As the bus passed it, I pulled the cord to stop but that damned driver just kept going. On these buses, there was an enormous emergency brake near the back steps (this thing was about three feet tall and built like the ones on our old Model T Fords, except it was three times larger). Both of us grabbed it and pulled with all our might. All the wheels locked up, throwing people out of their seats. The driver came running back raising hell in French, but we ignored him. As we walked away, Bardouche said, "I wonder what he called us?"

As we entered this little restaurant, which had live music and good looking waitresses, I said, "Bardouche, I have already eaten. What to you want? How about a good steak?"

He said, "That sounds fine but how about a drink while we are waiting?"

While we were waiting, the discussion again turned to the rapidly-ending European war. He said that most of the fighting had stopped with only isolated pockets of resistance, and even these were giving up without a fight. He also stated the rumors that he had heard, that the 32nd would be one of the first units sent home to start preparing for the final invasion of Japan.

Before our food was served, in came two of the nurses that I had known from my physical therapy treatments when I first arrived here from England. I asked Bardouche if he minded if I ask them to sit with us, and he replied, "Of course not." By this time, our food had arrived and we had ordered drinks for the girls. From the looks of things, we were headed for a great afternoon. The girls were both off duty so we asked them if they would like to hang around with us for the rest of the day. They also had heard the rumors that the war was close to over, so they too were ready to celebrate.

We left there and went on back to the Bouy LaFayette Club in my hotel. One of the girls said she needed to freshen up and use the rest room, so I told her to take my keys and use my bathroom upstairs and ask Bardouche to show her where it was. By this time, the place was really becoming a madhouse. I think everyone in Paris was in there. The couple left, and judging by the length of time it took them to get back, I think that they must have become lost or else were just having a good time.

We were still sitting there drinking when Bardouche and the girl finally returned. It must have been a great relief for them to use the bathroom for they each walked in with a smile that you couldn't have wiped off if you wanted to. I don't think that they were worrying about tomorrow, they were living for today! I turned to the nurse who had remained with me and said, "From the looks of things, I believe that I should have shown your friend the way to the bathroom."

She looked at me and replied, "You can show me now."

So we went up to my room, and after about an hour, we did get around to using the bathroom. By the time we got back to our table downstairs, I knew why both the nurse and my friend had a smile on their faces when they returned.

We sat at the table and discussed the progress of the war. The second nurse said that their future, like ours, was so uncertain that they had decided they were going to celebrate and just live for today and let tomorrow take care of itself. They both agreed that they were lucky they had run into us, as what they had done this night, they wouldn't want to do with just anyone. They were both married but thought that they knew me well as they had spent so much time with me during my therapy in their hospital. They had no intentions of becoming romantically involved with anyone, but with all the hell that they had been through taking care of all these poor boys coming back from action with missing arms, legs and other body parts, they just need someone to hold them, love and comfort them and make them feel like a woman again, not just for sex alone.

The way they felt made me feel a lot better. The few letters that I had received from my wife had made me lose faith in women and in marriage. I now realized that what I had thought was love in my marriage must have been lust, because she liked plenty of sex. After what I had been through, I realized that what I needed was a friend, lover and companion. Someone that I could talk to and help me purge the horrible things in my mind that I had been subjected to during combat. These things, after almost sixty years, are still there, but the wonderful caring person in my second marriage (my friend, lover, partner and companion as well as wife) taught me to have faith and to live with this problem.

I learned a lot from those two nurses, or, I should say, the one that was with me. She gave freely of herself and her love in the very short time we had together. I had been about to lose it like a boiler about ready to explode. The wonderful part about it was that the experience did as much for her as it had done for me. I was still ready to do a lot of crazy things, and with my friend Bardouche, there was no limit to what we would do. Anyway, we were having a wonderful time.

We left the club and went back up to my room. We were all hungry and all had to use the bathroom, for real this time. Everything was becoming more crowded all the time, so we decided that we would go to the mess at Place St. Augustine.

There was only one problem with this decision. It was an officers' mess and the nurses could go, but Bardouche, as an enlisted man, was not allowed to eat there. We were still in my room, so I had him try on one of my officer's jacket with bars and everything. Although the sleeves were a little too short, one of the nurses remarked, "You make a good looking officer!"

As we were heading to the mess, I told Bardouche that he was going to have to behave himself because I didn't want him to get in trouble for impersonating an officer. I had no sooner got his assurance that he would behave when a Frenchman pulled up to the curb in a car and said, "You people look tired. This is a great time for us. You have freed us from the Germans! Why don't you take this car and enjoy yourselves?"

I said, "How would we get it back to you?"

He replied, "Just leave it anywhere. I'll find it." With that, he got out of the car and we took it and proceeded to the officers' mess.

When we arrived and got out of the car, an enlisted man standing there saluted Bardouche and stood there holding the salute. I whispered to Bardouche that he had to return the salute. He did, but said, "I don't think I like being an officer."

We went on in and got a table by a window on the third floor that had a great view of Paris. I don't remember what we had to eat, but I do know that whatever it was, along with a bottle of wine, it was great.

We finished and went downstairs, and now that we had a car, we decided to see some more of Paris. We drove out to a park that had a lake where rowboats were rented. After rowing around the lake for awhile, our interest waned and we decided to go back down town. We were almost there when the car ran out of gas. We parked it where it had quit and left it and proceeded on foot. We were all getting a little tired by this time and the streets were becoming jam packed with everyone in a festive mood and celebrating. All this and the war was not yet officially over.

We found a bar that had entertainment, so we decided to have a few drinks. The only table that we could find that had seats for all of us was occupied by a lonesome-looking Scotch soldier wearing a Scotch kilt. I asked him if we could join him and he replied, "Yes, 'tis wonderful."

We sat down and bought him a drink. The poor guy was lonesome. We were having a good time and the girls were teasing him about what he wore under the kilt. He was enjoying every minute of it and just smiled when I asked him what it was like to wear a kilt. We were all having a good time and he seemed to love our company.

Finally I said, "I have to go to the restroom," and the Scotch man said, "Me too." When we had relieved ourselves, he looked at me and said, "Me lad, you asked me what it was like to wear a kilt. Why don't we just trade and you will know for yourself what it is like." I had consumed enough drinks that this sounded like a good idea, so I gave him my officer's pinks and I took his kilt and put it on. When we arrived back at the table, you should have heard Bardouche and those girls laugh. In fact, everyone in the place was getting a kick out of it and were trying to buy us drinks until the kill-joy MPs came in and made us trade back, but by this time, it was time to go home anyway.

We walked the girls back to the hospital where they thanked us for a wonderful afternoon and evening. One girl winked at me, smiled and said, "I know what was under that kilt when you were wearing it." With this, I told Bardouche that we should head back to our hotels and get some sleep and that I would see him the next morning. I told him that I would come by and pick him up.

I had just got back to my hotel and settled into bed when I heard a key in my door and the door slowly open. It was my friend, WAC Sergeant Eleanor.

"I hope I didn't wake you," she said.

I told her that I had just got to bed.

"I haven't seen you for some time. Do you mind if we talk for awhile?"

"That's fine," I said. "Do you have a problem?"

"No. It's just all the excitement now that the war is all but over." She sat on a chair near my bed and said, "At the HQ where I work, they say this should be the last day of the fighting. I thought that you would be interested in hearing that, but now I have to get to bed." And with that she headed for my window to return to her room.

After she left, I fell into a deep sleep and slept like a log, then woke up the next morning feeling relaxed and with only a slight hint of a hangover. I got dressed and headed down to Rainbow Corner to wake up Bardouche. I remembered how hard he was to get up when we were not in combat.

When I finally got him awake, I said, "Since you still have my jacket and bars, we might as well go back to the officers' mess to eat and find out what the latest war rumors are this morning."

We arrived at Place St. Augustine shortly, and who should be sitting there but my good friend Roger, the MP. He looked up and asked us to sit down. As we were being seated, he glanced at Bardouche and said to me, "I thought your friend was a sergeant."

I said, "He was, but I promoted him."

"That's fine, but with all this excitement, that old a--hole Provost Marshal has put a lot of extra MPs on and is going to be meaner than ever. As a friend, I am going to suggest that you get him back in his sergeant's uniform because that old bastard would be in seventh heaven to get hold of a friend of yours or mine."

Turning to Bardouche, he went on to describe the shoot-out we had in the hotel hallway. He also told us that there was a message received at MP headquarters early that morning that the war would officially end at midnight that night. The official papers would be signed the next day and the war in Europe would be over. THANK YOU, ROGER!

Hearing this news, I said, "Come on, Bardouche! Let's get back to my place and get you back in your correct uniform. We have a lot of celebrating to do and to do it right, we don't need to worry about you being picked up for impersonating an officer."

While he was changing back to his correct uniform in my room, I looked in my closet and came up with a bottle of Vat 69 scotch and a bottle of Champagne. With these reinforcements in tow, we headed out to do some serious celebrating. We anticipated nothing but fun for the whole day.

Bardouche had never seen the Eiffel Tower up close and he really wanted to see it, so that was the first place we headed. It was a long distance away and we were on the Champs. This is a main street, six lanes wide with a space between the street and the sidewalk about five feet wide. This space contained bicycle racks about ten feet long. Bardouche suggested that we make a road block with these racks, then bum a ride with the first car that stopped. The suggestion was all it took. We lined them up all the way across the street and soon had all traffic stopped. The first car was occupied by two French girls. We told them that we needed a ride to the Eiffel Tower and they were more than happy to grant our wish. We were glad that they spoke a little English.

While the car was stopped waiting for Bardouche to move one of the racks out of the way so we could proceed, the girl in the passenger seat got out (I think her name was Alesia) and held the front seat forward so that I could get in the back, and then she squeezed in beside me in that small back seat. In the process of doing this, her skirt was pushed up around her hips but it didn't seem to bother her. Man! Did she ever have beautiful long legs! They went all the way up to her hips!

Bardouche jumped in the front seat next to the driver (I think her name was Maria). After giving him a big hug and kiss, she took off. It looked like this was going to be an interesting ride!

Glancing back, I could see that the people had piled out in the street from the sidewalk and the cars behind us could not move at all. This didn't hold my attention for long. This French car was so small that Alesia was practically sitting on my lap. She gave me a big hug and kiss and said, "You American guys are heroes." And all the while her skirt was creeping higher up with her bare legs pressing against me and both of us being constantly jostled about due to the starting and stopping and trying to avoid bicycles.

I thought she might try to pull down her skirt at any time, but she seemed completely unaware of it. I could feel the warmth of her bare legs against me as she squirmed around to get more comfortable in that small space. The only thing she accomplished with all that squirming was to cause her skirt to ride up even higher and higher on her hips. I glanced down again at those beautiful long legs and the skirt was high enough now that I could see that she was wearing no panties. She saw me look but didn't seem concerned and started telling me about herself and her friend. They were both twenty-year-old college girls and were ready to celebrate the end of the war and have a little adventure.

By this time, I was getting pretty uncomfortable. We had been only moving at a snail's pace, but as we got away from downtown, the traffic moved a little faster. Thank God for this. I didn't know how long I could contain myself with this beautiful young lady's constant squirming around to get more comfortable. I never in my life thought I would find myself in such a predicament as this. It was almost worse than combat!

We at last arrived at the Eiffel Tower and I had no idea what would happen now. When we left my place, Bardouche had wanted to go to the Eiffel Tower's restaurant on the 2nd level and have something to eat and a few drinks. After playing with Maria's legs for the whole trip, he had changed his mind. We asked the girls if they would like to go with us to celebrate and they answered with a resounding, "Yes! Yes! Up to now, we have only had a ride with two nice guys. When we leave here, we will be ready for a big adventure."

Very few people realize just how large the frame work on the Eiffel Tower really is. It is so large that it contains a big restaurant reached by a lift (elevator). As we got off the lift, we were shown to a table where we had a wonderful view of the River Seine and the excursion boats that were practically overflowing with people who looked as if they were having a wonderful time. We ordered our lunch and drinks and sat there enjoying the view of Paris from this height. Both girls kept pointing out places of interest and we were all laughing and having a wonderful time in general.

As usual, the conversation turned to the war. The girls wanted to know how difficult it had been to defeat the Germans. We both related several of our war experiences and they seemed so intrigued by some of them that they would look into our eyes and hold on to our hands, squeezing tightly. During our conversation, we learned that both the girls came from very rich families and had been sent out of the country to school when it appeared that the Germans would occupy France. They had only been allowed to return after France was liberated.

They said that they wanted to do something special for us when we had finished eating. I think that they had been drinking before we met them because they were acting a lot like a couple of children. Although they had been to a Catholic School in Switzerland, they both spoke English well, but when they got excited, they would lapse back into a mixture of French and English. It was a delightful sound that I wish I could put into words.

Finishing our meal, we took the lift back down and located the car. As we were getting in, Alesia said, "Now it is time for your surprise and adventure! Our families are in Cannes down in southern France for a three weeks stay, mixing with all the celebrities there." She added, "My family has a Chateau on a private lake a little way outside of Paris. We would like to take you there. There will be no one there but the caretaker and the four of us and I will send the caretaker away for the day.

"That sounds great," I said, "but can we get Bardouche back to Rainbow Corners in Paris by 11:30 tonight so that he can catch his transportation back to his unit?"

"Oh no!" Marie said, "We wanted you to stay all night. Among other things, we planned to cook a meal for the four of us. The nuns taught us to be real good cooks."

"We'll just have to have an early dinner so we can get back in time," I said.

Alesia answered, "We're both ready to go, so let's not waste any more time." And off we went.

When we arrived at the Chateau, it looked more like a large palace to me. The moment Alesia was out of the car, she sent the caretaker away for the rest of the day. She said, "Now we can relax and I sure need to after that long ride in the back seat of that little car."

Believe me, I needed to, as she sat on my lap almost all the way with her skirt riding almost up to her hips, and those long, long legs burning against mine. The only place that I could find to rest my hands was on her bare legs and neither her legs nor my hands would stay still, but she didn't seem to mind. I think she really loved it.

"After that trip we need a bath to relax," Alesia said. She took my hand. "You can bathe with me." With that, she led me up a huge winding staircase, large enough to drive a tank up. Marie had already led Bardouche by the hand up the same stairs while Alesia was getting rid of the caretaker. Now I was only worried about me.

From the top of the stairs, Alesia led me through a door to the biggest bedroom I'd ever seen in my life. It had a canopied bed that was larger than my entire bedroom back home. Taking me by the hand, she led me to the bed and started to undress me. All of a sudden she stopped and said, "It would be a lot more fun if we undressed each other."

I agreed, although this was a first for me. I had never undressed a woman before. The exquisite thrill of removing clothing a piece at a time, exposing more and more of a beautiful young woman, is almost unbelievable.

After we were both undressed, again she took me by the hand, and as she was leading me to the bathroom, I glanced at her. I then realized that those long legs were not the only thing beautiful about Alesia. The rest of her was "unbelievably beautiful."

She opened the door to an enormous bathroom with a tub the size of a small swimming pool. She filled this tub with warm scented water. Drinking in her beauty with my eyes was exciting enough, but when she started bathing me, I became so excited that I told her that I wanted to make love now.

"It will be much better if you wait," She said and she kept right on washing me.

We finished and dried off with huge fluffy white towels.

Once again she took my hand and led me through a door into a room with a massage table with scented oils and creams close by. She told me to get on the table on my stomach. "I give a very good massage," she said.

She started on my neck and shoulders and worked her way down to my waist. With fingers like magic, she started with my feet and worked her way up to my waist. She smiled at me and said, "Turn over on your back."

I hesitated because I knew a certain part of my anatomy would be sticking up like a flag pole, but it didn't seem to bother her. Again, she again started with my neck, then arms, shoulders and chest, down to my waist. Starting with my feet, she worked back up to where my legs joined, working around my crotch area. I became a very embarrassed boy.

She just smiled at me, got a warm wash cloth and cleaned me up.

After I recovered, she said, "You should be OK for a while. Now it's my turn!" She climbed up on the table and lay on her stomach (Man, was she beautiful). I started with her neck, arms and back down to her waist. I then started with her feet and worked up her legs and thighs to that cute little rear "I'm not very good at this," I said. "I've never done this before."

She looked at me and said, "It's wonderful."

"Would you like to turn over?" And she turned over.

I looked at her lying there with her arms at her sides, looking like an angel, her magnificent firm breasts pointing at the heavens like twin volcanoes ready to erupt, and a little mound of hair where her thigh's joined, hiding who knows what kind of unknown delights. I hoped I could control myself long enough to finish this massage with this gorgeous young lady spread out innocently before me in all her glory. For an innocent small town boy from central US, it was unbelievable. (Just looking at her gave me goose bumps, among other things).

I started to massage her neck and arms. When I worked down to her perfectly formed breasts, she looked at me and smiled. As I touched them and worked the cream and oil into them, the nipples became like little stiff pink buds. She softly moaned, squirming and twisting. As I worked down across her flat stomach to that little mound of damp hair where her thighs joined, she almost went wild. She jumped off the table, grabbed my hand and practically dragged me to that enormous bed.

She said, "I need you now," as she pulled me on top of her, wrapped her arms and those beautiful long legs around me, those firm breasts trying to poke holes in my chest. We were so wild, our excitement level was so high, we didn't last long. She looked at me with tears in her eyes, still breathing heavy and said, "I wanted this gift to be special for you, something you would remember for the rest of your life. Wonderful as it was, it was too quick. Let's try again."

This time we made love very slowly, savoring each other's body and feelings. I think for a short time, we became a part of each other as our souls seemed one.

After we had settled down a little, still joined together, I pulled her over on top of me, with her head on my shoulder and arms around each other. She started talking to me. She told me she and Marie wanted to celebrate the victory and do something for the soldiers who gave us our freedom back. "When you stopped us at the road block, we thought this would be a great adventure. What more could we do than to share our love and that private part of our body we hold most dear with you. Although we were not virgins, the very few times it happened with young boys, it was not good; we didn't like it. Our sole purpose was to do everything in our power to make you boys happy, even if it was something we really didn't like. We wanted to give you a special fun time and something you'd remember for the rest of your life. In trying to give you this, I found this was the most exciting time of my life, as this sharing of body and soul, I think I received much more than I gave. I also realized physical love is wonderful when shared with someone you love, even if only for a day. I want to thank you for the love that you gave me and for sharing a part of yourself with me. I will remember you and this day for the rest of my life."

"Alesia, I will remember you and this day for the rest of my life." (If she only knew, I'm writing this account 60 years later).

After lying there together enjoying the closeness, we had a bath and went downstairs without dressing. Alesia looked at me. "This also is part of your gift, something you'll probably never get to do again—have the freedom of not having to worry about clothes. Tell your friend not to worry about clothes. I'm hungry, so Marie and I will fix dinner. After we finish eating, we will go for a nude swim in the lake. My family does it all the time. We French are not shy about being nude around family and close friends."

While the girls were in the kitchen fixing dinner, Bardouche and I sat at the table drinking a glass of wine. The girls both came in and joined us while the food was cooking. This was a first for Bardouche and me— sitting, having a glass of wine, all of us nude.

By the time we'd finished eating, it was almost completely dark. The girls went to the kitchen to clean up. We went to help. With four nude people in the kitchen, I think the girls would've finished much sooner by themselves.

By now it was completely dark, so we all headed for the lake for a nude swim. There is a great feeling of freedom, swimming in the nude. The water was cool but not cold. The girls kept saying it was cold. Alesia called, "Come over and keep me warm." Feigning cold, she grabbed me around the neck, kissed me deeply, and when she pressed those firm pointed breasts against my chest, I don't think either one of us was cold. I stood like that for a while. She suddenly held my neck a little tighter, lifted those beautiful long, long legs, and hooked them around my waist. She kissed me deeply and said, "I feel something down there. I need to sit on so it doesn't get cold." She wiggled and squirmed and all at once I felt a very private part of me enter what felt like a furnace.

She started a circular motion with her hips. I had never felt a sensation like that in my life. I held onto that cute little rear. It was like having a hold of something wild. We were getting so close my legs were getting weak. She was moaning, "Oh! Oh!"

I said, "Don't stop," as my knees folded. Our heads went under the water as we tried to untangle ourselves from each other. We came up sputtering and laughing and spitting up water. We said if we had both drowned, we would've died happy.

We climbed out of the water and headed back for the house. "Alesia, where did you learn all these things?" I asked. "Surely not from the nuns."

She looked at me and said, "When I was young, my parents gave me belly-dancing lessons. In France, mothers are much more liberal and teach their daughters how to please a man. Then they keep us restricted in a private school until we're old enough to marry."

"Alesia," I said, "I don't think you need any more lessons. I think you could probably kill a man with love right now."

She just smiled and said, "I've never done those things with anyone but you. You were the first, thank heaven. I will remember you always."

We reached the house and Alesia called the caretaker to return. I yelled for Bardouche to come down and bring Maria so we could get to Paris in time to catch his ride back to his unit.

"Alesia," I said, "Why don't you drive and let Bardouche and Marie sit in the back?"

We had just got underway when she reached over and pulled my head down in her lap. She reached my shirt and started playing with my nipples. I had never had a girl do this before. It must have affected her, as it felt like my head was lying in a furnace. I could even smell her excitement. I sat up—traffic was heavier as we got closer to Paris. We were talking about war in Europe. The official treaty being signed tomorrow. Traffic was so heavy I began to think we might not make it.

We made it in time for Bardouche to kiss Marie a tearful goodbye. (That was a couple of very sad people.)

We returned to our car. "I'll take you back to your hotel," Marie said.

When we got there, Alesia said, "I want to spend the night with you. I want to know what it's like to sleep with someone you love, holding you close. To wake up the next morning, put our arms around each other, feel our hearts and body become one."

In the end, it didn't work that way. I received a tearful kiss like my friend. Marie gave me a hug and kiss on the cheek.

They both thanked me for sharing a short period of our lives with them. It was the most Satisfying! Exciting! Wonderful! Experience and Adventure of our lives. As they walked out the door, I wondered if I would some day be sorry that I let Alesia go. If I had let her stay the night, I'm not sure I would have been able to ever let her go.

Later on in life with my second wife, the sharing of mind, body, soul, togetherness and physical love was even greater, maybe not quite as wild. We shared joy and sorrow together for fifty-five wonderful years before God called her home. I think this was because we were friends as well as lovers. Never were we not there for each other when one needed the other. The sorrow of the loss of a beautiful baby girl who only lived a short time. Then the joy of having the blessing of a wonderful son who became the joy of our lives.

I sometimes wondered if I should have shared my experience with this young lady with my wife after we were married, as I learned so much from her about sharing and I know it helped make my marriage a success.

Alesia and Marie had been gone only a short time when Eleanor came running up. She was shouting, "THE WAR IN EUROPE IS OVER! TODAY, MAY 7TH, 1945, AT EISENHOWER'S HEADQUARTERS IN RHEIMS, FRANCE, REPRESENTATIVES OF GERMANY SIGNED THE UNCONDITIONAL SURRENDER OF ALL GERMAN FORCES, EFFECTIVE AT ONE MINUTE PAST MIDNIGHT ON MAY 9TH, 1945."

With this news, I went on up to my room, which suddenly became a very lonely place. Tomorrow, for the first time in years, Europe would be at peace and the war would be officially over. People would be wildly celebrating (any kind of p-i-e-c-e would be available), probably for days to come.

As I lay on my bed waiting for sleep to come, I thought about the wonderful day that I had spent with Alesia and how she had taught me to feel and care again by loving and giving herself so freely and unselfishly. Other thoughts running through my mind was of Captain Ruth Morgan, (my CO when I was with Patients at Large) and what a hard time I had given her because she would not sign my transfer back to my old combat unit. After I transferred to the CID, we had run across each other several different times. Once we even had a drink together and talked for awhile. After I had taken a closer look at her, I decided that she was not the monster that I had thought she was. In fact, aside from having a sad look on her face most of the time, she was an attractive, mature, dark-haired woman (probably in her late twenties or early thirties).

As I lay there waiting for sleep to come, I thought that I should go see her and apologize for giving her such a hard time. I now knew that had she approved my transfer, that I would not now be alive and would not have met Alesia and had one of the most satisfying and wonderful experiences of my life. With these thoughts running through my mind, I finally drifted off to sleep.

I awakened the next morning to the blaring of horns and the shrieking of sirens adding to the screaming and yelling of all the people. It would have been impossible to sleep, even if I had wanted to. I quickly dressed and went down to the Bouy LaFayette Club and there sat my friend Eleanor with some soldiers. She waved and motioned me to come over and said, "These guys are looking for you!" They were guys from my old unit (some of the replacements we received after the Bulge) but none that I knew well.

I sat down with them and made my first mistake of the day. I ordered a Bouy LaFayette Special.

"Oh no! Not again!" Eleanor said. That's the way it all started out.

The guys were telling her stories about me and my nickname, "Mad Dog," and some of the crazy things I had done (exaggerated?). All the time that they were telling the stories, they were buying me drinks. After all, this was the first day of PEACE. As I have already mentioned, the French girls and many of the American girls had made it clear that any kind of P-I-E-C-E was available. The wilder of the WACs were singing their "theme song," "Roll Me Over in the Clover, Lay Me Down and Do It Again." We finally left this wild scene for me to show the guys around.

First off, we went to the Metro (Subway) Station. I really do not know what happened. I remember starting down the stairs, but the next thing I remember, we were in the cab of the subway train and I was operating the train. I looked around and there on the floor sat the motorman all tied up.

Astonished, I exclaimed, "WOW, who did that?"

One of the GIs looked at me and said, "You did. Your friends back in our unit told us that you were crazy and now I believe them." By this time I was beginning to get worried. I had been in the central control room at another time, and I knew it had an enormous control board running across the whole room. It had a red dot that showed the location of each of the trains at all times. It must have set them crazy because our train was not where it was supposed to be.

They shut off the power to our section, but thank heaven, the train stopped near one of the emergency exits and we were able to escape. We were lucky.

Even after our lucky escape, we were still ready to do some more celebrating. You just couldn't believe some of the crazy things people were doing, and it seemed to be contagious. We arrived at Place De La Concorde, and in the middle of this huge square was an enormous pool surrounded by a wall four or five feet high. In the middle of the pool were two big fountains. While we were standing there, two very attractive French girls climbed up on this wall and slowly disrobed in front of the whole crowd. When they were completely nude, they jumped in the pool and went swimming while thousands of people watched. It was not long before they were joined by several more girls.

After we had enjoyed this spectacle for awhile, we decided to move on. It was getting so crowded that one could hardly move or breathe. In trying to move against the crowd, I was knocked down and stepped on.

A young lady leaned down and said, "I am tired too. Can I lay down with you?"

I finally managed to get the young lady and myself up and we walked on. (This was supposed to be a friendly crowd, but it was dangerous.)

I finally found some much-needed food and ate and was doing much better and having a good time. I had a few more drinks, and then began looking for a side street where I could get away from some of the crowd so I could get a little air. I suddenly realized that I had again drunk too much and was beginning to feel bad again. I didn't know what had happened to my friends. I had lost them somewhere in the shuffle of the crowd. I located a bench and lay down and must have gone right to sleep. I don't know how long I slept, but when I awoke, still groggy, it was near evening.

While I sat there rubbing my legs to bring a little life back to them so I could stand up, a French man on a motorcycle stopped and said, "Soldier, you sure look tired. Here, take this thing. I am tired of trying to fight the crowd riding it. When you are through with it, leave it anywhere. I'll find it."

By this time, I was feeling better and I remembered that I intended to see my old CO, Ruth Morgan, to apologize to her for the hard time I had given her. I hopped on the bike and headed to her WAC hotel, but when I arrived there was no one there. I went to a bar that was nearby and had a few drinks, then went back to Ruth's hotel. There was still no one there, so I decided to go on up to her room.

I rode the motorcycle right on through the main entrance and then on up the five steps to the check-in desk. I could hardly believe how easy it was to ride up those stairs. Her room was 203, and I decided "What the hell." Since I'd had no trouble getting up the five steps to the desk, I'd just ride on up to see her. I remember riding up the first flight of stairs and starting on up the second flight, but the next thing I remember was knocking on her door. I knocked but received no answer. My front wheel was pressing against her door, and as I leaned over to knock again, I must have hit the throttle because the next thing I knew, the door popped open and I was inside.

Just as I shut off the cycle and leaned it against the wall, I got the sudden urge to go to the bathroom. I was very hot and I felt bad. I made my way to the bath room, and as I was getting up off the stool, I rested my hand on the bath tub. It felt cool to the touch, so I went to the bed and got a pillow, took off my clothes and proceeded to lie down in the tub, where I must have immediately gone sleep.

The next thing I remember was the door opening and someone coming in. It sounded as if they were undressing. I decided it was the captain and she must've had to go bad, because she came on into the bathroom without even turning on the light. At that point, I must have gone back to sleep. The next thing I knew, there was a bright light shining in my eyes. I looked up and there, standing with hands on her hips with arms akimbo and with legs slightly parted and resting against the tub, was the completely naked (Captain) Ruth Morgan. With a horrified look on her face, she exclaimed, "What are you doing here?"

I was in complete shock, and all I could answer was, "I was hot and crawled into the tub to cool off. Now I'm scared."

Still lying there on my back, I looked up, and just above my head where her legs came together, was the most luxurious mound of silky black hair that I had ever seen. This was contrasted by a rather flat stomach over-shadowed by two firm, slightly larger than normal, well-shaped breasts. Neither of us moved until I raised my head and said, "Wow."

At which point, she looked at me and laughed.

"Captain, you are one attractive woman!"

She looked at me again and said, "From your point of view, that is quite a compliment. What are you going to do about it?"

I looked down and saw that a certain part of me was already standing at attention.

She was still looking at me with that hungry look, which was shocking to me. She went on to say, "I went out to celebrate at the officers' club tonight. There were several crude, higher-ranking officers there that kept trying to get into my pants and they probably couldn't have satisfied me if they succeeded. You know, women have needs too. When I first saw you in my tub, I was going to call the MPs, but when I saw your 'manhood' standing at attention, I changed my mind. You are the first man that I have seen naked since my husband was sent to the Pacific two years ago. Two years is a long time and you sure look good! With the future looking so uncertain, I am ashamed to admit it, but I need someone to love me, not just for sex."

"Ruth," I said, "what I really came over here for was to apologize for giving you such a hard time when you were my CO in the DOPAL. Tonight, you are again my CO. Why don't we just go to bed and hold each other and see what happens? If I do anything you don't like, just tell me."

With that, this kind and loving woman and I proceeded to her bed. After talking for awhile, she told me how lonely she was and held on to me like she was scared to death. I teased her and jokingly asked, "You're not a virgin, are you?"

She laughed and answered, "NO."

I told her to turn on her stomach and then started to massage her gently on the neck and proceeded on down her arms and back on down to her well-shaped rear. I then started with her feet and worked on up her legs and thighs.

"That's wonderful!" she said. I asked if she wanted to turn over on her back. The question was hardly out of my mouth, and she was on her back. While I started to massage her shoulders, I kissed her on the neck and breast. As I moved on to massage her breast, I could feel them respond to my gentle touch by her nipples getting as hard as little knobs. I worked my way down over her stomach and to that very wet mound of black silky hair. She responded by moving her hips against my hand.

She finally pulled my hand away and said, "I need more." She pulled me over on top of her and raised her knees as she parted her legs for me to enter her. Slowly she started moving with me. Abruptly she stopped moving and was absolutely still and said, "I want to enjoy the feeling of fulfillment and make this last a long, long time." She repeated those abrupt stops several times. She was making it last.

I said, "You are teaching me a lot of things that I didn't know. Would you like to get on top?" She smiled at me like a child about to receive an ice cream cone, so I turned over and she climbed on top of me and settled down and began a rocking motion with her hips, this time no longer stopping. I massaged her breast while she continued this rocking motion and she began moaning and bent over, grabbing me around the neck and pressing those hard nipples against my breast hard enough to poke holes in me.

"Oh, yes. Yes!" she said as she kissed me wildly. We quietly held each other tight.

When she finally turned over on her back, she looked at me and smiled as she pulled her knees up to her breast and hooked her legs over my shoulders. "I want to be wild!" she said, and wild we were. I think only her shoulders and my knees were touching the bed. Each time I made that deep penetration, it seemed to me that the mound of silky hair (or what was underneath it) was going to devour me completely. It just couldn't last too long and we peaked together and slid down into the valley of satisfaction. With an "Oh, wow" from her as we wrapped our bodies around each other, we fell into a deep, relaxed sleep.

How long we slept, I don't know. As it was beginning to get light, we gave each other a long deep kiss and then started to get dressed. We each noticed the motorcycle at the same time and Ruth said, "My God, what are we going to do about that?"

"I don't know," I said, "but I guess you know that if I am found here, we will both get a court-martial. You could get out of it by saying that I broke in here and raped you."

"After what we have had together, I could never do that."

I went to the door and opened it a crack. Peering out into the hall, I could see no one. I told Ruth that it would be impossible for me to ride that motorcycle back down the stairs. With some fast thinking, I said, "Ruth, you go out to the elevator and punch the button. As the door starts to open, if no one is coming, I'll run out and shove the motorcycle in and hold the override button all the way to the loading dock in the basement." Complying with my instructions, she went to the elevator and quietly said, "It's coming."

I went running out as the elevator door opened but when I reached it, there was no car, just an empty space and I couldn't stop the cycle. Down the elevator shaft the cycle went. I threw my hand up and caught the edge of the door frame and Ruth grabbed my other arm, or I would have followed it down the shaft. With knees so weak and shaky that we could hardly stand, we made it back to her room. All we could do was sit down on the edge of the bed and hold each other very tightly till we caught our breath.

After catching my breath, I said, "Ruth, I have to get out of here, but I did like the way you let me apologize to you. I have never apologized to a woman like that before and I sure would like to apologize more often, if it's going to be like this."

Smiling, she looked at me and kissed me softly on the lips and said, "Lindy, this was a one time deal and as precious and wonderful as it was, I love my husband dearly and I will never tell him about this. I don't intend to ever leave him. With the future being so uncertain, this was something I needed to go on with my life and once again feel like a woman. Your gentle patience with me in the beginning and the wildness at the end, climaxed with quietly lying there holding each afterwards, made me feel as though you knew exactly what I wanted. I had always dreamed of being on top while making love to a man, and when I saw you there nude on your back in my tub, it all came rushing back. I had often wondered how it would be to put my legs on a man's shoulders and wrap them around his neck and go completely wild. You made it happen!"

"Ruth, maybe it's because I have always wanted the same thing. I never realized that the physical part of making love could last so long. I, too, am facing a very uncertain future and as you know, there is plenty of sex out there just for the taking, but it is just the wham, bam, thank you, ma'am kind. The time we spent together will allow me to face the rest of this war and hopefully return home and live a normal life." I took her hands in mine. "Ruth, I have to get out of here. We could still get our rears in a sling if I'm caught in here. I know that this was a one time deal, but I hope that we can still see each other and be good friends."

"Lindy," she answered, "I do want to see you again and to be friends. Let's have dinner together tonight. I want to tell you why I wouldn't sign your transfer."

With an "OK," I started toward the window to make my way down the fire escape. She caught me and gave me a soul-satisfying kiss, to which I answered, "Ruth, if you don't turn me loose quickly, those wonderful parts of you that are pressing against my chest are going to make it impossible for this to be a one time deal." With that, she let go and down the fire escape I went.

After I had made my way down the fire escape without getting caught, I breathed a big sigh of relief and headed for Place St. Augustine to eat. I badly needed to replace the energy that I had expended during the night, although, I must say, it was one of the best ways of expending energy that I had ever experienced and also one of the most satisfying.

I ate, then went home and crawled into bed and enjoyed one of the most restful sleeps I have ever had. I slept through the morning and into the afternoon until about four o'clock when the phone rang.

"Lindy, this is Ruth and I just wanted to see if you made out OK. After you left, I was so completely exhausted and hungry that I went out and ate, then returned and hit the bed for one of the most restful sleeps that I can remember in a long time. I am tired of celebrating, but I would just like to buy you dinner and have a long, quiet talk and if you feel like listening, just pour my heart out to you."

"Ruth, my answer is yes. I am also tired of celebrating. A quiet dinner with you sounds real good."

We met and she took me to a small, out of the way restaurant that had excellent food and a small string band playing softly in the background. After all the noise and partying that had been going on the past few days, this was a very restful treat. We ordered a drink and our food, and then she began to relate some of her experiences to me.

She began, "I was married to my husband about a year before he was sent to the Pacific and we had a fantastic relationship. Everything was wonderful and the physical side was unbelievable. When he had to leave, I thought I would just die. I hoped that I was pregnant so a part of him would always be with me, but it didn't happen that way. To add to my misery, I was sent over here, far away from my friends. In my mind, I knew that I was going to miss him terribly but I didn't realize that the loss of physical love would be almost as painful. I had women here that I could talk to, but I needed a male or father figure. I worked with two men and they both seemed real nice. One asked me out to dinner and I thought just to be around a man would be enjoyable, but was I ever wrong. The first thing he did was try to figure out some way to get in my pants and start an affair. That was the last thing I wanted. I loved my husband, who I might never see again, and wanted no part of a 'sordid affair' and just having something stuck between my legs for his gratification. What I needed was someone to talk to and understand what I was going through.

"When I came home last night and saw you lying naked in my bathtub, I thought to myself, that's what a man still looks like. My husband has been gone two years and, like I told you, at first I was going to call the MP's, but as I stood there watching your manhood rise, I changed my mind. I was standing there just as naked as you were with most of my private parts right in your face. Then you raised your head and exclaimed, 'WOW, you're a very attractive woman!' I thought, that from your point of view, that was a great compliment. As I stood there looking at you, it was almost like placing a plate of food in front of a starving person. I suddenly had an urgent need to fill that empty space inside of me and felt very ashamed of myself when I said, 'What are you going to do about it?'"

She continued, "When you led me to the bed and told me that we could just lie there and talk if that was what I wanted to do, I was lost. With that wild need inside of me, I knew how it would end no matter how ashamed I was. I had to tell you this because I don't want you to think badly of me."

I told Ruth that she had no reason to feel ashamed and went on to tell her about the two French girls, one of whom (Alesia) wanted to give me a special gift, a gift of herself, a gift for helping free her country and something special that I would remember the rest of my life. I went on to tell her how Alesia had taken me in her arms, loving and sharing with me, if only for a day, her body, soul and her most precious parts, giving me the innocent love of a young and beautiful twenty-year-old girl. I told Ruth that I had not been ashamed of taking that gift.

"Dear Ruth," I said, "I was a gift to you and I received just as great a gift in return. I'm a very lucky man! In just two days, I have shared the gift of love with two remarkable ladies. Not just physical sex, though it was fantastic and almost unbelievable. Those memories I will hold in my heart for the rest of my life." (This statement has proved true or I would not, almost sixty years later, be writing this account.)

Ruth said, "Lindy, now I want to tell you why I wouldn't sign your transfer, even though I knew how bad you wanted it. After reading in your service record that you had a wife and a child that you had never seen, I just wanted to make sure you got home to your family. In my job, I have seen case after case of young men getting out of the hospital and coming through here and in just a short time, be killed in combat. Maybe I was doing this because I had hopes of someone doing the same to keep my husband safe. I realize now, just how much you must have hated me. When you asked for a transfer to the CID, I thought that it would be a safe place, so I immediately signed it. Then later when your friend, MP Roger, told me of the hotel lobby shoot-out and how you had to stand there and be shot at by this man because Roger was in the line of fire, I realized that some greater power had to keep you and everyone else safe."

I answered Ruth by telling her that life works in strange ways and our future is always uncertain. I went on to tell her that I thought that in the war in the Pacific, if the island of Japan had to be invaded, the US would suffer 3,000,000 casualties and that the Japanese, 12,000,000. The chance of ever getting home to live a normal life was going to be slim for most of us. I told her that I could hardly wait to get home and see my baby, but that I thought my marriage would be in name only just for the sake of my daughter. I continued on to tell her that I thought that the relationship in my marriage was based on lust instead of love, especially in the case of my wife, as she was the first woman I had ever slept with.

"Ruth," I said, "Now, I would like to pour my heart and soul out to you. My wife and I did not make love, we just had sex. That high plateau of love was thrilling but was never completely fulfilled. I was not her first, although I didn't learn this until much later. I was thrilled that she wanted to have sex with me after only one date, since she was a very, very religious person. I thought that I was the luckiest man alive, as I had never had a serious relationship with any girl. She used me like a man would use a whore and loved the physical side of our relationship, but there was no sharing of heart and soul or closeness to each other.

"At my young age, I thought that this was love, especially when I was assigned to Camp Livingston, Louisiana training camp for a year and she came down to live with me until we could get married. I know now that what I thought was love, was only sexual lust. I was just something to be used for her sexual satisfaction. I also realized that she was a very mean and uncaring person.

"I was shipped out of the country for almost two years and then came back to Camp Maxey, Texas, where we were outfitted with new equipment and training preparatory to being shipped on over to Europe for the D Day invasion. It was at this time that she came down to be with me, and during her stay, she became pregnant, which made both of us very happy. We both wanted a child, because if I didn't come back, a part of me would live on. This was the first time in our marriage that there was more to our love than just physical satisfaction. Now I thought there was hope. In celebrating the end of the war over here in Europe, I decided to live just for today, and if I ever make it home, to try to keep our marriage together for our daughter's sake."

I continued, "You see, Ruth, I really understand and appreciate what you were going through. It's too bad that we couldn't have met at a different time and place. You asked if we could still be friends without having an affair, and that this had just been a one time deal, and I accepted that. I'm sure that we both wished that this one time could have lasted much longer. You were up and down the mountain more than once. When we did make the last one together and slid down into the valley locked in each other's arms, I could not believe we had been physically together so long. As for remaining friends, I can see no problem with that. We can have an understanding to have an outlet to share our feelings, and as you well know, there is no limit in this town, if all you want is cheap sex."

"Lindy," Ruth said, "I don't think we will have a problem at all unless I come home sometime and find you asleep in my bathtub. I want to thank you for all you have shared and given of yourself to me and I want you to know, I received much more than I gave. Thanks again!"

After this wonderful evening, we both headed to our respective homes for a restful night's sleep.

The Victory celebration in Europe was winding down and was almost all over and things in Paris were beginning to settle down. Now they were only celebrating eighteen hours a day instead of twenty-four. It was still hard to get anything done in my job, though. It was almost impossible to find the people that I needed to see. I would sometimes have to wait at least three days or more to locate them. I was anxious to get started back on my big case of the major and the two French girls, but there was not much to do except wait. I did want to keep my case load as low as possible, just in case, through some miracle happening, the war with Japan came to an end and I would be sent home. They had been setting up a point system on sending men home, and the way things looked, I would have the maximum. I had been ready to give up, but now there was hope again.

Reflecting back on things, I had been lucky the last several days. I had seen my old commanding officer after each of us had thought the other was dead, and then there were the two nurses who had shared so much with Bardouche and me, companionship and physical release that they needed just as much as we did. (I feel bad that I can no longer recall those girls' names.) Then there was Alesia, who bestowed on me the greatest gift any beautiful innocent young lady could give to any man for helping to free her country. She made me realize that there were some people who really cared about the hell that we had gone through. She drove away from my mind that unbelievable horror that I had seen and had dimmed it forever. Then there was Capt. Ruth Morgan, my CO while I was attached to the Detachment of Patients at Large. I had hated her with a passion because she would not sign my transfer back to my old unit. I now realize that all she was doing was trying to keep me alive.

When I went to apologize to her, I pulled a crazy stunt which she could have had me thrown in jail for the rest of my life. Instead, she gave me a mature love and became a dear friend for the rest of my stay in Paris. She had taught me much and sharing that short period of life with me, gave me much more than I could ever return. Indirectly, I would have not have been able to share the gift that Alesia gave me had it not been for her effort in trying to protect me. She may have even given me back my life. Two other ladies had helped me through some very difficult times. They were Gloria Clark and Sgt. Eleanor Stein, and they had been like sisters to me. I was indeed a very lucky man.

I don't think I would have had much of a marriage when I got back home had it not been for the wonderful understanding of these ladies and what they had taught me. I now intended to go home and try to make things work for the sake of my little girl, Linda. Tomorrow was going to be another day and the people were all still half crazy.

The next morning, things appeared to be starting to return to normal. I was getting ready to head down to breakfast when my friend Manual phoned. He told me that he had to fly a load of material into Switzerland and he thought that I might like to ride along. He added that wristwatches were selling in Paris for $250.00 and that he thought that they could be bought in Switzerland for $25 to $35 each.

I wasted no time in saying, "I'm ready. What time do you want me to meet you?" He asked if I could meet him in a couple hours, and I said I could. I scraped up as much money as I could in those two hours and we made the trip. While Manual was unloading the material, I took his money and mine and found that by buying more than one case, I could purchase the watches for $25.00 each. Loaded down with watches, I returned to the plane.

We managed to get them all loaded aboard the plane and headed back to Paris. It was hard for Manual to believe that we had bought so many watches. When we arrived back in Paris, he somehow managed to round up a Jeep for us to use and we took all of the watches except a few he wanted to keep back to my apartment, where we locked them up in my closet. It was secure because that was where I kept all the important papers pertaining to my pending cases.

After stowing the watches in my closet, we proceeded to the officers' mess for dinner, where we discussed the ending of the war and with its end, how the French were returning to their normal nasty selves. As usual, we were concerned about the war in the Pacific and how slowly it seemed to be progressing. We thought for sure that we would both be sent there. Finishing dinner, I cautioned Manual about sending too much money home at one time. Although what we were doing was legal, there was no point in taking the chance of having someone question it. We were both going to make a considerable amount of money if we had time to sell all the watches. He went back to the air base and I returned to my quarters.

I was in no mood to fight the crowds and all the noise, so I just went down to the club for a drink. My friend, Roger the MP, came in and asked me if I would like to help him escort several French troops down to the Glare de L' Est train station, where they were to catch a train to southern France. Having nothing better to do, I agreed to help him.

When we arrived at the train, there was a big party in progress on board the troop train. We sat down with them to relax for a little while, and somehow, we ended up in southern France. Somehow trouble just seems to follow one around. Anyway, after a lot of finagling, we got back to Paris late that night with our honor still intact. I didn't even stop at the club, but just went straight up to my quarters and hit the sack.

After the trip Manual and I made to Switzerland and then getting those French troops down to southern France, it was time for me to hit the road again and get a little work done. I went to the office and started working on the case of the major and the two French girls.

With this case, I had been really lucky. We had the good luck of catching the major with a truck load of US Army property and he was arrested on the spot. The Judge Advocate's department, in going over his records, discovered that he had been falsifying them. All I had to do now was to locate the two girls and get them back to Paris to testify at the trial. After three days of looking, I located the girls and had them return to their apartments in Paris. Now all that remained was the wait for the trial to begin.

In the meantime, Toni and I went over her testimony for the trial. Her testimony alone was enough to bury the major. When I called on her, she was dressed in a short pajama outfit that, again, left nothing to the imagination. I don't know what she was trying to prove, but it looked like trouble incorporated to me. Once again, I got out of there--fast.

After the interview with Toni, I proceeded to the department store to interview Aletta. As we sat in her office, she had one of the girls bring us coffee. She had followed my advice in getting rid of anything even resembling Army or US property. I asked her if she had done the same thing in her apartment. She replied, "Yes, but I would like for you to go and look it over with me just to make sure. (We did this and there was nothing there.)

She told me that she had not talked to the major since I spoke with her the first time. She also added that the major had paid her apartment rent at first but now she was paying it herself. He had been forcing her to sleep with him, but after the store was in her name along with the bank account, she had refused to sleep with him.

I suggested that she include in her testimony the fact that he had tried to sell her Army supplies for her store but that she had refused. When she had a cash flow problem, he paid for her apartment rent only to force her to sleep with him.

As I mentioned earlier, this strikingly attractive lady was dressed in a trim business suit, not like a prostitute. She had worked hard to make her department store a success. Although I didn't expect anything from her, I was sure that she would share anything she had with me, including herself, so I was doing everything I could to help her. Again, I cautioned her not to accept any Army or US material, new or used.

After her interview, I went back to the office where I went over the testimony of both girls with my CO and discussed the truck that we had picked up. I hoped they would set a trial date soon so we could get it over with. With the overview completed, I headed to dinner and back to my quarters for a good night's rest.

Two weeks went by since I had interviewed the two girls and then the case went to court. I will not go in to a lot of detail as it would soon grow boring. I'll only hit some of the high spots. The major was found guilty of trying to sell the truck load of US property and of some of the smaller deals. Then Toni testified that she had been in the apartment when he sold U.S. property like shoes and jackets to different people. She told a pretty convincing story, helped along by the way she was dressed and the way she crossed and uncrossed those pretty long legs set off by her short skirt. She also displayed some of the presents that he had given her, most of which were government property. He was found guilty on all of those charges, but Toni had to return the gifts or she would have been charged with receiving stolen property.

Aletta arrived in court wearing a very conservative suit and testified that he had tried to get her to sell US government property in her store but that she had refused. In regard to paying her apartment rent, it could not be proved that it was not paid with money other than his own. She also testified that he had met with several different people in her apartment to have them pick up stolen US property. On all of these charges, he was found guilty. She had to pay back the money that he had given her, although they found her guilty of nothing. Her only problem was that of being taken advantage of by a senior Army officer.

It took them only a short time to find him guilty on all the charges and sentence him to a life term in the stockade. This made me very happy, as he had been selling food, clothing, gas and ammunition when soldiers on the front line were freezing, starving and dying because of a shortage of these materials.

I was sure happy to see closure to this case and also very happy to see Aletta come through it all without losing everything that she had worked so hard for. Through all her suffering, she had come out smelling like a rose. She still had her store and a rather large bank account. Because she had been forced to prostitute herself, I think she deserved every bit of it. As for Toni, she had to return her gifts and had lost her golden nest. The way some of those old goats on the court martial board were looking at her as she crossed those long legs during her testimony, I knew it would not be long before she found another "sugar daddy" to pay for her apartment.

I headed back home after the trial to call Ruth to see how she was doing and to ask if I could take her to dinner. I knew that she had been having a rough time. What had taken place between us was now history and we both needed a close friend that we could talk to and confide in. Things work out in strange ways, but I now knew that we would always be nothing more than good friends.

On the way to make the call, it seemed to me that Paris had settled down somewhat and was almost normal again. I was really glad that the black market case was over. It had been a real pain.

I called Ruth as soon as I arrived home and she seemed very happy to hear from me. I asked her if she would have dinner with me and she replied that it would make her very happy.

I went by and picked her up and we went back to that same little, out-of-the-way restaurant that we had gone to before and again enjoyed their excellent food and quiet atmosphere. It was a place where we could easily talk and enjoy each other's company without a lot of interference.

As we started our conversation, she told me that she was doing a lot better now and I told her that I too was doing a whole lot better. I went on to describe to her the case of the two French girls and the major. When I had gone through the details and how it had finished, Ruth said, "That is exactly what the old goat deserved. I don't feel too sorry for Toni; I believe she got what she deserved. I am glad for the other girl, Aletta. She came out of the whole ordeal in good shape, even though she did have to prostitute herself to that no good major to keep from losing her store but, thank goodness, it was only for a short time. Sometimes bad things just happen to good people."

201

We sat there and continued to talk and the conversation turned to home. It was then that I told her about flying with Manual to Switzerland and buying up all those watches to sell and then sending as much as possible of my part of the money home to my wife. My service allotment would only take care of the normal everyday expenses and I thought that this extra money would make a good nest egg to buy furniture, etc. when and if the war was ever over. I asked her if she thought that I was doing the right thing by sending this extra money home to have a little start in getting our feet on the ground. I told her that if I was lucky enough to get back home, I was going to do my best to make my marriage work if only for the sake of my little girl who I'd not even seen a picture of. She agreed that it sounded like a great idea.

Ruth talked along the same line, saying that if her husband ever made it home, she thought they would have a wonderful life, as she was desperately in love with him. She went on to say that she wanted to have a child as soon as possible so that if ever again they were separated, they would have a part of each other to cling to.

All this talk of home and family made me feel that life might be worth living after all. It did make me feel a little sad, but having a good friend to talk to helped a lot. What we had done together now seemed just like a dream. Maybe it wasn't right, but the friendship that resulted sure helped us get by day by day. We understood each other and could say almost anything to each other and not get involved in a nasty sexual affair. That eased our minds when things got too bad. After a great meal and relaxing evening, we called it a night and went home. I don't know about Ruth, but I slept great.

I woke up the next morning feeling rested and relaxed, but it seemed that time was just creeping by. I realized that more than a whole month had gone by since the war in Europe had officially ended. It was early June 1945, and from the looks of things, it would only be a matter of time until I was sent to the Pacific for the invasion of the main island of Japan. The chance of a great number of our troops surviving the invasion was slim. At this time, I could see no way that I was going to make it home. The only way that I could see my family and friends would be a delay in route to the Pacific.

Some of my wild escapades in Paris had helped me to understand women a lot better and I now thought that I could get along with any woman. I was finally beginning to face reality more. I told you about going to Switzerland with Manual after the close of the European war and purchasing and flying out a load of Swiss watches on a C47 that we sold for a terrific profit in Paris. I thought that sending this profit to my wife in the States, she would be able to take good care of our baby Linda even if I didn't make it back home. This, at least, gave me something to work for, even though I don't think she had even sent me a picture of the little girl. If she had, I didn't receive it. Anyway, at this time, it seemed the right thing to do. I would learn later that I should have sent the money to my mother and my life would have been much better. At least I would've had our money (more about this later). I didn't realize all the problems that I was going to have.

Returning to my room at noon, I checked my messages and checked to see if any of my old friends from the 32nd were in town. Much to my regret, none were. I suppose the entertainment in Germany was just as good as it was in Paris now that the war was over. I had a surprising message from Aletta, the second girl in the black market case. She wanted me to call her, and that worried me. I thought something must have happened and that maybe I had missed some loose end in some part of the investigation. I decided to go directly to her department store.

When I walked in, Aletta was tied up with a customer, so one of her clerks showed me to her office to wait. She brought me the usual cup of coffee to enjoy during my wait, but it was only a short time before Aletta joined me. She told me that there had been no need for me to come all the way to her office. I told her that I thought she was in trouble.

"On the contrary," she said. "I was doing some paper work and I realized just how much work and effort you had put in to protect me in this case, and I decided that I wanted to do something to partially pay you back for your kindness. I would like to invite you to my apartment tonight for a home-cooked dinner."

I told her that a home cooked dinner sounded fine (my last home cooked meal was with Alesia at the Chateau, but at that time food was not the main thing on my mind). After I made a weak protest saying it was not at all necessary, she said, "If seven p.m. is OK, I'll see you then."

I arrived at her apartment promptly at seven and knocked on the door. When it was opened, I thought I was at the wrong place. Standing at the door was this vision of a beautiful lady dressed in a formal off the shoulder evening gown of a pale blue color looking at me through almost hypnotic smoky brown eyes. Her dark hair fell loosely over her bare shoulders, and as I looked, I could see the slight swelling above the gown indicating that it concealed a marvelous pair of breasts. Lower was a waist that I could have spanned with my hands and hips that flared softly into legs that could only be perfect.

I finally realized that I was staring and stepped into the room. Taking her by the hand, I lifted it to my lips and kissed her fingertips and told her how incredibly beautiful she looked. You must remember that in the several weeks during the black market trial, this lady had always worn a rather severe business suit. As attractive as it had been, I could hardly believe that this beautiful creature who had answered the door was the same person.

She took my face between her hands and with a touch so light that I could scarcely feel it, she softly kissed me on the lips, then showed me into the dining room with a candle-lit table set for two.

She called for her French maid to bring in the ice bucket, which already had wine chilling in it. She said that she had hired this maid just for the occasion so we could have an uninterrupted dinner and conversation. She told me that if the maid was a distraction, she would have her leave, but I told her that it didn't bother me at all.

We sat there with our drinks and enjoyed a seven-course meal (a first for me). She was treating me like I was the most important person in the world and more importantly, making me feel that way.

"Without you," she said, "none of this would have been possible, so I want to share a small part of it with you. I could have easily ended up in prison because of my forced association with that major."

When I looked into the depths of those smoky eyes, I knew she was speaking from the heart. She continued to look at me and said,

"I have something to say to you that I just don't know how to put into words. As you know, France has a lot of different customs and is a lot more liberal than your country. This dinner is so little to share with you that I would love to share much more. Here in France, it is the accepted custom for most of our important men (even those who are married) to have a mistress. Being a mistress in France is to be respected as much as being a wife."

Leaning forward, just inches from me and looking directly into to my eyes, she said, "I would like to share your life and myself with you and become your mistress for as long as you are in Paris. We can live in this beautiful apartment and hire the maid full time so we can spend all our spare time making each other happy. I don't think that I am in love with you at this time, but I think that as time passes, love will come easily. As for the physical side of love, my need for that is just as great as yours, but only with the right person." As she leaned even closer, those eyes penetrating even deeper into mine, I knew she was speaking from her heart.

Looking back into her eyes, I replied, "I could probably easily fall in love with you, but it would be forever and I have a wife and child waiting for me back in the States. I've had a couple of short affairs here in Paris, but I do not intend to get involved again. Once this war is over and I have survived, I intend to go back and make a life for my little girl. I don't have much of a marriage, but I do have a responsibility. Aletta, you will never know how great a temptation this is for me, but it would be unfair to you, my family and myself. You are a beautiful lady and I know from my investigation that you are honest. You deserve much better than this. I think you want security and a lifetime commitment, and that is something I cannot give you. I want to remain your friend. I need a friend as much as you need a friend, and I think this common friendship will become very important to both of us."

We continued to sit in front of the fireplace with our drinks for a long time. I listened as Aletta told of some of the hard times that she had endured during the German occupation. I think we had a meeting of souls, relieving and easing some of the things that had been burdening our minds.

205

During our conversation, my mind wandered back to those Swiss watches that I'd gotten in Switzerland and how I had sent the profits back to my wife in the States. I had many of the watches left and I asked her if she would be willing to sell them through her store for a profit of $25.00 each and send the money directly to my wife, thus allowing me to send much more money than I otherwise could. She readily agreed to this and I told her that she would be doing something that was very important to me.

As we continued to talk, she still treated me like I was the most important person in the world, but occasionally I noticed a small tear in the corner of her eye. The time came when it was necessary to bring to a close this wonderful evening with this beautiful lady.

At the door as I was leaving, I took her hand in mine and kissed her fingertips. She took my face in her hands and again gently kissed my lips softly like one would a baby, and with a tear in her eye, she said, "Goodnight, good friend," which made it even harder to leave.

Returning to my room, I lay awake for hours thinking of this delightful evening that I had spent with this lovely young woman – but still sleep did not come. She was, without a doubt, the most beautiful woman I had ever seen. Considering the suffering and hardships that she had been through and as intelligent as she was, she certainly did know her own mind. What I couldn't understand was why she would want to share her life and even her wealth with me, as my chances of staying alive were very slim. On the other hand, I wondered if I had made a mistake in turning her down. I was beginning to believe that the time I would have spent with her would have been the happiest and most satisfying time of my life. After much contemplation, I figured that I was right in saying no, and was very lucky to have gained a wonderful friend in Aletta.

As I lay there in my bed though, my mind kept wondering back over the emotional gauntlet of combat and the loss of so many friends. Being cut off behind enemy lines, fighting my way out half starved and frozen, my bad marriage at home, and being stuck in Paris unable to rejoin my unit. I had almost reached the breaking point and was ready to give up. Finally happier thoughts pervaded, the kindness from the young WAC who kept me from being robbed, the WAC Captain trying to keep me safe, finding my old CO in Paris after I thought him long dead. After that there was the young adult French girl who gave me so much of her innocence and love, even if for such a short time. Ruth, the mature lady who had really made all of it possible. And finally, just today, this beautiful fantastic lady offering to share her life with me.

Remembering all of these things and those dainty hands on my cheeks and that soft goodbye kiss on my lips was like telling me, "Everything will be all right." I thought, "How lucky can I be!" It seemed as though someone was looking out for me. With all these thoughts still running through my mind, sleep finally came.

By now things seemed to be going well and my day-to-day cases with the CID were mostly small and getting boring. I was just keeping busy enough to help the time pass faster. My morale, after being down to rock bottom, had improved greatly and I was beginning to see a little light at the end of the tunnel, even though my commanding officer still wouldn't approve my transfer back to my old outfit. Even the war in the Pacific was going much better. I had seen in the papers where the Marines had taken the island of Okinawa and the Army had taken several of the other islands. This made me feel much better. I thought that perhaps the war would end and I would make it home in one piece after all.

When I got a little ahead on my cases, I found transportation to my old unit and went to see and visit a lot of my old friends. They asked if I would like to see the Buchwald Concentration Camp. This was the camp where 50,000 innocent people lost their lives and only 20,000 were found alive. The visit to the camp was an enlightening experience that I would not like to repeat.

This was where the prisoners, mostly Jews, were used as human guinea pigs for medical experiments. They were placed there for six weeks, during which time their food was restricted and they were supposed to lose forty percent of their weight. Among other things, they were forced to use untried drugs. Many had surgery on arms or legs or other operations performed on them without the use of anesthetic. Those who survived this six weeks ordeal were sent to the gas chambers and the bodies were sent to one of the six incinerators, each of which held three bodies. All that remained was a small pile of ashes. At one time, they ran out of coal for ten days and there were almost 2000 corpses stacked like cord wood outside. Although the camp had been liberated, there were several bodies still around and the stench was horrible. There was probably more meat on some of those corpses than there was on some to the prisoners that were still alive.

After looking at all this, I lost some of my guilt about killing an enemy soldier. (Let me tell you, there is a feeling of guilt. Not at the time it happens, but later, when you try to sleep, especially if the soldier was young. You wonder about his mother, father, sister, brother, and even his girl friend. It's a horrible thing to take someone's life, even if he is trying to kill you. Even now, sixty plus years later, I still see some of those faces in my sleep.)

Returning from the camp, I went back to the rest of my old unit and told my buddies goodbye. It had sure been great to see old friends that I had lived with for years. They all agreed with me that it now appeared that the war in the Pacific was progressing much better and it seemed as though the ETO units would not be sent over there. I headed back to Paris, thinking that I was lucky to live a life of comfort in Paris, "The City of Light."

The next morning after my visit to the 32nd, I was awakened by a telephone call from, of all people, Gloria Clark. She said, "I have been trying to call you for several days. I am stationed in Nice and I have a couple days off and I would like for you to come down. I would like to return the favor of your showing me around Paris. Nice is only a little distance from Cannes, which is, as you probably know, the place were celebrities from all over the world go to soak up the sun and be seen. I would sure like to show you around."

Since I was still ahead with my cases, I said, "Just name the time and the place."

I caught the train out of the Gare de l'Est Station in Paris and headed for Nice. When I arrived, Gloria was there to meet me with a hug and a kiss, exclaiming, "I'm sure glad to see you. You have become almost like family to me. Even my brother has been asking about you. I have managed to scare up some transportation, so let's go!"

As we crawled into the car, she told me that she had rented adjoining rooms in a hotel in Cannes, as that seemed to be where all the action was going to be for the next few days. We headed out on the beautiful drive that took us along the coast of the Mediterranean Sea. The closer we came to town, the more beautiful the already fabulous scene became. When I caught sight of the hotel, I said, "I don't know whether I can afford this!"

"Don't worry," Gloria said. "It's already taken care of."

As we walked into the hotel, I couldn't believe all the important people I saw. Several movie stars milled about in the lobby. Even with all those celebrities in the lobby, we did not tarry long there, but went on up to our rooms to freshen up.

After about forty-five minutes, Gloria knocked on the door that adjoined our rooms and asked if I was decent. I told her that I was and she came in and we both sat down and ordered a drink and relaxed. We proceeded to bring each other up to date on the news from home and family and of our jobs. Presently, she asked me if I was ready to go out to eat. By this time, I was beginning to get a little hungry, so I asked her if we couldn't just eat here at the hotel. She answered that she had eaten here before and the food was good, so we proceeded to the dining room.

Arriving at the dining room, we were shown to a fine table and, thank heaven, Gloria spoke French, because I wouldn't have had the slightest idea what to order. To this day, I do not know what I ordered, but with the soft music in the background, I know that it was good.

Glancing around the dining room, I couldn't believe some of the low cut evening gowns and beautiful clothes some of these stars wore.

Gloria said, "If you think this is something, just wait until you see the bathing suits on the beach tomorrow."

We finished our meal and then took in a few bars and other entertainment places. Everything was exciting and we had a wonderful time, but as the evening grew on, I was beginning to grow tired.

"Let's go back to our rooms and rest," Gloria finally said. "I have a full day planned for you tomorrow."

Arriving at our rooms, she said, "I would like to talk some more." We took off our shoes and lay down on my bed and continued to talk for hours till we both drifted off to sleep.

I awoke to someone shaking my shoulder. It was Gloria, who said, "Lindy, I am going to my bed. Sometimes I wish I wasn't so shy!"

We were both up bright and early the next morning and had an early breakfast, after which we proceeded to the beach. On the way, she said, "I hope you brought your swim suit." Even with all the excitement, we both remembered to bring our suits, which we donned and strolled down the beach. Compared to all the others on the beach, I thought that we were overdressed by about ten years, style wise. It seemed that most of the stars and starlets (especially the pretty younger ones) were trying to outdo each other as to who could wear the skimpiest suit.

We swam in the sea and lounged on the beach until I became concerned about getting burned. When I expressed my concern, Gloria suggested we go back to the hotel. Arriving back at our rooms, we put on our uniforms, which the hotel had cleaned and pressed while we were swimming. We ate an early lunch and then took in some of the sights. After awhile, Gloria said, "I don't know exactly how to tell this, but do you remember that club with the nude waitresses? Well, here they have an island with nude beaches and it is only a little distance off shore. You can't even leave the building on the dock with any clothes on. I know that I have led a pretty sheltered life, but I would like to try that. In fact, though I wanted to see you terribly bad, that is one reason I wanted you to come down. I didn't want to try this without a man to protect me, and you are the only man I trust. "

I told her that I wasn't sure if I could look at all those naked women without a certain part of my body embarrassing the both of us and asked if she was willing to take that chance. When she answered, yes, I decided, "why not?"

This is one experience that I would probably never have the opportunity to experience again in my lifetime. We made arrangements to take a boat out to the island, and on the way, I tried to put the picture of Alesia out of my mind.

We arrived at the island dock and went into a building with a lot of stalls along the inside, some of them large enough for two people. Looking at Gloria, I said, "You take that one and I will take this one."

She replied, "If you think that I am going to walk out of there naked by myself, you're crazy!" We both went into one of the larger stalls and started to undress. All the while, I was trying to think of anything that would keep my mind off standing there in that small space and undressing with a young woman just inches from me. When she was partially undressed, she said, "I can't do this!"

She had her back to me and when she turned to me, I said, "You have to now. You've already seen me." With that, she finished undressing, grabbed my hand, closed her eyes and ran for the beach and into the water up to our chins. Somewhat elated, she said, "There certainly is a feeling of freedom, isn't there? I heard some of the girls talking about how wonderful it was, and I just wanted to try it, but not without a man to protect me."

We played around in the water trying hard not to touch each other, especially me trying not to touch her. For me, this was a hard chore because she would not let me get more than an arm's length away. We observed the men and women strolling up and down the beach and drinking soda pop at a stand, seemingly unconcerned with all this nakedness. By now, Gloria had her eyes open and seemed to be interested in the action.

The water was warm and the feeling of freedom was great. I asked Gloria if she was getting this same feeling of freedom. She answered, "Yes. It almost feels as though you are floating. I believe you could float on your back in this water, but wouldn't part of me stick out of the water?"

I said, "You're going to have to walk out of the water with those parts sticking out anyway, so why don't you go ahead and try it?" She turned on her back and floated with no problem at all, and commented that it felt great. Even I floated on my back and I didn't embarrass either of us.

When we had both become accustomed to seeing nude people, Gloria said, "You know, some of these people don't look too good, but this is quite an experience. I'm the only one to have seen myself nude and that was in a mirror, so I wonder what I look like to others."

I told her that there was only one way to find out and that we were going to have to find out sooner or later, so I took her by the hand and we slowly walked out of the water and onto the beach. When I observed her looking at me out of the corner of her eye, I took her other hand and turned her to face me. She looked me over so closely that I was almost embarrassed. As she stood there, she wanted to know how she looked from a man's point of view.

I said, "From the front, you look great. Turn around. You can't see your backside in the mirror." When she turned around to face me again, I told her that if she looked any better, I wouldn't be able to keep my hands off of her. To this she replied, "If you weren't married, I don't think that I would want you to."

"There is something about being nude that gives you a lot of freedom," I said, "but I don't think I would like it all the time.

"Neither would I. You know, this has been one of the greater experiences of my life. I have never seen a naked man before, and although some of them look different, they don't look good to me."

We returned to the water for another swim, and by this time, Gloria was running around like a small child and not the least bit inhibited. We were enjoying each other and it was getting to be late afternoon when we returned to the dressing room, dressed and caught the boat back to the mainland.

We had a light dinner, and while we were eating, I said, "Now that we have our clothes back on, I want to tell you what a beautiful body you have. You are a beautiful person."

After finishing our dinner, we returned to our rooms, since we wanted to get an early start the next morning. We were both tired. I took a shower and went to bed, but it was only a little while before she knocked on my door and asked if she could come in. "Sure," was my answer. She entered wearing her pajamas and, thank heaven, I was wearing mine.

She asked if it would be OK if we talked some more and she lay down on the bed beside me. "You won't tell anyone about this will you?" she said. "I'm just lonesome and homesick tonight and I don't want to be by myself. If, while we are talking, we both go to sleep,

I would like to stay with you till morning. Ever since my brother talked about you and when I later met you on the Metro, I have felt safe with you."

We lay there talking and we both must have fallen asleep. I was startled awake in the morning by the faint fragrance of perfume. When I opened my eyes, there was Gloria with her eyes closed in peaceful sleep with her face framed by her dark hair spread out on her pillow only inches from my face. It was hard to resist the urge to run my fingers through it. I must have moved a little as I lay there looking at her, because she opened her eyes and smiled at me.

"I slept like a log," she said. "I guess we both must have. I don't think we touched each other during the night." Looking at me, she touched my hand and continued, "This is the first time since I have been over here that I have been able to feel close to anyone."

With that, we decided it was time to get moving, but just as I started to get up, she looked at me and said, "I need you to hold me close before we get up."

I turned to her and she put her arms around me and held me tight, placing a kiss on my lips. This was not the usual sisterly kiss that we had shared before. "Whoa!" I said.

"Thanks for not taking advantage of me. I have had several weaker moments since yesterday and I just needed someone to be close to. If anything had happened, I would have been sorry afterwards."

We had breakfast, then began our drive back through this beautiful country to Nice. Talking as we drove, she tried to explain to me why she was terribly lonesome. She told me that she had not been out with any man that treated her like a lady since she left me in Paris. Every one of them had tried to take advantage of her. This made me happy that I was able to behave myself. Her brother told me what a sheltered life she had led before she met me.

We arrived at the train station in Nice and sat in the car until it was time for my train to leave for Paris. We commented about how much we had enjoyed our stay. That was probably the only time either of us would ever enjoy a nude beach. She looked at me and said, "It's kinda sad that I won't be able to tell any of my family about this wonderful adventure and sharing this closeness."

As the train pulled into the station, we got out of the car and she walked with me to the station platform. As I got ready to board, she put her arms around me and kissed me deeply on the lips just like she had in bed earlier that morning, all the while holding me tight and molding her body against mine. She looked into my eyes. "Don't hate me. I will never be able to repeat that experience with anyone until I find a man that I want to spend the rest of my life with."

I boarded the train, and as the train pulled out of the station, I sat in my seat watching her as she stood there waving. Never knowing if we would see each other again, it was sad for me and I am sure it was for her. It was almost like leaving one of the family. As I have often said, all good things have to come to an end sometime. I arrived back in the Gare de l'Est Station in Paris and took the Metro home.

After my return from Nice, things at the office were rather quiet, just a few small boring cases, but as I said before, keeping busy made the time pass faster. I would clear these up in a couple of days and then I would take some more time off.

I enjoyed relaxing and "hanging out" around the Bouy LaFayette Club with several of my friends, like MP Lt. Rogers, with whom I always had a good time. Then of course, there was Eleanor, the WAC sergeant, who was there almost every night. When she was sure that I was going to be there, she would join me for a drink, but she would rather go to a quieter place where we could sit and talk uninterrupted. Even though I enjoyed good company, I tried to hold my drinking down to two drinks.

Ruth didn't seen to be having such a hard time of it now, although she hadn't heard from her husband for a long time. She was much more upbeat now that the war in the Pacific seemed to be moving along at a much faster clip. According to all reports, the Pacific fleet was shelling the main island of Japan daily and the B29s were bombing around the clock. With all this, if it came to a land invasion of Japan, we would suffer millions of casualties, so our feet were not out of the fire yet. The outlying islands of Japan were falling one by one, but the main island was the one where we would have the high casualties. The Japanese people made the comment that should such an invasion take place, they would fight to the last man, woman and child.

All we could hope for was that a miracle would happen. Stranger things have happened, but all we heard now was just talk. It appeared that they may not have to send but a few troops from Europe to Japan, only a few special troops. I hoped it would not be the reconnaissance and intelligence units because that would be me.

I hadn't had any letters from my wife for a long time. I got more from my folks than anyone else. I know it was much harder for them to write than it would be for my wife. Even though my morale is low, for some reason it seems like time is passing much faster, I just wish I would have some more interesting cases—the more interesting, the faster time goes.

Eleanor just walked in and sat down with me

"Let me buy you a drink," I said.

"Fine," she said. "I've missed you. What have you been doing?"

I told her I'd been down in southern France to Nice and Cannes. "You remember Gloria? She invited me down for a couple of days to watch all the celebrities."

"What did you guys do interesting?"

When I told her about going to the island with the nude beach, she said. "You guys have all the fun."

"Are you asking me to take you?"

"I don't think so, but it does sound like fun."

We had another drink. "I'm tired," she said. "Let's just go up to your room. I need to talk and it's hard to find a man you can spend quiet time with without him trying to get in your pants."

"Are you saying I'm harmless?"

"No, but you're my good friend and I trust you, so I'm safe." Eleanor looked at me and said, "It's early. I think I'll go check in, make bed-check and come back. I feel like company." About a half hour later, my window opened and Eleanor stepped through in her pajamas. She walked over to my bed, said, "Move over," and lay down beside me. "I just wanted to be comfortable," she said. "'There are not too many times I can get in a compromising position in a man's bed without it leading to something else."

"Eleanor, you're a pretty girl and you look very sexy in those old G.I. pajamas. If it wasn't for spoiling a wonderful friendship, I might be tempted."

"The same goes for me," she said. "I don't want to change a thing. Sex is plentiful; a good male friend is hard to find. Lindy, you're the only man I'd feel comfortable with like this."

I looked at her. "I'm beginning to think there's something wrong with me. This is the second time in a few days I've ended up in bed with a pretty sexy girl in pajamas and all they want to do is talk." I then told her about Gloria and our trip to Cannes. "Do you think I'm too shy?"

"I think you're an honorable man," she said. "I came over to talk to you about the war in Europe being over and it looks like it will end in Japan shortly. My thoughts were pretty much the same as yours, if we had to invade the main Jap islands, very few of us would ever get home.

"As you know, I've talked to you about a lot of things. I've had several affairs since I've been over here, including sex with one who was very special. I was madly in love with him. He was my first. We were looking at a future together after the war. You met him—he was a fine young man. He was killed in combat about a week after our last date. I was broken hearted.

"After that I was afraid. I had two affairs that led to sex. I knew I should never have let things go that far. I just felt that I was missing out on life and with the uncertain future at that time, I thought that the fulfillment of that sex need was love. The feeling of satisfaction at the end of the sex act left me empty. What I want to know, do you think that I'll ever find a love like that again with someone else?"

I looked at her lying there. I saw the misery in her eyes, even a couple of tears. I said, "I don't know what to tell you. I think it's possible to find love again, maybe even a greater love than what you had. I myself think it's much better to have loved and shared love deeply with someone even for a short time, than to have never known love." I told her about the French girl, Alesia, who gave me the gift of love for freeing her country, even if only for a short time "I was down at rock bottom; I saw little chance of ever making it home. That part of herself she gave me filled a spot that gave me hope again. You also have received that hope. Somewhere inside you is a spot that young man filled for you. There will be a time down the road when that will give you the courage you need.

"I care about you. I'll never forget the night that a young WAC sergeant who had never seen me before took a young lieutenant, drunker than a skunk. Took his billfold loaded with months of back pay, rented a room, paid for it, managed to get me up to the room, got me undressed, put me to bed, hung my uniform up because you knew I had to report to that Colonel in a class A uniform the next morning."

I looked at her. She seemed to be feeling much better. I thought a little teasing might help, so I said, "I've wondered ever since that night you put me to bed. I woke up the next morning completely undressed. You didn't take advantage of me, did you?" With that, I leaned over and kissed her very lightly on the lips. "You know I am doing this because if you did, I wouldn't want to get screwed without getting kissed, even if it's a little late."

She started laughing. "You think you are smart. If I'd done that, I would have taken at least 50 English pound notes out of the billfold, not just enough for the room."

This put everything on a lighter note. Suddenly she looked at me. "You're an honest man. You kissed me. Do you know what that means? Since I didn't screw you that night, that means after that kiss you owe me one good 'screwing' any time I demand it!" She smiled. "Gotcha!"

"I would do that to you, just to be mean, except it would spoil our precious friendship," I said.

"Do you realize how few of these young adult women over here, most of whom are lonely and homesick WACs, Red Cross girls, nurses and even some civilian girls, who have no father or brother figure they can talk to or depend on? Usually if they do try to talk to someone, most soldiers think it's a come-on and all you want is sex. I'm a very lucky person, I'm more than lucky. I couldn't talk to either my father or my brother like I talk to you. Not even my mother. I told her, I trust you too. I wouldn't trust many people with a key to my room."

We lay there and talked into the small hours of the morning. It made me feel good that I was able to help her. It was good therapy for both of us. We both decided it was time for her to go to her own bed.

When I woke up the next morning, I remembered one of the things Eleanor and I talked about. On April 12th, 1945, the President of the United States of America, who was the Commander in Chief of the United States forces, died. This was shortly before VE day in Europe.

We now had a new Commander in Chief in the middle of the war, Vice President Harry S. Truman. Most of us had never heard much about him or what kind of a man he was. That was one of the reasons everyone was a little down, not knowing how he was going to perform taking over command. With the war going much better in the Pacific, we just hoped that he would keep going in the same direction. We had finally began to believe we had some chance of getting home alive.

Manual and I were going to get together soon and have a meeting with Aletta. He thought he might be sent back to the U.S. soon and we had to make different arrangements for his money from the watches. I took care of a few minor cases in the next few days, but nothing exciting.

I got a call from Eleanor to check my headquarters memo.

MEMO
FORCE HEADQUARTERS – APO -887

On August 6, 1945, President Truman ordered the 1st Atomic bomb dropped on Hiroshima, having the power of 20,000 tons of TNT, destroying sixty percent of the city.

On August 9, 1945, the second bomb was dropped on Nagasaki, an industrial city, completely destroying the steel and iron works necessary to their war effort. The Japanese called this weapon inhuman. The Vatican issued a statement that it deplored the use of the atomic bomb.

> *Truman told Emperor Hirohito, "This is just a warning. Unless you surrender, I will continue to drop these bombs until you can no longer make war." Emperor Hirohito accepted an unconditional surrender.*

World War II was over.

I said earlier that maybe some miracle would stop this war before we lost millions of men in the invasion of the main islands of Japan. Looks like our prayers were answered. This weapon was something we'd never heard of. There were rumors of German secret weapons, one of which was an Atomic bomb. They'd had jet planes since 1943, V1 and V2 rockets and etc. If we hadn't brought this war to a quick end, we could have very well been on the receiving end of one of these horrible weapons. They had already tested a V3, which would reach New York. This rocket had a speed of over 3,000 miles per hour.

It was now mid-August and now that World War II is over, it looked as though I would soon realize my hopes of going home. They had set up a point system for sending soldiers home, and they were leaving for the U.S. by the thousands. Points were received for time spent in service, time overseas, awards and more that I can no longer remember. 140 points was the most you could have, and I had much more than that. I'd have to finish up all the cases I had in my file. That shouldn't take long.

I no longer needed to get back to my old outfit. I would be shipped directly back to the States and discharged there. After spending so many months with almost no hope of ever getting home, this was almost unbelievable, but now, the waiting was going to be hard. I just hoped that I could keep busy enough for time to pass quickly.

After finishing up a small, easy case, I decided to relax a little so I called Manual. He told me that he would be in Paris late that afternoon. It was not long before Ruth called and she suggested that we get together. I had no sooner hung up from that call, then Eleanor called and she too wanted to get together. Anticipating all these friends getting together, I called Aletta to see if she wanted to eat with us. She said that she would like to invite all of us to her place for dinner that evening. I checked with all the others and they thought it sounded like a splendid idea.

We all met at my hotel and then went on to Aletta's place at 7 p.m. She greeted us at the door, again wearing a beautiful dress and looking wonderful. As we all stepped in, she took my face in her hands and kissed me softly on the lips and said, "I'm so happy the war is over for you." As I introduced her to each of my friends, she kissed them all, boys and girls alike, on the cheek and told them how happy she was that they could come.

She was a wonderful hostess and treated us all like royalty. We had a wonderful meal in a delightful setting. The French maid took care of everything, leaving the whole group to eat, talk and be happy. With the war being over, everyone was practically bubbling over with happiness. We finished off the dinner with a fancy desert that I had never seen or enjoyed before. It was unbelievable.

After desert, we moved to the living room in front of the fireplace to enjoy an after dinner drink of fine French brandy. While the rest of us were enjoying our brandy, I suggested that Manual and Aletta go to the dining room and make arrangements for sending his camera money back home. A short time later, we thanked her for a wonderful dinner, to which she said, "Thank your friend Lindy. He is responsible for it all. Have him tell you the story, how this came about." We all headed home.

The next morning, following the dinner and delightful time the five of us had at Aletta's' place, I awoke in a great mood ready to hit the road and get something done. The first thing, before even thinking about a new case, was to discuss the point system for going home with my commanding officer. I had already reached the maximum required, which was 140. When I asked him how soon I would be able to go home, his discouraging reply was, "I don't have time to train anyone to take your place."

I replied, "But regulation states that anyone who has 140 points or more should be sent home immediately."

He reiterated, "I still just don't have any one to replace you!"

Not ready to give up, I said, "There are hundreds of thousands of soldiers over here that don't even have 40 points."

His stubborn reply was, "I am still not going to sign your papers."

Here I was, stuck again. The war was over and I had my points to go home but I am still here. I thought the main reason was that my CO was a low timer on points and he was just being mean, but I was still a soldier and I would fulfill my duty.

There were several cases that would take me to some of the other countries in Europe, so I started taking every one that I could, hoping that it would make the time pass more quickly and I could meet some new people and see new places, but most of the cases still proved to be boring. Without going in to detail, the traveling did make the time go faster and before long it was the middle of September, 1945. I had been flying to most of my assignments, so I had seen a lot of beautiful countries. I was still trying to keep as busy as possible, so I took any case that I thought would prove interesting.

For one case in particular, I had to fly to Helsinki, Finland, and from the looks of things, it would last for several days. Another thing that made it more interesting was that I would have to have an interpreter. Guess what? They assigned me a very attractive French girl named Jean who spoke five different languages. This was a great surprise for me.

Thank heaven for this girl, Jean. When our plane landed in Helsinki, I don't think I could have found my way out of the airport without her. Helsinki was a beautiful city, parts of it located on several islands. We located our hotel, and I would like to add, it was one of the very best, as we were on an expense account. This would be another case of having a very attractive girl next to me in an adjoining room. (Sometimes things are just hell.)

At any rate, after we got settled in, we decided to eat and get an early start the next morning. This suited us both just fine. Since she could speak the language, she was able to find us a great place to eat. We enjoyed a couple of drinks and a great meal and floor show, both of which were much different from those in France. We finished our meal and went back to our rooms and went over the paperwork for the case, talked for a few minutes, then went to bed (in separate rooms).

221

Feeling refreshed and ready to go the next morning, I called Jean and we proceeded down to have breakfast. After breakfast, we met with and interviewed two men and one American soldier. The case turned out to be much simpler than I had anticipated—just some screwed up paper work that we were able to straighten out by noon.

When my interpreter and I went out to lunch, I found I had been mistaken when I assumed that she was French. As we were eating, I made the comment, "You don't act very French." She answered, "I'm not. I am Finnish. I was raised in Finland and only recently moved to France to accept this job as an interpreter." She added, "If we didn't have to return so soon, I would show you around. I have a lot of relatives here—aunts, uncles, cousins and a lot of other acquaintances."

This sounded good to me, so I replied, "I have a week to ten days to finish this case and as we are already finished. If you want to visit some of your relatives, that will be just fine."

"Oh, no!" was her reply. "I couldn't do that and leave you here by yourself. I could take you with me, and I am sure you would enjoy it as most of my cousins speak English well, and even the rest know some English."

This sounded like a great chance for me to see a lot of different country and meet different people that I otherwise would not see. Seeing how eager I was, she wasted no time in calling her uncle, who lived outside the city, to come and pick us up.

He took us from the city to a small, lovely farm in the country. The people that I met there were completely different from the French, very open and friendly. Not only that, her aunt was a wonderful cook. In all, it reminded me of the small farms in Kentucky where I have a lot of relatives. In addition, Jean treated me just like one of the family—as a matter of fact, all of them did.

When bed time arrived, the both of us were shown to a third floor attic-like room with twin beds. I was rather shocked at this arrangement, but Jean said that this was just a normal thing in their country. Again, this was a learning experience for me. She was friendly and definitely not shy. We undressed in the same room and went to bed, just like we were part of the family. The next morning, she was up early to help her aunt fix breakfast, then came back up to call me to come down and join them at the table. We spent three lovely days in this manner before her uncle took us back to town. I don't know when I have enjoyed anything so much. It reminded me of home.

Jean spent that first afternoon and the next day showing me around the town. That evening, I called Jean to my room and we finished up our paperwork and then went out for a late dinner that night.

She was a lovely young lady. I suppose I should say, a very, very attractive young lady, which became very apparent when I observed her in the revealing dress she wore to dinner that night. Everything was just in the right place and was the right size. Though I tried not to be so apparent, she noticed me looking at her and said, "You have sure treated me like a lady. I half expected you to try to get in my pants and I'm not too sure that I would have objected." I told her that it had been a temptation. We went back to our hotel and went to bed (again in separate rooms). I was justly proud of myself.

Rising early the next morning, we had our breakfast in the hotel before heading to the Helsinki airport, where we caught an early flight that got us back in Paris that afternoon. As we parted, I thanked Jean for her assistance and the wonderful time she had shown me while we were back in Finland. She gave me her telephone number and address and replied, "I have enjoyed working with you and I want you to give me a call if you need me again." With that we parted.

I turned my papers in at the office, but the commanding officer was not there. I still had some of my allotted time left and I didn't want to start a new case quite yet. It was getting on toward the last of September 1945, and I was growing more unhappy with my delay in getting to go home, but I didn't know what I could do that would help. I decided to take a couple days off to see a few of my friends and try to get myself in a better mood. After spending those three days with the family in Finland and being reminded so much of home, I was even more homesick than ever. I tried to call Manual, but was informed that he was on a flight and that they weren't sure when he would return, which left me even more down.

I called my old CO, Ruth. She said, "Thank heaven you called. I have been trying to get in touch with you. I received my papers to go home and I have been trying to get in touch with you to thank you and tell you how much I appreciated your helping me over some very rough times. I have also received word that my husband is in the hospital back in the States and is going to be all right. I would like to see you before I leave and I want you to bring your friends along. They are a great group. That dinner at Aletta's was just wonderful and I would like to thank her."

I was beginning to feel a little better by now, so I suggested, "Why don't we take her to that little out of the way place you took me to? Maybe Eleanor could come too, but my friend Manual is out of the country."

Ruth thought that this sounded like a great idea, so I got on the phone and started making some calls.

It was a very happy group that met at my hotel for a drink before going to dinner. Even I was feeling much better now. Aletta showed up in another of those beautiful dresses, but maybe all dresses would have looked beautiful on her. She seemed very happy that we had asked her to join us. I couldn't understand why men were not falling all over themselves to take her out. I think every male head in the place turned when she walked in.

Finishing our drinks, we left the Club and walked to our favorite little restaurant. The four of us, Ruth, Eleanor, Aletta and I, ordered our food and drinks and then just sat there reminiscing.

Ruth said, "Aletta, that dinner at your lovely apartment with all these wonderful friends was the closest thing to having a family since I've been over here in France. I want to thank you!"

Aletta leaned across me and kissed Ruth very lightly on the cheek and said, "I'm so happy you're going to be able to get to see your loved one soon. I hope someday that I can have a love like that too. It seems that I have been so mistreated by men that I am afraid to trust any man. The only man that I really trust is sitting at this table with us, but he is married and has a family and will be going home soon." She looked straight at me and continued, "I am sure you have heard what he did for me when I was entangled in that black market scandal."

The other two girls replied that they were well aware of what had happened. Eleanor added, "Lindy came through for me also. When the young man that I intended to spend the rest of my life with after the war was killed in action, Lindy was like a father, mother and brother to me."

At this point, Ruth said, "He also came through for me when I had almost given up all hope, so you girls are not the only ones." Looking at Aletta, she went on, "Aletta, the only difference is that you are in love with him, aren't you?"

She answered, "Yes, but I didn't realize it at first, and I think when I did realize it, it was because he did not try to take advantage of me when he could have easily done so. Through all this, I can in the end say that I did gain a good friend and that I was able to help him out in a couple of small ways."

Somewhat self conscience about all these positive comments, I said, "You girls will never know just how much the friendship with you wonderful ladies has helped me. Eleanor saved my a-- one night. Ruth gave me a part of herself and showed me that someone really cared for me and was trying to keep me safe. "

Turning to Aletta, I said, "I hope the friendship that we have had with each other will someday help you find someone you can love." Continuing on, I said, "I am again having a rough time of it and I am ready to go home after spending almost five years in the Army. As you all know, the military has set up a point system where the more points you have, the quicker you will be sent home. This system only goes to a maximum of 140 points and I already have more than that, but my commanding officer will not process my papers! He says he doesn't have anyone to replace me, but there are many soldiers being sent home with only 30 or 35 points. Here it is, almost the end of September, and I am still here when I should have been home a month ago."

Eleanor looked at me and said, "You know that I work in headquarters and I am doing this type of paper work everyday. When we leave here tonight, I'll stop in your room, and if you have your personal records there, we will get all the forms filled out and I will send them down from higher headquarters and your CO will HAVE to sign them." I guess you know that I was elated and could hardly believe this turn of events!

A feeling of festivity returned to our small group with the addition of these few words. Everyone was very happy for me and, as for me, it looked like I would be on my way home in a few days. We all decided to go back to my room and have another drink while Eleanor looked over my records to make sure that I had the required number of points.

The gathering in my room was just a little sad, as this was probably the last time that this group of good friends would be able to get together. Ruth already had her papers and thanks to Eleanor, I would have mine the next day. I suddenly felt very sad. We would all be leaving soon and only Eleanor and Aletta would still be here. Things brightened a little when Eleanor said, "It looks like I will be getting my papers in about two or three weeks, so the wait won't be long for me."

When Aletta looked at me with tears in her eyes, I said, "This is your home and you own your own store here. You have a good bank account and the occupation is over, so I want you to try to be happy."

She smiled a sad little smile and replied, "I know and that is all well and good, but I still will not have you and your friends."

We all hugged and kissed each other a sad goodbye, but Aletta asked me if I would walk her home, as this would probably be the last time we would see each other. When we arrived at her apartment, she asked me if I would like to spend the night. I told her that if I did, I would probably not be able to leave, and with that, she placed her arms around my neck and kissed me goodbye. It was not one of those gentle kisses that she usually gave me. I think maybe it even made my toes curl a little.

She said, "Part of my heart was in that kiss. I hope you will remember it forever. Thanks for giving me back my life! Goodbye, good friend!"

On the way back to my room, I wondered to myself if I was a damn fool for leaving one of the most beautiful women that I had ever known up to this point in my life. She was not only beautiful on the outside, she was beautiful on the inside too. Deep in my heart, I knew I was doing the right thing. I had a mother and father, two brothers, a sister, and a little girl that I had never seen, as well as a wife that I seldom heard from. (Sometimes, I wondered if she was still there.)

I went up to my room and lay on the bed thinking about and wondering if Eleanor would get my papers pushed through. When I awoke the next morning, I wondered if all the things that happened last night were really true or if all of it was just a dream. I decided to treat this day just like any other.

I had no cases so I decided to go to the officers' mess at Place St. Augustine, thinking that I might find someone there that I knew. I had no such luck, so after finishing breakfast, I decided to go back to my room and go through all my belongings just in case my papers went through. I knew that I would not be able to take everything with me. As I went through all my equipment and personal effects, it seemed that my whole lifetime was contained in this one room. I felt that if I left anything it was going to be like leaving a part of myself. To add to these sad thoughts, I was scared, because having been in the military the biggest part of my adult life, I had no idea how I would react to civilian life. Thank heaven I had spent part of that time in Paris to semi-adjust. Even though most of my contacts were military, I did come in contact with a lot of civilians.

While I was in the process of getting everything in order, I received a call from Eleanor. She had all my paperwork finished and wanted to know how to get it to me. I named a sidewalk café that was nearby and said, "Meet me there and I will buy lunch."

After we had a pleasant lunch, she said, "I'll come by tonight and help you pack. I read your orders, and you will have to report to Camp Wings on the coast tomorrow."

After our lunch, Eleanor went back to her work and I took my orders, and with my heart in my mouth, went to see my commanding officer. This was a confrontation that I was really dreading. I knew he would be very unhappy. When I did present him with my orders, he exclaimed, "How did you get these! I am supposed to sign them and send them through channels."

I told him that they came in the inner office mail with a notation stating that, with the points this man has, he should have been given his travel orders over a month ago. With a look of resignation, he said, "I didn't realize that you had so many points. I'm sure going to hate to lose you."

With that, I saluted him and ask if there were any problems with the last case to which he replied, "No." (The meeting had gone well.)

My travel orders called for me to find the first available ground transportation to Camp Wings located at LeHarve, France within the next forty-eight hours and to report to Commander of Troop Movement RE-3222-32 from E.T.O. to the zone of the interior (which means The European Theater of Operations to the United States).

I called around and finally located transportation to Camp Wings for the next morning at 10.00 hours.

I went back to my room and started laying out all my worldly possessions. You can't realize how hard it was to start getting rid of things that were part of the only security that I had for months and even years. I, of course, kept my Colt 45, my Luger, my P-38, my 7.65 Belgium Browning automatic along with a pair of German Field glasses and another special Luger in a walnut case that had been manufactured for a German general. I waited until Eleanor got off work to finish packing my two dress uniforms, two pairs of fatigue boots and one field jacket.

I was wanting to go home so bad that I could taste it, but on the other hand, I was scared to leave the only home that I had known for months. The only way that you could appreciate how I felt was to have been there and to have experienced it for yourself. I was afraid I was leaving a part of myself there.

When Eleanor arrived, we went on out to dinner then returned to my room to finish my packing. I tried to thank her for pushing my paper work through but she said, "You are a friend, and had I known you had so many points, I would have pushed them through even sooner." We finished the packing and spent the remaining time we had together talking about the good times that we'd had together and even some that were sad. She told me that she had checked her paper work and thought that it would only be a week to ten days before she would be heading home.

"I'm very happy for you, but it is sure going to be lonesome without you," she said. "You are like family to me." I was glad that she would only be by herself for a short time. We were both tired and nervous about what the next few days would bring. Before returning to her room, she put her arms around me and held me tight. With tears in both our eyes, we kissed each other goodbye before a very sad parting.

For the last time, on September 26th, 1945, I left the Bouy-LaFayette Hotel. I had my travel orders to report to Major Green at Camp Wings, LaHarve, France. (All these camps were named for different brands of cigarettes.) It was with great sadness that I left the hotel that had been the only home that I had known for months and months. No one was even there to say goodbye.

When I caught my transportation (a 6 x 6 truck), I was given a list of ten soldiers and was told that I would be responsible for seeing that these men reported to Major Green at Camp Wings. It was mid-afternoon when we arrived, and I reported with these troops to Major Green. The major put a sergeant in charge of the men and assigned them space in the enlisted men's area. He assigned me to the officers' area and told me to get rid of my equipment, then to report back to his office. His office was the only permanent building in the camp. All the others were tents with the sides rolled up and four folding cots for sleeping. I put my equipment on my cot and reported back to the major.

He said, "Lt. Fancher, you are the only line officer who has commanded men. According to my paper work, all the rest of these enlisted men are individuals from different outfits. I want you to appoint a first sergeant for these men. He will keep a morning report and you will report the status of these troops to me each morning at ten a.m. in my office. The rest of this packet will consist of a medical detachment made up of doctors and nurses.

"On the other side of my office will be the nurses' quarters, and it will be off limits to all personal except for the inspection that you will conduct on my orders. We are short on trained officers, so I am going to have to assign you an awful heavy load. You will be custom inspection officer, custodian of records, and the finance officer. As custom officer, you will inspect every piece of equipment that is to go aboard the ship. You can assign anyone you want to help you, but you will be responsible when your signature is on the custom inspection certificate. It may be spot checked by a higher ranking officer.

"Watch for live ordinance. As custodian of records, you will responsible for seeing that all records are loaded on the ship with the proper troops and then dispersed to the proper troops when they disembark in the U.S. As finance officer, you will collect all foreign money, and this will be exchanged for U.S. currency. The limit of the money that can be exchanged will depend on their pay scale. All this will be accomplished by October the 5th, and you will depart on the ship, the *Thomas H. Barry*, for the United States of America on the 6th."

GETTIN' READY

The day was September 27th 1945. I was at "Camp Wings" near La Harve, France, the staging area for people getting ready to return home to the States. I had already started to check everyone's equipment and war souvenirs. I had appointed a detail of six men to help me accomplish this task. Before I started down the line of tents, I had three men place a table and chair in front of the tent and another spread a GI blanket on the left side of the table. All the men in each tent would line up outside the tent with all their equipment. When they were lined up, another man in my detail would go into the tent and make sure that everything was out.

One man at a time would place all his belongings on the blanket and then proceed to the right of my table to sign a custom inspection certificate verifying that he was the owner. Another of my detail would hand me each item from the blanket. All that was approved, I passed on to the owner, who placed it in his pack or bag. All the enemy equipment was left on the table until I had inspected each item to make sure it was disarmed and safe. I then had the owner list it on the certificate. I would then sign my name as custom inspection officer.

No one would be allowed to board ship without this certificate that was prepared in duplicate. I also had them fill out their tags for their hand baggage. Any item that I had found to be unsafe, I had another of my detail take to a pit a short distance from camp. (I had a guard posted on it so that nothing could be removed.) I had all these procedures set up like a production line and all seemed to be going well. When Major Green came by, he agreed that it was a good idea. I asked the major if it would be OK to have my first sergeant make the report to him in the morning so that I could keep my line going.

He said, "That's fine, as long as you sign the report." I can no longer remember how many soldiers we had, but I do know that I signed my name many, many times. As everyone grew more accustomed to their jobs, including me, I began to think that we would be able to make the deadline and board the ship on the 5th of October. I finished up the day with satisfaction. All I had to do now was to make sure someone in the tents not yet checked didn't slip some unauthorized item to the ones that had already been checked.

I went to bed early, as I wanted to start checking more of this equipment early the next morning. We did get up early and made an early start and by evening, had finished checking all the enlisted men and had only the doctors and nurses left to check. The following morning, September 29th, we started the checking of the doctors and the nurses. It also went well and fast. Some of the underclothes of the nurses proved not to be GI issue and were pretty skimpy. As you know, at that time I was pretty shy and was known to blush a little at times. These girls seemed to enjoy showing them to me just to make me blush. We finished up the check that night and I was looking forward to having a little break the next day.

I awoke the next morning, September 30, 1945, thinking that I would have a day of leisure and be able to take it easy. It would be only five days (evening of October 5th) until we could board the ship and sail for home. My hopes of taking it easy were dashed the moment my feet hit the ground. I was ordered to get a list of all personnel along with the amount of their pay. I also had to get a list of the exchange rate of all foreign money. As custodian of records, I had to appoint a man in each package (the whole ship was divided into packages) to be responsible for the records in his package. Each package determined which distribution point they would be assigned when we arrived in the States. (Mine was Fort Sheridan near Chicago.)

After making these preparations, I had to get all the lists and forms made up for the money exchange and I knew that with this, I was going to need help. I finally located a doctor and a nurse who agreed to help me with this task, but I was still sweating blood because of all the counterfeit money, both foreign and American. Once I had signed my name, I would be responsible for every penny. Finding the doctor and nurse, both of whom were familiar with foreign currency, was a great relief for me. After getting all my "ducks in a row," all that was left to do was wait for orders to pick up this "damn" foreign currency.

I reported to Major Green that everything was ready except for the money exchange, and that due to the large amount of counterfeit money that I expected, I had enlisted the aid of a doctor and nurse to assist me. He said, "That's fine, but remember, when you sign your name, you're responsible. You will start your exchange at 0800 tomorrow, October 1st." He directed me to go into town to the paymaster at the finance office and get a list of the exchange rate of all foreign money. He even issued me a Jeep and a driver.

In addition to carrying out my orders in town, I managed to buy a case of Cognac Four Star Hennessey. All that I would have to do now was to figure out some way to get it home. At any rate, I dropped the cognac off at my tent and returned the Jeep to Major Green.

After returning the Jeep, I made up the list for the exchange for the foreign money. The following were for the main exchanges.

> French Francs---1000 francs = $20.00
> English Pound---1 pound = $4.00
> German Deutsche-mark--Can't recall
> Dutch Guilder---Can't recall
> Russian Ruble--Can't recall

I guess you know that this dumb, small town farm boy was getting pretty damn nervous. I didn't have any idea how much money there would be, but I did know that it was going to be more money than I had ever seen in my life and I didn't like the idea of being responsible for someone else's money.

The morning of October 1st came and I appointed a detail to set up tables in front of my tent. I had a roster in alphabetical order of all the men along with their rank. All that remained to be done was to find something to put all this money in. The solution to this was a trip to the kitchen tent to talk them out of a few boxes. I had already picked up a box of rubber bands at the paymaster's office.

With all the preparations made, I picked up the roster and started calling out the names. As each man came up to the table, the doctor and then the nurse would take each bill and check it to see if it was counterfeit, then they would pass it to me for a final check. After I had checked it, I would enter the foreign amount in one column and the equivalent amount in the last column. This procedure went on until about three p.m. that afternoon.

I called Major Green and we went over the roster and he announced that the exchange was closed. He then called the paymaster and told him the amount of US currency he would need to make the actual exchange and that he was sending his finance officer in to pick up the money. The total was $219,878.37.

Once again, he assigned me a driver and this time, a ¾ ton truck. I arrived at the finance office and turned in all this "damn" foreign money to the counting room. They, of course, had to count it, but, thank heaven, it came out right. They brought out two wooden boxes stamped with the words U.S. Mint. These boxes contained all new bills, 1s--5s--10s--20s, along with some change. I had to count all this money, but it didn't prove to be a great task, as all had been packaged at the mint with the exception of a few loose bills and some change. The boxes were heavy enough that it took two men to carry each box out to the truck.

Arriving back at Camp Wing, I reported to Major Green, who informed me that due to the black-market, he had received orders that I couldn't pay the men until we had boarded ship and were well out to sea. This really threw me for a loop. I asked him, "What am I supposed to do with all this money? Do you have a safe?"

His answer was, "Not big enough for all that."

Then I really did start to sweat! I had all this money, and even though I had a gun, I had no ammunition and I was sleeping on a cot in a tent and the sides were rolled up. The only place that I could put the money was under my cot and even then, both boxes were so big, that they stuck out. I had the doctor and the nurse watch over them while I made a trip over to an old pillbox near the shore. There I found some 9mm ammunition for the German P-38 that I had captured earlier in the war. Getting this ammunition at least made me feel a little better.

I had sure been looking forward to getting rid of the responsibility of caring for this money, but that had all gone down the drain. The next morning when I went to the latrine, I pulled the side of the canvas down so I could keep my boxes in sight. The same held true when I went to the mess tent to eat. I am sure you know that I slept very lightly for the next few days, but the time was slowly but surely passing and October 5th finally arrived. This was the day we boarded the ship and sailed for home. This day I lucked out. We were to board the ship in the afternoon, but as custom inspection officer, I had four men carry the two boxes to the purser's office on board early. Here it was placed in a large safe in the office, leaving me free to go about my other duties.

What a relief!!!

The ship, the *Thomas H. Barry*, was a small luxury liner and we would have only 1500 troops on board, and most of these would be doctors and nurses. After securing the exchange money, I returned to Camp Wings and appointed a detail of a couple men to take care of the records of each "package" of enlisted men. I took these men on board and showed them their men's quarters, then returned to the camp and appointed leaders for each "package" of doctors and nurses and returned them to the ship to assign their quarters. I first took the doctors and then the nurses. I didn't have to worry about keeping track of their records, as all officers carried their own. The "packages" determined where they would be sent when we landed in the States.

After completing all this, the morning was almost over. I returned to Camp Wing and had lunch. What a relief not to have to worry about that money. I was able to sit down and actually enjoy my meal. Finishing lunch, I got my personal stuff together at last.

Major Green called me to his office and thanked me for the good job, then told me to go aboard ship and appoint a detail to see that each "package" found their correct quarters. I took my "stuff" to my stateroom and stored it under my bunk, then proceeded to help the men find their team leaders and quarters. The boarding went much smoother and easier than I had anticipated. After all were boarded, we had an early dinner. Since the dining room space was limited, we had to eat in three shifts.

I had just got good and relaxed when I received a call to report to the ship captain's quarters where Major Green and the ship's purser informed me that everything seemed to be in order. The only fly in the ointment was that the purser informed me that I would have to remove the money from the safe so he would have room for the personal effects of the passengers. I was greatly relieved when the captain said that I could pay the men the first day out. He went on to say that he would like to hold a spot check of equipment to be sure that there was no live ordinance on board. Major Green again thanked me and departed.

It was beginning to look like I would be able to relax and not have to spend the rest of my life in the Army trying to repay the money, should I have made a mistake in that damn foreign exchange money. I had a detail place the pay back under my bunk again, then hit the sack. I wanted an early start.

Early the next morning, I had my table set up again and enlisted the aid (starting the payroll) of the same doctor and nurse who had helped me before. This was all new money, so you can just imagine how it would stick together. As I went down the roster, I would carefully count the money, then pass it to the nurse who would also count it, then pass it to the doctor and he would count it. When he had completed his count, he would pass it to the soldier, who would then sign, verifying that he had received it.

This worked like a charm and with the three of us working, it was going much faster than just one checking. We went through the whole thing in record time, and I must have been living right. I was only short $2.35 in change. I took this amount out of my own pocked and paid the last man and we were done.

I kept two sets of records. Some of the soldiers had very little money and some had none at all. Others had more than they were allowed to take home. I hated to see these men lose their money, but it could be spread. This worked out all right for which I was thankful.

Having disbursed the payroll, I felt like a great weight had been lifted from my shoulders. I had hated having the responsibility of caring for all that damn money.

I thanked the doctor and nurse for all their help and told them that that I had a bottle of Four Star Hennessey Cognac and would be more than happy to have them join me for a relaxing drink. They both answered with a resounding, "Yes," and the nurse added that she had a bottle of Champagne in her bedroll and that she would bring that and we all could relax. Due to a "directive" that stated that there was not to be any men in the nurses' quarters nor nurses in the men's quarters, we headed for some tables and benches on the top deck. We sat there drinking cognac, washing it down with champagne, and it wasn't long before we were all so relaxed that I think we were limp.

The dinner at night was always early, as movies were shown in the Persian Square dining hall. As I mentioned before, the meals were served in three shifts due to the shortage of space. Meals were served from four p.m. until seven p.m. and the movies started at 7:30 p.m. and ran for the rest of the evening. I went back to my stateroom to rest a while.

I forgot to mention that I had left the German Luger 9 mm with a 22 caliber adapter kit encased in a walnut presentation case on top of my money boxes, and it had been stolen just before we picked up the money. This special gun had been made for a German general. The same gun today would probably be worth eight to ten thousand dollars. I was really unhappy.

I thought that I might be able to find it the next day while I was doing the live ordinance check. After finishing that inspection, I anticipated having the rest of the cruise to enjoy myself and I certainly intended to do just that. I didn't know any of these nurses, but I did know that one of them was the friend of one of the nurses that I had known in Paris, so I was looking forward to finding her.

I got up early the next morning (October 7th, 1945), had my breakfast, then contacted the ship's captain to see if we could get the live ordinance inspection started. He said, "Lt. Fancher, you can start the inspection any time you are ready."

After the strict inspection that I had performed on shore before boarding ship, I didn't anticipate any problems, which proved to be true after picking and inspecting the first stateroom. After the first inspection, I thought to myself, this is going to be a piece of cake. Next I picked a storage room that was used to store all the bags and gear. The first bag that I opened contained an enemy mortar shell (souvenir) with its nose pointing straight down. With this discovery, I almost turned white. It was live with no safety, so all it would have taken was a six inch drop on its nose to detonate the mortar. The first thing I did was to rig a safety so that I could get the thing to the rail and heave it overboard.

After disposing of the mortar, I immediately contacted the captain and explained to him that if that mortar had gone off in the storage room (which was at the waterline), it would have in all likelihood sunk the ship. We made an announcement over the ship's communication system that anyone having mortar shells, grenades or any other kind of explosive devises, should notify me immediately. Failure to do so would mean confinement in the brig until we reached stateside, where a court martial would be conducted. This meant that going home would be out of the question.

A flood of soldiers contacted me to report explosives in their gear, and I had a very busy day checking out all these reports. I found one live enemy grenade and a few 20mm shells, all of which I threw over board. In every case, the soldiers had been told that these objects had been disarmed. I don't know where they had them concealed when I made the inspection on shore at Camp Wings.

After checking out everything that had been reported, the captain and I made a few more random checks but discovered nothing else dangerous. The captain and I discussed whether or not to bring charges against the soldier who had the live mortar shell. I informed him that the soldier in question had a good combat record in action and since no one had been hurt, I would like to drop the charges and forget the incident.

"That's fine with me.," was the captain's answer, and he added, "How would you like to have a drink with me in my cabin? You sure do look like you could use one."

"I sure would," I replied. While enjoying our drink, he told me that he had been fortunate to have me aboard to handle this scary situation. I told him that explosives had been my specialty in the Army.

While we had been performing the inspection, I was always on the lookout for my German Luger, but it was of no avail. I finally decided it was some civilian among the ship's crew that had taken it. The captain gave me permission to search any place on his ship and that if I didn't find it, to leave my name and address and if it should show up later, he would send it to me. I thanked him for his kindness.

With no more duties to perform, all I had to do now was to relax and enjoy the rest of the voyage. During the inspection of the doctors' and nurses' quarters, I had met several nurses and a few of us planned later to have a few drinks together. This sure sounded good to me.

After dinner, I looked up some of these nurses. Most of their quarters, I should say, staterooms, were located around Persian Square (the dining area), where after the last meal was served, the lights were turned out and the movies played. Several of us guys took a couple of bottles of cognac with us, and when the lights were turned out, the nurses let us into one of their larger rooms with six nurses and we proceeded to have a party. With the cognac and treats, we had a great time. No hanky panky, just a lot of fun. The room had a port hole, which was a handy way to dispose of dead soldiers (empty bottles). We were having so much fun that the movie was over and the lights had been turned back up before we knew it, so there was nothing to do except wait till the next show began. It was a fun party and we all got out without being caught.

After wandering around the deck enjoying the fresh air for a while, we called it a night and went to bed. The next morning, I awoke with no duties to perform. What a wonderful feeling. I went up to the top deck and just sat there enjoying the cruise. I noticed that the wind was beginning to kick up a little and a few of the waves were beginning to have white caps on them. That did not bother me at all. It was wonderful not to have anything to worry about.

This didn't last very long. A short time later, a message came over the ship's communication system that I was to report to the ship's captain.

When I reported to him on the bridge, he told me that he had received a radio message that we were heading into a severe storm and that we had neither the supplies nor the fuel to go around it. He said that it would be no problem except we would have a rough ride. He asked me to send a detail around to inform everyone and to have everyone fasten down any loose objects. He said that if I needed extra personnel for the detail, to use the doctors and nurses and that he would also announce it on the intercom. I said, "Yes, sir!" and got the project started. It turned out to be a fun job. I got to talk to a lot of the nurses and during the process, I ran across one that I knew in Paris.

Even though it was my third day on board ship, I was still getting stuck with jobs, but I finally got the message out to everyone. It was about the middle of the afternoon when the ship began to ride some pretty rough waves. It didn't bother me too much, but a few people were getting seasick, so after the evening meal, the movies were canceled and it was suggested that everyone remain in their quarters.

I went to sleep and slept well throughout the night until the main part of the storm hit early the next morning. I dressed and proceeded to the mess hall. There was only a doctor, a chaplain and myself, and who should come in next, but the nurse I knew from Paris. I asked her to sit with me and we ate and enjoyed ourselves, but I guess most of the other people were seasick. When we finished eating, we went on up to the bridge to see the ship's captain. He said that it was going to be a rough ride but that it was a good solid ship, so there was nothing to worry about. The storm would last for about three days.

As the morning wore on, the storm increased in intensity and the ship labored just to make it to the top of each wave, where it would pitch down again and slide to the bottom of the next. No sooner had it leveled out than it would begin its laboring accent to the top of the next wave. I remained in the pilothouse watching the captain, as he was doing one hell of a job jockeying the speed and heading the bow into the next monstrous wave. After watching him for some time, I figured that there was no need to worry. He finally asked me to assure the passengers that everything was OK, even though the going would to be a little rough.

I went below deck, where I found some of the nurses were pretty upset. I went on back to my cabin and picked up a couple bottles of cognac and started making the rounds of the nurses' cabins, assisted by the Chaplin and the nurse that I'd known in Paris. After a few shots of cognac, most of them settled down pretty well. Locating a doctor, I asked if they had anything in their supplies that would combat the seasickness. He located a medication and had a couple of the nurses help him administer it, and before long, several of the nurses were completely over being so sick.

Meanwhile, I was getting a little tired and hungry from running all over the ship. Just trying to walk was pretty rough. I went to the mess hall, and by this time, about two dozen had shown up, including the nurse that I'd known in Paris. At least some of the people were getting used to the rough voyage.

The nurse asked me if I had any more of the cognac left, and I replied that I still had one bottle. She suggested that we take it up to the sheltered deck beneath the pilothouse and drink it while we watched the storm. To me, this sounded like a wonderful idea. As we sat there watching the storm, each time the bow dipped, it looked like we were heading into a solid wall of water.

Within a few moments, the waves that broke over the ship had us drenched to the skin, but with the few shots of cognac we had, we didn't notice the cold at all. It was so much better up here than it was below deck where all the people had been so seasick, that when I became concerned that we might be washed overboard, I just roped us to the bench and huddled closer to keep warm. I don't know if it was more exciting to watch the storm or cuddling so close together.

I did find out that a girl could hold you awfully tight under these circumstances. As pleasant as it was, we finally got cold enough that we returned to our cabins. After getting into some dry clothes, I met the nurse in the mess hall and we had a leisurely cup of coffee. As a whole, we had a wonderful time.

Returning to the mess hall the next morning, I had breakfast with the same nurse. After breakfast, we headed back up to the same deck to continue our storm watch, taking the cognac with us. The ship was still pitching and rolling, and as it nosed over an exceptionally large wave, we were pitched up the last three steps to the deck above.

WWII: Through These Eyes

We slid head first into the door of a stateroom, breaking our bottle of cognac. The stateroom door opened and there stood the chaplain that had joined us during breakfast.

He laughed and asked, "What are you guys doing down there on the deck?" We told him that we were headed up to the deck to have a drink and watch the storm to get away from some of the sick odor below deck, but we had been thrown off our feet and had broken our bottle. He replied, "You poor children! Wait just a minute." He went back in his cabin and returned with a 5th of Vat 69 Scotch, which he gave us and said, "Have fun!"

We had borrowed a couple of heavy rain slickers (similar to what the firemen now wear). We found our seat again and as we enjoyed our drink, watched the storm. It was great to get away from the sick people below. We continued this routine everyday until, on the fourth day of the storm, I awoke and could detect no movement of the ship at all. The ocean was like a sheet of glass. We had weathered the storm with no damage to the passengers or the ship.

It seemed that all had now recovered from the seasickness and were getting anxious to get back to the good old USA.

Toward afternoon on the last day of the voyage, the ship's captain called me to the pilothouse again. He wanted me to appoint a leader for each package when we docked. I told him I had already taken care of it. He also told me we should be able to sight land in about a half hour. He said we had made a record crossing (seven days), the fastest the ship had ever made.

As we entered the harbor, no one will ever be able to describe the feeling of seeing that great lady, "The Statue of Liberty," holding up the torch of freedom as we sailed slowly past. There were many aboard who never expected to see the USA again.

Now that I had finished all my jobs, I only had to take care of myself. What a relief! I stood on deck and watched as the troops debarked. Some who lived in that area were met by wives and family. They couldn't go home yet as they still had to go to camp for processing of their discharge. At least their loved ones could see they were alive.

At last it was my turn. I headed for the gang plank. The captain shook my hand and said, "Thanks." I walked slowly down, and as I stepped off the boat my feet were on the old USA. I had survived.

HOME AT LAST

It was the 13th of October, 1945. My orders were to report to a camp outside New York City (I can no longer remember the name). We remained there until the 24th of November while troop trains were being readied to transport the various packages to all parts of the US. I boarded a train headed for Fort Sheridan near Chicago. When I was released, I couldn't get a train for Lincoln until the next day, so I had to spend the night in Chicago. I arrived in Lincoln about noon on December the first, 1945. I had called my wife the night before, so she and my little girl, Linda, along with my mother were there at the station to meet me.

As the train pulled into the station, the excitement that I had expected just wasn't there. I had been such a long time away that the town where I had worked and spent so much of my life, prior to the war, made me feel like stranger in a strange place. My wife was standing there, holding a little baby girl that I knew must have been mine because she looked just like me. Before I knew it, I was off the train and my mother was hugging and kissing me and commenting, "I thought I would never see you again!"

Turning to my wife, she said, "Hand me the baby and say hello to your husband!"

My wife seemed reluctant to give her the baby, but she finally did, so I grabbed, hugged and kissed her, but the kiss had no depth or feeling. I am not to sure any of her kisses ever did. She almost seemed afraid of me. I was not the same boy she had married a few short years ago. I figured that it would take time to adjust to each other, and if just the three of us could get to our duplex on Pekin Street alone, all would work out well. All I wanted was a home and security, something we could call our own.

My first surprise was not long in coming. My mother said, "I'll drive you home." I answered, "It's only a couple blocks, so let's walk." My wife injected, "No. We've moved out on College Avenue out near the Lincoln College. To save money, my folk's family and I rented a big two story house there." (When I had gone overseas, her mother, father, brother and sister had lived on a farm outside Middletown, Illinois.) I didn't know what to think of this move. When I'd left, my Sergeant's pay and allotment was enough to pay for our apartment and all the everyday expenses, and then when I got the Battlefield Commission, there was another big increase in pay. With all this extra money being sent home, I just couldn't understand the need for this move.

We finally arrived at what I guessed was my new home. It was a nice two story house in a very fancy part of town. There was a bedroom downstairs with a double bed and a baby bed. It had a small closet, which was almost full of my wife's clothes, and that is where I was told to put all of my clothes and worldly possessions. My wife said that this would be our room. This was not my idea of coming home to try to rebuild our life together. As it turned out, the whole family would eat together and share all the expenses. (A family of four adults and ours, just my wife, baby and myself) The only good thing was that the bathroom was just off our bedroom. The bad part was that we would have very little privacy and privacy was what we needed if our marriage was to succeed. I thought that the first thing I needed to do was to find a house or apartment of our own, but for right now, all I wanted was some food and rest. Tomorrow would be soon enough to start looking.

Out of habit, I awoke early the next morning, only to find that someone was in bed with me. It was my wife. She had evidently come to bed after I was asleep and didn't bother to wake me. I had hoped that after everyone had gone to sleep for the night, we could have had a discussion on how we ended up in a house with all these people. She was still asleep, as was our sweet little baby girl. I stood there looking at my daughter. She looked so much like me. I heard people moving around in the bathroom and the kitchen.

I dressed, then went into the kitchen where my wife's sister was having breakfast and preparing to go to school. I sat down and had breakfast with her, and when we had finished, I walked the several blocks to school with her. This young girl talked to me all the way and told me how much she had missed me. I only wished that I had received the same kind of reception from my wife. Young as she was, this girl became my best friend in that family. After she went on into the school, I went on downtown to see the people that I had worked for before the war.

Carl Maurer seemed happier to see me than anyone so far with the exception of my mother. He wanted to know when I wanted to go back to work and I told him that I really didn't want to do anything for awhile. While we were talking, Young Coonhound Johnny, whose father had died while he was in service, came in. Young Coonhounds' real name was Vince Schwenoha, and as many of you know, his father, "Coonhound Johnny," was in the slot machine and pinball machine business as well as operating a tavern just north of Lincoln on old Route 66 with his wife. With Vince in the Army and his father dead, Vince's mother, Minnie, was operating the tavern and trying to keep the slot machine and pinball route operating until Vince got home. She had caught her service man stealing and had fired him. Before he left for parts unknown, he practically destroyed a whole warehouse full of machines by cutting and pulling out wires.

Vince was trying to repair the machines, but was having problems and was seeking Carl to help him. Carl told him that he didn't have the time to assist him, but suggested that he ask me to help. I told him that I wasn't ready to go to work yet, but would help him out until I decided what I wanted to do.

This was how I started working for Coonhound. I went down to his shop and we got the machine he was having a problem with fixed up. I looked at several other machines and told him that I was sure that I could repair most of them with the exception of a few that had too many parts missing. He told me that he didn't know how much he could pay and I told him not to worry about it. I still had money coming from the Army and had a bonus coming from the state.

We seemed to hit it off from the first moment and went out to eat. I told him that I had several personal things to take care of, but would be in the first thing in the morning. (I wanted to see if

I could find an apartment or a house to rent. This turned out to be almost impossible, as there were close to 12,000,000 men across the country already discharged and looking for homes.)

I went home, if you could call it that, for supper. It sure didn't feel like home, but it was all I had for now. The whole family had the evening meal together, but there was little conversation except from the younger sister. She told me all about school and inquired about places I had seen, etc. After the meal, I went into the bedroom and played with my little girl, Linda. She was a real sweetheart. When my wife finished in the kitchen, I asked her if we could get her sister to watch the baby so we could go out and have a little time to ourselves.

We went out to one of the better places in town and found a secluded table where we could talk without being interrupted. I told her that I had been trying to find a place to rent, either a house or an apartment, because I thought that we needed a place to ourselves. With the allotment money and the extra money I had been sending home, we should have been in good shape financially.

She gave me a strange look and told me that almost all the money was gone. Shocked, I asked what had happened to it. She replied, "I don't know, but this new house is more expensive to rent and, of course, we needed new furniture."

I could hardly believe this. There should have been enough extra money that we wouldn't have had to worry about a single thing for a year.

Remember earlier in the story, I told you about my cigarette rations and the money I made on them as well as the cameras that Manual and I bought in Switzerland and sold for a huge profit, all of which I had sent home to my wife. I let all of this drop for the time being and I had another drink before we went home to bed.

By the time that we got home, everyone seemed to be asleep, so she wanted to have sex. I thought maybe everything would work out after all, but as it turned out, it was about the worst physical relationship with a woman that I'd ever had in my whole life, even with her before I went overseas. There was no love or sharing or closeness and she was constantly cautioning me to be quiet. I don't think she even kissed me the whole time. The whole affair left me with an empty feeling and I had a hard time going to sleep.

The next morning, I was up early and went downtown to the Post Office and rented a box. I proceeded to the telegraph office and sent a message to Aletta in Paris asking her to send any money remaining from the sale of the cameras to Post Office Box 172. If it had not been for our little girl and my family that I had not yet spent anytime with, I think I would have caught the first plane back to Paris and taken my chances with Aletta. I was feeling mighty low. It seemed as though I had traded the hell of a war that I knew how to fight, for a kind of hell that I didn't know how to combat. I worked for part of the day, then continued to hunt again for a place to live.

Vince had a pickup truck that he said I could use to go see my folks that night. With my wife and little girl in the truck with me, I headed to see my folks in Mason City. The road looked very familiar to me as I had traveled it many, many times when I worked in Lincoln before I had enlisted. When we pulled up, my whole family was there and even Dad hugged me when I got out. There was Dean, who was no longer a baby, and Irene, who had grown into a young lady, and Dale, who was a young man in high school and now working. This all seemed impossible. After all the greetings were over, Mother went back into the house and started fixing something to eat.

Now I was starting to feel like I was really home. This felt like a real family and I felt like I belonged, not like an outsider like I had when I entered that fancy house on College Avenue in Lincoln with my wife's folks. I can't even begin to tell you how wonderful this little house of my folks felt. Everyone was trying to talk at once, even my dad, who was ordinarily pretty quiet.

We sat down to a simple meal of good old solid food with a huge platter of hot fluffy home made biscuits and real butter. Of all the fancy places where I had eaten all over a large part of the world, this tasted better than any of them. Another of the great things was that Mom enjoyed fixing such a meal just as she always did. We sat around and talked until about eleven o'clock that night. Dale had gone to work earlier, since he worked at the theater, but we did get to visit until he left.

By eleven, I decided that we had better head back to Lincoln because I didn't want to get in too late and disturb my wife's folks. I felt like an outsider as it was. When we got in, I fed the baby while my wife got ready for bed. Again, she kept cautioning me to be quiet. By the time I got to bed, my wife was already asleep. I snuggled in close, hoping for a little closeness, but she just moved farther away. I guess she didn't want any sex. She didn't want anything, but with what I had been through during the war and the horrible things I had witnessed (the inhuman treatment of many civilians as well), I really needed someone to talk to and to unburden my mind of all these recollections. I needed love and sharing, not just the physical relationship of sex. I finally turned over and went to sleep. I wanted to get an early start looking for a home and trying to get more machines fixed.

Vince had let me keep the truck all night to drive into work the next morning. He had told me that I could keep the truck unless we had deliveries to make, and this sure helped me while looking for a house. He also told me that I could take it home and use it at night. Before he went home, he told me that he would have to go to Chicago to buy parts the next day and he gave me the keys to the shop and all the machines.

I was in the shop bright and early the next morning and had started to work on the machines that still needed repairs. I had hardly got started when Vince came in and told me that he was heading for Chicago and that if I should have to make a service call, to be sure to let his mother know when I returned. I went through all the machines and marked all the ones that would be easiest to repair so we could get them out of the shop to make more room.

I had been working for about an hour when a man came in and said he would like to talk to me. He was an official of Logan County and even at this late date, I will not repeat his name or the office he held. He informed me that if I wanted to stay healthy, I had better not continue to work for young Coonhound. He said, "This is a personal warning to you!" I informed him that I was only helping out for awhile. He looked at me again and said, "You have been warned!"

When Vince returned that evening, I told him what had happened. He explained to me that after his dad had died, his mother continued trying to operate all these machines and the business, and that another group was trying to take over all the operations in Logan County and trying to force her out of business. He went on to say that if I was worried, I didn't have to keep helping him. I said, "Just let me ask you one question. Do you need me?" He answered, "Yes!" so I said, "I will work for you just as long as you need me."

I went home that night and unpacked my two shoulder holsters and then cleaned and checked both my Colt 45s. Both holsters were under my coat when I went to work the next morning. I called the man who had given me the warning and asked him to come in and explain just what he had meant. He came in and repeated his warning, and this was just like waving a red flag in front of a bull. I looked him in the eye as I removed my coat so that both 45s were in plain sight. I told the man that Vince had spent four years in the service of his country doing just what they asked and was now trying to run his father's business, which had gone to hell while he was away serving his country. I went on to add that I had served over five years in the service of my country and over four of those were out of the country, and that I had not spent this hell to return home to be threatened by a some "little" man.

Continuing, I told him that I intended to work for Vince for just as long as he needed me and that if he thought he was scaring me, he had better think again. I told him that I had fought in one battle where we were outnumbered fifty to one and that I was still walking around. I added I had been shot at more times than he could count. I said, "Now, my advice to you is to stay away from me. I will bother no one unless I am forced to defend myself. This is my warning to YOU!"

This was very upsetting to me, just getting home and having marital problems on top of it all. I'd had problems before and still came out on top, but I did go out and try to sharpen up my combat skills. I would just have to see what the days ahead would bring.

After the man had left, I started again to work on these partially destroyed pinball machines. This was a job that kept my mind completely occupied. I had been away from this sort of work for over five years and there were miles and miles of wire in each of them, to say nothing of all the hundreds of contact points, relays, solenoids, transformers and electric motors. I was amazed at how fast tracing all this conglomeration came back to me. Most of the machines had schematics which made the job much easier.

About mid morning, Vince came in and asked me to go with him on a service call to repair a couple of slot machines. This was an opportunity for me to get out of the shop for awhile and to get reacquainted with many of the people who operated the restaurants, filling stations, and bars where our machines were located. I had met almost all of them before I went to the Army and they all seemed glad to see me. This part of my life was beginning to make me feel like I was home again.

Returning to the shop, Vince said, "It looks like you are getting along real well with these machines. Why don't we eat, and then you can take the afternoon off and look for a place to live." This made me very happy because, unless you have been in my position, you do not realize just how hard it was to find a house during the housing shortage that existed at that time.

I finally located a lady who had a house on North McLean Street that was not livable because she could get no one to repair it. I made an appointment to see her anyway and we went together to look at the house. It was a big two story house, and from all appearances, it seemed to be a very solid house. There was a huge upstairs, but there was no bathroom in the downstairs part. The downstairs had two bedrooms, a living room, a dining room and a very large kitchen. There was a pantry off the kitchen that was large enough to install a downstairs bathroom. I was very impressed with the house and she told me that if I would make the repairs, she would rent it to me for $30.00 a month and that she would pay for all the repairs and equipment.

I told her that I really didn't need a place that large and I was a little concerned about repairing a six foot square place in the downstairs plastered ceiling where the plaster fell due to a leak in the bathroom above it. She said that if I would repair the leak and patch the plaster, then close off the inside stairway and install a door to the outside, she would rent out the upstairs and rent the lower floor to me for $20.00 a month.

249

I looked the whole situation over and noticed that there was a big two story barn out back. When I inquired about it, she said that it would go with my part of the house. All that remained now was to agree on how much she wanted to spend. She said that it needed new kitchen cabinets, sink and stove, as well as the new bathroom fixtures that I would have to install. She said that she would also pay for all the paint and material for the inside of the house. I explained to her that it would probably take me about six months to make the repairs because I would have to do them during my spare time. We both agreed on this and I was greatly relieved. I now was beginning to see the light at the end of the tunnel.

When I had finished talking with the lady about the house, I figured I might as well go to the so called "home." About the only good thing about going home was being able to see my little girl, Linda. She almost always had a smile for me. Madeline, my wife's sister, was in high school and she also seemed happy to see me and talked to me about school and liked to hear about all the far away places I had been and seen. She was also curious about what it was like living the Army life. As for the rest of the family, including my wife, they had little to say to me. This made me feel like an outsider in my own home. It was very upsetting and I just didn't know how to handle it.

I went on in to eat dinner with the rest of the family, and as usual, there was little conversation except with Madeline. When we had finished dinner, I went in and played with our baby before heading back to the shop to discuss my house plans with Vince. I wanted to see what he thought of the whole deal.

On the way back to the shop, I dropped my wife off at church and then picked up Vince and we both went out to look the house over. He thought it was wonderful if I was able to do the repair work. I told him that I didn't think it would present any problems.

As it was still cold, one of the first things that I would have to do was to install a gas conversion burner in the old coal-fired furnace so I could get the lights, gas and water turned on so I could paint and keep the water from freezing. I talked to my old friend, Carl Maurer, and he said that with his connections, he could get me a burner at cost. My first project was on its way!

I had mixed feelings about discussing the house project with my wife, so I decided to just keep it to myself for a while. She would probably not want to leave the fancy part of town on College Avenue. I didn't want them to know that the house I would be repairing was even bigger than the one they had for fear they would want to move in with us there too. What I was looking forward to was privacy so that my wife and I could maybe work out our problems.

The next thing that I needed was to buy a car. I would need one so I would have a means of getting around and to pick up parts and supplies to get started on the house. I had sent home enough money to be able to afford a pretty nice car, but from what I gathered from my wife, there was very little of it left. This was something that we would have to discuss later. All my thoughts now were focused on my work and repairing the house, and anyway, I needed to give myself a chance to get more settled before I even thought of having this discussion.

The next few days, I kept busy at work and spent my evenings working on the house. I got the conversion burner installed in the furnace and the leak in the upstairs bathroom fixed and had all the utilities turned on. Now I would be able to work on the place anytime of the day or night when I had extra time. Things were beginning to get squared away pretty well and my job kept me busy.

I was discussing some machine problems with Vince one day and he said, "I'm glad we have a few minutes. I have been going over my books and finances, and I've found that due to getting additional machines that you have repaired and gotten back in operation, I will now be able to pay you a good livable wage. When you get an automobile, I will pay your car expenses when you use it for work, but you can still use the pick up truck and take it home at night. It will help a lot when you need to pick up things for the house."

Things were looking bright for me again.

Speaking of using the truck, I was spending more and more time on the road making service calls. I liked this because it sure made the time pass faster and I was meeting many of the people that I knew before I entered the service. Although my home life was not great, the time I spent in the evening with our baby before I went to work on the house was wonderful. My wife and I just seemed to coexist, and by the time I returned home, she was usually already asleep. I would try not to awaken her, but I knew that sooner or later we were going to have to have a long talk about what happened to all the money that I had sent home and several other things.

For the time being, I had a lot of other things on my mind, such as trying to bring myself up to date on my complicated technical work that I had been away from for over five years, to say nothing of trying to get the house repaired. With all this on my mind, I didn't want to have a "blowup" with my wife. It was best to wait until I had the house finished to have this discussion away from all her family.

I did receive some good news. The suppliers were going to deliver the hard-to-get fixtures for the downstairs bathroom. I was going to have to hurry and get the shelves removed from the pantry and get all the plumbing roughed in and the dry wall up. They were also going to deliver the kitchen cabinets and sink, so I was going to have to get the new hot water heater installed in the basement. It appeared that I had my work cut out for me, but with my unhappy marriage, all this extra work bled off some of my extra frustration before I exploded. I was sometimes afraid of what I might do. I had never experienced having someone who was supposed to love me, lie to me and treat me with no consideration.

One of the bright things about coming home from overseas was learning that Mom seemed to have made a complete recovery from her cancer. It was the happiest news I'd had since coming home. In addition, having the use of Vince's truck, I was able to get home to see everyone quite often. I was still looking forward to getting a car, as it would make things much easier.

It was not long before I finally received money from Aletta in Paris for the watches she had sold for me. I now had money enough to buy a good used car. Even if I could have afforded a new car, there were none available at that time.

I was finishing up some work at the house a few nights later when I received a service call from the Maple Club to repair a slot machine. I decided to go ahead and make the repair that night instead of waiting till the next day. It had been a long time since I had a drink, so when I finished the repair, I decided to have one. On entering the bar, I saw several old friends, one of whom was a car salesman. I joined them for a drink and mentioned to the salesman that I was in the market for a car.

He said, "You are in luck! I just got in a 1939 Hudson Terroplane." When I asked him if it was in good condition, he told me that to the best of his knowledge, it was. He said, "As soon as we finish our drinks, we will go have a look at it."

We got in his car and went to the lot. It was a big car and very clean with a big straight eight engine in it. It even had a fold out bar in the back of the front seat with places for glasses, a bottle and ice. There was also a little electric shift on the steering wheel. When I asked the price, he said, "$450.00." I jumped at it and told him that I would take it and would pick it up the next day. With the money that I had received from Aletta, I would be able to pay cash for it. We returned to the club and sealed the deal with a drink.

When I finished my drink, I returned to my so-called home, being very quiet when I entered so that I wouldn't wake anyone up. I was hoping that my wife would be awake, but no such luck. If she was awake, she was pretending to be asleep. I looked at Linda and she was sleeping soundly and looked like a doll. She made me feel good just looking at her. I crawled into bed and went to sleep.

I was so excited about getting the car that I was up early the next morning. Just as I went out the door to get in the truck to go to work, Madeline asked if she could have a ride to school. I told her sure, and then dropped her off at school before going to the shop. At the shop, I left a note for Vince, telling him that I had taken the service call last night and was going to pick up a car this morning. I then called the salesman to pick me up and we went down and I signed all the papers and paid for the car.

When I drove that car out of the lot, I realized that I was home at last and finally had something that was all mine. I thought to myself, "If I can get all those repairs made to the house, I will have a home as long as I can pay the rent." Just this thought gave me a feeling of security, even though I still had loads of work to do to get the house in a livable condition. It would be wonderful to have a place that I could call my own. It had been five years since I'd had a place that I could really call home. The Army had been my only home all those years and even before that, when I was working in Peoria and Lincoln, I was living in a hotel or a rented room.

I had to return to work, but now I felt as if I had something to work for and I could hardly wait until evening so that I could drive over to Mason City to see my folks in my own car. It was unbelievable how wonderful it felt to have something I could call my own.

My work with the machines was going better and easier all the time as my skills returned. I had been able to get most of the equipment repaired and placed in service locations where it would make money. Of course, when this happened, there were a lot more service calls, so I was spending much more time on the road, but it made my job more secure. Vince told me that just as soon as he could find one, he was going to buy me a service car so I wouldn't have to put so many miles on mine.

We really got along well together. He also told me that as soon as I had a phone in my house where he could get in touch with me, I could take off work any time I had my shop work caught up, so I could work on the house. This was great because it would enable me to get the house ready much faster. What a blessing.

I had a very busy day with a lot of service calls, so the day seemed like it was almost over before it hardly began. I locked up the shop and went back to my so-called home and had dinner with her family as usual. (Of course, I was paying for most of it.)

After dinner, I showed the car to my wife and asked her if she would like to ride over to see my family. She replied, "Yes!" and even looked like she was happy. She got our baby, Linda, and when she got into the car, she looked around inside and remarked that it was beautiful. On the way to my folk's house, the car rode like a dream, and in no time, we were there.

When we got there, it was like coming home, but naturally, baby Linda got all the attention from Mom and Dad, which made me feel real good, and I had more of chance to talk to Dale, Dean, and Irene. Even my wife seemed as if she were enjoying herself. This kind of reception gave me a little peace of mind and drowned out some of the horrible memories of the war that were still there. We had a wonderful evening, and as we sat there and talked, it was eleven p.m.

before we knew it. Dad had gone to bed around 9:30 p.m., as he had to go to work early in the morning.

By the time we arrived back in Lincoln, it was nearly midnight. We got into our room and put Linda to bed, and she didn't even wake up. My wife and I got to bed at the same time for a change and I was expecting the same cool reception as usual. I had already turned over and was ready to go to sleep when she put her arms around me and pulled me over on top of her. We had quick sex, after which I wanted to just lie close to her and get to know each other better. Much to my disappointment, she got up and went to the bathroom, and when she returned to bed, she turned her back to me. I might as well have been a stranger. I lay there thinking of the friendliness she had shown me earlier that evening that had made me think that things might be changing. Sleep came slowly.

The next morning, I went to work as usual, but there was not much to do with the exception of a few service calls. (We didn't even receive many of them in the morning.) Vince suggested that I go work on my house until about 10 a.m. He went on to say, "One week I will take the service calls in the evening and the next week you take them."

This schedule went on week after week and before long, the repairs were nearing completion. The biggest thing that I had to get done was to patch the big hole in the plastered ceiling where the plaster had fallen off. I went down to the Union Hall to see if I could get someone to do the job. I had never done any plastering. The head man there told me that it would be nine months to a year before they would have anyone with time enough to do it. This was a shock and I didn't know what to do until I finally remembered that my dad had a friend, Jake Sexton, who did plastering.

The next time I went to see my folks, I went to see Jake to see if he would do the job for me. He told me that he too was snowed under. He looked at me and said, "Lindy, I have known you since you were a kid. I have some extra tools that I will loan you and I will write down the instructions on how to mix the plaster. I am sure that you can do the job." This was a great relief to me. Now all I would have to do was wait until I had time to do the job. Each phase had to be completed once it was started.

At work, things were going about the same, but as business grew, more night service calls and money collections were occurring. This was good, as it kept my mind off my own problems. I was just too busy to think of them. Time passed quickly in this manner. I worked, went to see my folks, spent time with Linda and some with my wife when she felt like it. Spring was almost over and the house was finished except the plaster repair in the ceiling.

Late one night, I had been out on a collection and service call and was returning from the "Old Pioneer" at Lake Fork (a tavern, dance hall and gambling joint at the lower end of Logan County). I had only gone a few miles when I noticed that a car was following me. I had over a thousand dollars cash with me that I had collected during my night's work, so I was very concerned. I slowed to let him pass several times but he wouldn't pass, and this made me very nervous. I turned off on a country road and he turned off right behind me. He still followed when I repeated this procedure several times. I then knew I was in trouble.

I rolled down my window and started looking for a low ditch along side of the road that I could pull into and still drive out of. When I found one, I took one of my 45s in my right hand and wheeled over. This car, with four people in it, pulled over and the window rolled down and they shouted for me to get out of the car. I think the one doing the shouting was the same one who had threatened me at the shop. I didn't say anything. I just picked up my other 45 and placed both of them on the window frame and put six rounds of 45 slugs in the lower part of their car. They took off, throwing a hail of gravel behind them. I pulled out of the ditch and went on back to the shop and called Vince to tell him what had happened. I told him that we would get together the next morning.

When I arrived at the shop the next morning, Vince was already there. We proceeded to discuss the episode that had taken place the night before. I told Vince that I thought we should report the event to the sheriff's office, if he had no objections. He agreed with me and thought it would be a good idea. We drove on over to the court house and went on up to the sheriff's office on the second floor. After he invited us in, I told him what had transpired the night before and how I had reacted to the episode. He was quick to tell me that I shouldn't have shot at the car.

To this I responded, "I really didn't shoot at the car. I did hit it, but I had no other choice." I then showed him my Federal Identification and permit that I had at that time. I also gave him the number to call the FBI should he have any problem with it. After this, he quieted down somewhat. I then told him that I thought he should see to it that this sort of thing didn't happen again.

After we had returned to the shop, Vince asked me what I had shown the sheriff. He said that he thought that the sheriff and some of his friends were in on the confrontation. I agreed with him, but I told him that I didn't think it would ever happen again as I still had friends in high places. After this discussion, we returned to our routine work.

With all the routine work caught up, Vince told me that he had a friend in car sales and that this friend had a good used Plymouth for sale. He suggested that we go over and have a look at it and take it out for a drive, and if it worked well, he would buy it for my service car. We picked up the car and drove it down to Springfield and ate, then drove back to Lincoln. The car worked just fine and Vince bought it. That night after dinner, I was over at the house working and Vince brought the car by and told me that this was my service car. He asked me to drop him off at home and that I could keep the car at my home and use it as if it were my own. This was a great deal for me, as I wouldn't have to put as many miles on my own car.

After dropping Vince off at his home, I returned to the house and continued to work for a while. I could now see an end to all this extra work. About the only major thing left to be done was to patch the hole in the ceiling and do some more painting. I had transformed it into a very attractive house. I thought it was going to be a much nicer place than that so called "fancy house" on College Avenue.

The next project was to line up some furniture so we would have it when we got ready to move in. I didn't think my wife was very happy about making the move, but I had made up my mind that we would move just as soon as it was ready. I didn't intend on paying rent on that fancy house. It sure was not worth what I was paying when we were only using the one bedroom. If they wanted that big house, her dad and brother could pay for it.

Time was passing quickly and before I knew it, summer was here and the weather was turning hot. I had been home now for over six months. It was going to be wonderful to get into our own home and I had hopes that it would correct some of our marital problems.

Leaving the house that night, I stopped for a sandwich before going home. When I got home, I found that my wife had also eaten, so I asked her if she would like to go over and look at the house I had been working on. She said that she thought that would be nice, and when we went in, she looked over the whole place, the kitchen with its new sink, stove, cabinets and floor in addition to the completely new down-stairs bathroom. She even said that it was beautiful, but she still appeared to be uptight about something.

She finally told me that she thought for sure she was pregnant. This was a real shock to me and I could hardly believe it. I said, "We've only had sex twice that I can recall. The first time was just a few days after I got home on the 1st of December and the second time was when we returned home after visiting my folks after I bought the car."

I went on to say, "I think you should go to the doctor and find out for sure." We returned home and went to bed. I thought that if I held her and talked to her, it might make her feel better. When I tried, she just turned her back to me and said she just wanted to sleep.

I was very upset. I just couldn't understand how two unsatisfactory sex sessions (so-called lovemaking) could result in her becoming pregnant. Of course it takes two, and I should have been more careful. I guess I could have said no to sex, but that seemed to be the only thing she wanted.

If it were true that she was really pregnant, I knew that I would have to hurry and get the house finished, because there wouldn't be room for us all when the baby came. I really had hopes that things would work out once we got moved, but at this point in our lives, the last thing we needed was another child. As I lay there with all these thoughts going through my head, I just couldn't sleep. I finally gave up, got up and dressed, then went back over to the house and made a list of the material that I would need to patch the ceiling the next day. There were several small projects that had to be finished, so I spent the rest of the night working on them. At daybreak, I went downtown and had breakfast.

Finishing breakfast, I went out to see if my wife wanted me to take her to the doctor so we could find out for sure if she was pregnant. She said that she was pretty sure she was, but that she would appreciate seeing the doctor. I dropped her off at the doctor's and picked her up and took her back home later. The doctor would call us and let us know the results later that day. When I dropped her off at home, I asked her if there was anything that I could do that would help her or make her feel better.

She replied, "No, it's just that I'm not ready for this." She then looked at me with more feeling than she had shown me since I got home. I thought that maybe there was still a spark there like there had been when she was pregnant with Linda.

I went back to the shop and asked Vince if I could take the rest of the morning off to start working on the ceiling. As usual, he said, "Sure! Take the whole day off if you need to." I went on out and picked up the material that I would need over at the house, and by that time the morning was half shot.

As I started mixing the plaster, I realized that it was unreasonably hot for that time of the year. This was actually a two-man job and I was trying to do it by myself. One man should mix the plaster and hand it up to one on the ladder. I had to mix the plaster and then carry one batch at time on the mortar board, up the ladder along with the trowel. I had to almost run up the ladder to get the rough coat on before it began to set up. It was approaching midday and I had already made several trips up and down the ladder. I had just started up with another mortar board full of plaster when the phone rang.

It was my wife and she told me that the doctor had told her that she was five and a half to six months pregnant. I told her that I couldn't leave the plaster job at this point, but that I would be home just as soon as I could. I finished that batch of plaster and had just loaded my board and crawled back up the ladder with sweat running down into my eyes. As I assumed the very strained position to apply the mortar, I heard the screen door open and someone enter. Since

I was trying to apply the plaster before it set up, I didn't pay any attention to this interruption.

"You can't do that!" a voice shouted. "You are not a union plasterer!" I looked around and found that the voice belonged to the same jerk I had gone to see at the Union Hall several months before. He was the same one who told me that he could get no one to do the job for me for almost a year.

This interruption hit me wrong. With the bad news from my wife and trying to do by myself, as well as not knowing for sure just how to do it, I was intensely disturbed. I climbed down the ladder, and without a word, went into the closet and picked up my Colt 45. As I walked back into the room, I slid the slide back. I looked at him and said, "Mister, this is my house and I'll do any damn thing I please. Now I want you to not only leave this house, but to get completely away from this property and do not come back." He immediately left and to this day, I think that I would have shot him if he had given me a hard time.

It really scared me, as I had almost reached the breaking point. I had come back home from fighting a war, hoping for some peace and quiet, and the first thing that happened was marital problems. The next thing, I was warned that if I wanted to stay healthy, I had better not work for Vince. Then there was the attempted robber, which was only a cover up for the attempt to beat me up. I had made up my mind right then that I was going to fight to see that things changed, even if it meant I had to call some old Army buddies to help me. Thank God, it never got that far. In the next local election, there was a big turnover in local officials and most of the trouble makers were voted out.

I finished the rough plastering and returned to my so-called home to see if I could get my wife settled down. I would return to apply the finish coat of plaster the next day.

I arrived at home thinking that I would have dinner with the whole family as usual, but it seemed that everyone was a little uptight. I suspected that she had told her family that she was pregnant. I couldn't tell how her family felt about the situation except for Madeline.

When I went out to the car to get something, she followed me out. She said, "Another baby right now is the last thing you guys need."

I replied, "I know that. For just a kid, you're a smart girl. I'm just going to have to make everything work out."

She looked at me and said, "Good luck! Give me a ride down to the school to pick up some homework and I will come back and baby sit with Linda while you two go out for a while and see if you can get each other settled down. Or rather, you get my sister settled down."

When Madeline had picked up her homework and I returned her to the house, I picked up my wife and we went out and found a quiet place were we could sit and talk. I had a million things I wanted to talk about, the house and money among other things, but I didn't think that this would be the time. When I asked her how she was feeling, she replied, "Outside of being tired, I am fine." I said, "You sure don't look like you are five or six months pregnant." She responded, "I don't feel like it either."

During our conversation, we decided that she must have gotten pregnant that one time on the third night that I was home. I said, "We sure had gotten results for a few minutes of pleasure." She looked at me and smiled, which was, I think, the first friendly look I had received from her since I got home from the Army.

"May I talk to you a little without upsetting you?" I asked. "Things have been sort of strained since I came home. I've been through hell and I am sure I have changed. I have been threatened and had an attempted robbery among several other things since I returned home. What I need now is some closeness, friendship and sharing of souls. What I am trying to say without hurting your feelings, is that sex is not enough. I need to feel some love along with the physical act."

She looked at me and said, "I thought that was what you wanted, but you were so different. All I wanted was love and friendship. With the baby coming, why don't we try to be friends and try to help each other with our problems and let the physical part of it come out of a feeling of togetherness and love?"

I thought to myself, I think we are at last beginning to understand each other. From what I'd heard, I think that she might have had an affair or two while I had been gone, but of course I had a few wild flings while I was in Paris. I thought to myself that it was best to just let these things ride. What I didn't know and what she didn't know wouldn't hurt either of us.

We finished the evening, went home, got ready for bed and lay there talking and holding each other. She stated, "I didn't realize just how much I needed to be held and loved." This time, there was a real love as well as the physical love, and afterwards, we both slept like a log.

After sharing that fine evening with my wife, I thought there might just be hopes for our marriage after all. I went to the shop the next morning and told Vince that I needed to try to finish the ceiling that morning, and of course he told me to go ahead. I proceeded to 417 North McLean Street (location of our new home) and put on the finish coat of plaster. It went on much faster than the rough coat. When I finished up around noon, I decided that I might as well go back to the shop to work. As the day-to-day work was mostly routine, I will go into no long, drawn out descriptions. I'll only say that it was great to get back into the swing of things. Traveling around to all the different locations and getting reacquainted with old friends was a great therapy for me.

That evening, I located a bed and dresser for the spare bedroom, and as I had already paid for the furniture, including the baby bed, in the down stair's bed room in the house on College Avenue, I thought we would use it in the master bedroom. Things at last seemed to be shaping up.

My wife's younger sister Madeline was still the only real friend that I had in the whole family, and she went out of the way to be decent to me. She wanted to see the house that I was working on, so I took her over to see it. She said, "This is much nicer than the place we are living now! Once you get that dining room ceiling painted, you won't even be able to tell it was repaired. The smartest thing that you can do is to get your wife and baby moved into this new home as soon as possible. With just the three of you, there is a much greater chance of getting your problems worked out." (All this from a teenager)

We left the house and went to the store and purchased a refrigerator and a used washer and dryer. They would be delivered the next day. I received a service call, so Madeline went with me. It was at a drive-in, so I bought each of us a cheeseburger and a coke. I finished up my service call and we sat and talked for a while. She was very mature for a teenager and this was a pleasant interlude away from all my problems, probably the best I enjoyed since I returned from the Army.

When I returned her home, I picked up my wife and baby and took them over to see the house. I was surprised to see my wife's eyes light up when she saw the inside of the house, even though there was almost a full day's painting to be done in the dining room. She liked the house so well that I thought that maybe working my rear off was going to be worthwhile. Even for me, there was a great feeling of satisfaction to see a hopeless house turn into an attractive home. To add to that, the hard work had helped me rid myself of a lot of pent up emotions and frustrations.

After looking at the house, we went to a soda fountain and bought Linda and ourselves an ice cream cone. What a mess! But it was sure worthwhile watching her enjoy it as we fed it to her. We went on home and went to bed and actually lay there and talked and enjoyed ourselves. There were still a lot of things that I didn't want to bring up until we got settled in our new home, but all in all, it had been a very pleasant evening.

As the days passed I was still keeping busy with my work and putting the finishing touches on the house. Within a few days we would be able to move in. I now had a little more time to think.

FLYING!

With more time to think, a promise that I made to myself after we had fought our way out of Honsfeld after being cut off during the Battle of the Bulge, kept running through my mind. On the outskirts of Honsfeld, just north of town, were twin airstrips with planes all gassed up and ready to fly. I could have flown out of there and been to our own lines within ten minutes. The only problem was, I didn't know how to fly. I promised myself that if and when I got home, I was going to learn to fly and never again be in this position.

We had to walk and had no food except what we could dig out of the frozen ground with our bayonets. We had to sleep outside most of the time with just the clothes on our backs and in weather with temperatures often dropping below zero with snow up to our ass. Out of ammunition and always out-numbered, we had to fight the enemy with their own ammunition and weapons, keeping on a constant move to stay ahead of the enemy armor, as we had no heavy weapons to defend ourselves. After two weeks of fighting our way through one small town after another, half frozen and starved, we finally reached our own lines. I had LOST FIFTY POUNDS during those two weeks. That is when I promised myself that I would learn to fly.

With all the problems that I had encountered after getting back home, this self-made promise had been put on the back burner. Now that I was beginning to get caught up, it was again foremost in my mind. It gave me something to look forward to.

It was not long before we were in our own home at 417 North McLean Street in Lincoln. No one knows what a wonderful feeling it was to be in our own home after not having a real one for so many years. By this time, of course, little Linda was walking and now there was plenty of room for her to run and play. Even the back yard was large and roomy. I was now able to do a lot of the things that I had always enjoyed. I was even able to go swimming out at the Lincoln Lakes. I became a little more relaxed; it was certainly a great feeling and time passed much faster.

On June 21, 1946, my wife delivered a baby girl. We named her Marianne, and they were both doing fine. I took Linda over to Mason City to stay with my mother until my wife came home from the hospital. Marianne was just the opposite of Linda. She looked just like her mother, while Linda looked much more like me.

My wife finally got home from the hospital and was doing fine. We had already moved into our new home and things were going much better than I had anticipated. My wife asked her mother to stay with us for a few days to help with the baby, and against my better judgment, I agreed with her.

Several weeks passed after my wife and new baby came home from the hospital. Her mother had finally gone home and our household had begun to settle down. Regretfully, our relationship had cooled down again and reverted back to just a physical thing, but that seemed to keep her happy. Now that the baby was here, she didn't seem to need me anymore.

After we had moved into our own home and I no longer paid most of the bills for that big house on College Avenue, her folks moved back to the small farm house near Middletown. It was only after this move that I finally found out how we had all ended up in that big house. Her father had joined the Seebees (a civilian construction unit employed by the military to build camps, airstrips, etc.) When he left, my wife's mother moved in with her in our apartment. Of course, her father got home (as well as her brother after a brief time in the Army) a long time before I did, so the apartment wasn't large enough for all of them. I don't think either of them had a job for awhile. With all the extra money that I was sending home, I suppose my wife thought we were rich, so they rented that big house. Why they needed to buy all new furniture, I'll never know. I will also never understand why she also loaned her brother a large sum of money to buy a car. (Money never repaid). With that money alone, my wife and I and the girls could have lived for almost a year.

All of these things I found out as time passed by. Had she only told me the truth in the beginning, I don't think I would have been nearly so upset, but instead, she kept insisting that she didn't know what had happened to it. In addition to all this money, there was still a large amount unaccounted for.

Some time went by and I received more of the watch money from Aletta in Paris and I still had more to come. I went out to the airport to see about taking flying lessons. I could do this now without having to take anything out of our living expenses.

I had another thing that helped me a lot. The Maple Club just east of Lincoln had two armed robberies in a short time. The owner hired me as an armed guard and bouncer, mainly, as an armed guard. Most of my time was spent out behind a hedge in my car with a Thompson

Sub Machine Gun borrowed from the Sheriff's office. I also built and rigged an alarm system with a series of buttons all over the place. Once one of these buttons was activated, no one could shut it off but me. The money I received for this system was more than enough to pay for all my flying lessons.

The club was a popular place that drew people from all over the state to enjoy big name bands and gambling. The salary that I received for my eight p.m. to one a.m. shift was almost unbelievable. The management didn't want any repeats of the first two robberies, as there had been a threat to the customers who had also had all their rings and money taken. The robbers had also robbed the "Old Maple Club" next door. This smaller building contained a bar, restaurant, with the gambling "joint" on the second floor.

It so happened that at the time of the robbery four car-loads of car dealers with loads of cash were visiting the club. They were heading for a big car auction in Decatur. The robbers, of course, got all their cash too. They even threatened to cut off the owner's finger because he was having trouble getting off a big diamond ring.

They terrorized everyone and even shot holes in the floor, and either slashed or shot holes in the customers' tires. I was really hoping that they would come back while I was there. With all the problems that I'd had since coming home, it would have given me a great deal of satisfaction to be able to eliminate these terrible people from the face of the earth. I held this job until all the robbers were caught.

I didn't get a chance to rid the earth of this scum. I held this job (in addition to my regular work) for a little over two months. The gang of robbers was finally caught after killing a couple of people during another robbery. I received a call from the sheriffs' office asking me if I would take the owner's wife, along with two of the waitress who were working at the club the night of the Lincoln robbery, to the court house in Havana to see if they could identify them.

When the Havana sheriff brought the four men out for the lineup, the girls identified all four, so I imagine that all were a guest of the government for a long time, except the one who did the shooting, who if convicted would receive the death penalty. They were rough-looking cookies and the girls said that they were sure glad that they had been caught because they had scared the pants off of them when they had shot holes in the floor.

When we returned to the club, the owner had a little party for the girls and me. He asked me if I would like to stay on as bouncer for the club, but I declined, telling him of my dream of becoming a pilot. I told him that this was something that I had promised myself when I had been cut off, starved and frozen during the Battle of the Bulge.

Interesting as it was, I was glad when this job was over as those fifteen-to-eighteen hour days were getting to me. The great thing about it was that I not only had enough money to pay for my flying lessons, but also enough to buy an airplane that was for sale at the airport.

I decided that I would take a week off and do nothing but spend a little time with my daughters, Linda and Marianne. Working those long hours for over two months, I was stressed out. The mental and nervous strain of knowing that I was the only one to protect those customers from the potentially dangerous robbers, should they return, got to me. (As it later turned out, two or more of them were really killers.)

I spent the next week just resting and working regular hours and spending time with my family. When that week had passed, I made a trip out to Lincoln Flying Service on Route 10 just west of Lincoln. There I started to fulfill the promise that I made to myself during those bleak and horrible days of fighting in Germany from December, 1944 through January of 1945, trying to get back to our own lines. During that time we lost half of our troops but seven men and I had managed to fight our way out. And in that two weeks we only had the food we could dig out of the frozen ground. All the men including myself lost approximately fifty pounds during that short time.

When I arrived at the airport owned and operated by Henry Brock, he introduced me to one of his flight instructors, Stan Bright, an ex-Navy flyer. He took us into the office where I bought a log book, air map and a book of pilot regulations. Stan took me out to the flight line, and sitting there was the same type of plane that I had seen on that strip north of Honsfeld, Belgium. He told me to get into the plane and study the manual until I could touch any and every control in the plane with my eyes closed. An hour later, he came back and told me to close my eyes and touch each instrument as he called it out. He then asked me to start a pre-flight check of the plane, being very careful of fuel and lubricant levels.

I thought I was done and started to get out of the plane. He said, "No, stay in the plane." He then checked all my throttle and switch settings, then walked around in front of the plane and yelled, "Clear, Contact." Before I knew it, I was sitting in the plane with the motor running. He climbed into the plane with me and said, "Let's go," and instructed me to taxi up and down the runway a few times.

He finally told me to go to the end of the runway and turn the plane facing into the wind, then do a mag and static check, and finally to check the pattern for traffic. This completed, he said, "Now line the plane up with the runway and check the carburetor and trim tab. Now ease the throttle all the way forward."

About a third of the way down the runway, he said, "Ease back on the stick." As I did this, everything became very smooth. I WAS Flying!

At 600 feet, he said, "Pull your throttle back to 2150 rpm and make a left turn. Now make a 45 degree right turn to leave the traffic pattern. Now slowly add throttle and climb to 1200 feet." As I did, we headed out over Lincoln. At last, I was actually flying.

This was probably the greatest thrill of my life up to this time. As I looked down, the cars, buildings and people looked like toys. After flying around a short time, we headed back to the airport, where he explained the traffic pattern to me. I looked down and that runway sure looked awfully short. He followed through on the controls and soon we were back on good, old mother earth. I could hardly believe that in the short time we were in the air, I would've had enough time to have reached the American lines during the Battle of the Bulge instead of the two weeks it actually took.

That July the 10th day of 1948, I had taken my first flying lesson in a J-3 Cub, N-number 347OK powered by a 65 horsepower Continental engine. From then on, I started going out every night after dinner to fly. Not only was I flying, but time was also flying by. By July 19, 1948, after only six and a half hours of flying time, my instructor turned me loose to do my solo. I want to tell you now, it's a strange feeling to realize that you are up in the air all by yourself, with only you to get that wonderful machine back to mother earth. If flying is the second greatest thrill on earth, landing has to be the first. Again, I could hardly believe that in only eight days, I was able to fly the plane.

My instructor gave me a list of maneuvers to practice anytime that I could find the time at the airport, and I managed to get in a lot of flying time. I also found time to look over the plane that was for sale there at the field. It was a low-houred Consolidated Vultee Air Force plane built in 1942 that they had sold to the civilian market. I paid the $500.00 cash for the plane, but I wanted to get more flying hours on the small plane before trying this big, old plane. It had a big 450 horsepower, nine cylinder radial engine, and weighed four times more than the plane I was learning on. I also wanted Otis Morris, the aircraft mechanic for the field, to check it all over before I started flying it. In the meantime, I got in as much flying time as I could.

I was having no problem whatsoever with any of my flying until one day when my instructor was checking me. He suddenly flipped the plane in a spin and in doing so, scared the crap out of me. He said, "Now that was a spin. You'll have to do spins on your flight test for your license."

I hated to admit it, but that spin scared the hell out of me so I went up ever chance I had to try to practice them but I couldn't get that plane to spin. One day, I climbed to about 5000 feet and started a spin, but everything was past the red line and by the time I pulled out, dirt was flying all over and I was plenty shaken. When I landed, a friend of mine, Bob Buchanan, was standing there. I told him that I didn't think I was going to be able to get my license because I couldn't do spins.

"There's really nothing to it," he said. "Show me how you were trying to do it." When I showed him, he said, "No wonder! You are trying to do an inverted spin, and that plane just will not do one."

"Well, I finally got it to spin but it scared the hell out of me," I said.

"Come on, I'll show you." When we checked the plane out before going up, we found that I had popped the jury struts on both wings.

"We'll have to take another plane," he said. "You damn near tore the wings off of this one!"

To make a long story short, we took another plane and we went up and he showed me how to do a spin and there was nothing to it. After that, the next thing I had to do was get checked out in my own plane. I had already made my cross country and was very close to having enough time to get my license.

After solving the problems with my spins and finding out just how really simple they were, I was feeling great. I went back home to spend time with my family as I did every night. My daughter Linda was a joy, but Marianne was a very unhappy baby and cried a lot. My wife seemed to be more unhappy all the time. Maybe it was because we didn't have much of a sex life. Our physical relationship, especially for me, was very unsatisfactory. Marriage without sex (which seemed to be all she wanted) left us with very little going for us. We didn't have a togetherness of mind or soul. As for her part, I don't think we were even friends. Even though I was trying to spend time with the family for the sake of the little girls, I was getting near the breaking point and the meaningless sex left me feeling uptight and empty. I think she really enjoyed the physical part of it and reached her satisfaction from one to three times each session and then immediately turned over and went to sleep. I would lay awake for hours trying to figure out what, if anything, I was doing wrong. I was ready to give up, but I still wanted to keep everyone together for the sake of the two girls. Eventually, sleep would come and I would get some rest.

Along with my flying, working hard kept my mind occupied and I was able to get by. One morning, I had just arrived at the shop and realized that I had left some material on the back porch at home, so I returned home to get it. I pulled into the alley and ran up to the porch. My time in the Army had taught me to move very quietly. As I started to pick up the things I needed, I heard voices and looked in the kitchen window. There sat my wife and her mother. At that moment, I heard her mother say, "You should make him quit spending all that money on flying." I could hardly believe what I was hearing. I opened the door and said, "What's going on here?"

270

Everything got deathly quiet. I told her mother that she had better leave and told my wife that we needed to talk. She replied that her mother could stay. I answered, "This is my house and either she leaves or I will throw her out!" Her mother left, but my wife called the police.

When the officer arrived and wanted to know what the problem was, I told him. He explained to my wife that this was my house and that it was my right to ask anyone to leave. After he had told my wife this, I told him that I wanted him to get the hell out too. I told my wife to sit down because we had to talk. I explained to her that it was none of her mother's business how I spent my money as long as all the bills were paid to keep this household running. I added, "As long as this has all come up, I want to know what happened to all the extra money that I sent home."

It was then that I discovered that she had supported the whole family and had even loaned her no good brother even more that I had originally thought. To make matters worse, I found that her mother had rented a room in the house next door and moved in.

When I found out her mother had moved in next door, I knew there was no chance of our marriage ever working out. I said, "The best thing that we can do is to get a divorce just as soon as possible." She didn't seem to be unhappy about this at all and we agreed to an uncontested divorce on irreconcilable differences. In the separation, I would move out immediately and I would pay all the bills and living expenses until the divorce became final. At that time, I would be responsible for child support in the amount of a legal agreement in court. She would have custody of the children but I would have visitation rights at all reasonable times. I gave her all the household furniture and there would be no alimony. I also told her that I'd heard of other things that she had done while I was gone and one thing in particular, just before I returned home from the Army. I told her that if she tried to contest the divorce, I would have this made public. With that, I told her that I was going on to work and that I would have my belongings out of there after work that evening. This was September 9, 1948.

After renting a room at the hotel, I went back to work. I checked with Vince and he had a storage room at the shop where I could keep my belongings until I found a place to live. After all the hours of hard work fixing up the house, I was back in the same position that I had been when I first got home. Yet, no one could have realized the great pressure it had lifted off my shoulders. I would probably get to see the girls even more than before. I could hardly wait for the divorce to become final. I tried to go by to see the girls each day but most of the time my wife wasn't there. She had hired a twenty-one-year-old Lincoln Christian college student to baby sit for her. I don't know why she didn't have her mother baby sit.

After visiting, I would head out to the airport to get in some more flying time. I wanted to get in as much time as possible and to get checked out in more planes, but most of the time, they were not available when I had the time. It was a strange feeling not to have a home to go to after I had spent so much time fixing up that one, so I more or less made the airport my home. Those pilots out there were a great group of people, and not having my wife around, I didn't end my day not being able to get a good night's sleep.

I ran over to Mason City and told my folks about our separation and pending divorce, and they were very unhappy with me. I told them that if they had heard some of the things that she had said about them, they wouldn't be so unhappy. I guess they would just have to learn as I had. Such is life.

After telling my folks about our separation and the coming divorce, I was feeling pretty low, but after all the lies that my wife told me about various things, I was happy to get out of the situation. I did feel terrible about the girls, but I knew that she would never let me have them. I only hoped that someday my folks would know what I'd had to put up with. I was glad to get out of this unpleasant situation before I did something that I would have regretted for the rest of my life.

One evening when I was visiting the girls, my wife came in. She introduced me to the baby sitter, the Christian College student. She said, "This is Vada Compton from Norfolk, Nebraska. If you are going to the airport, would you mind giving her a ride home? She lives on Keokuk Street, about half way across town."

"That would be OK," I said. "I'll be going right by there on my way to the airport." As we started out, I didn't say much because she seemed a little afraid of me and I had no way of knowing what my wife had told her about me. Nothing good, I was sure. I did finally ask her how she liked Lincoln.

"It's OK," she said, "but I really miss my family and I'm having trouble finding my way around this town. I have to walk about two miles to get to the college, but I know my way there." About this time, she reached over and touched me on the shoulder. Pointing to a house on the corner, she said, "I have a room in that house over there." When I let her out, she said, "Thank you very much. It's a long way out here and this ride will give me much more study time."

I think this young lady was having a difficult time of it, but with my mind on flying, I thought little more about her. I spent the next hour flying, after which a group of us went to a nearby restaurant where I had my dinner while the rest of the guys had a drink. Finishing dinner, I returned to my lonely hotel room. After having had a home for a while, it was going to be hard to get accustomed to living in one room again.

The next day when I finished work, I stopped to see the girls, and as usual, Vada was babysitting. A short time later, while I was playing with the girls, my ex-wife's mother came over and said that my ex was going somewhere with a group of ladies and that she would stay with the girls. I prepared to leave as I didn't want to spend any more time around the mother than I had to. As I left, Vada had just started down the walk. As she had the long sixteen blocks to walk and I was going to the airport anyway, I asked her if she would like a ride.

She hesitated a moment, then looking at me with a shy smile, she said, "Sure would, if it isn't too much trouble!" This time she was much more talkative and told me that school was hard for her as she had to learn to read and write Greek and study from a Greek bible. I don't think she really had many close friends as she was babysitting and then working in a restaurant on Saturdays, many times a double shift. I dropped her off at her room, then proceeded to the airport.

All my days were about the same. I did move around all over the county in my work and I met many interesting people and had a lot of challenges. Some of the new equipment that was coming out in that post-war era was very complicated, but it always seemed that I would succeed in working out the problems. This gave me a great sense of accomplishment in that I was doing something useful. After work, I continued to stop and see the girls and almost always ended up taking Vada home on my way to the airport. As the days went by, she became at ease talking to me.

One day she said, "You sure seem to love those little girls and I don't believe all those things your wife told me about you." This made me feel better.

One morning on my way to work, I stopped in a restaurant to get my breakfast. As I looked for a place to sit, I saw Vada sitting alone at a table. I walked over and asked if she would mind if I sat with her. She nodded, but continued to count out her change to see if she had enough to eat on. I asked her if she would let me buy her breakfast, as I really appreciated the good care she was taking of my girls. When she looked at me and answered "Yes," I suddenly realized that she was a very attractive young lady.

As we talked, she seemed to understand me and I began to have the desire to know her better. I hadn't had a female friend that I could talk to since I'd gotten home from the Army, and I thought that she needed someone just as bad as I did. We finished our breakfast and I took her on out to the school. When she thanked me for the ride, I think there was a spark between us. I had never had this feeling before and I was sure she was feeling the same way. I had no desire to have an affair at this time, but I knew we both needed a friend.

From that day on, I made a sincere effort to be at the house when she finished baby sitting. I also started taking her to breakfast and then to school, as I had to go right by her house and besides, I knew there were many days when she wouldn't have had money enough to eat. As we shared these morning breakfasts, I began to realize that she was not just a young, attractive girl, but also a deep, caring young lady. There was a very definite attraction between us and I think that both our hearts beat faster when we were near each other. With my folks so unhappy about my divorce and more or less taking my wife's part, I really needed a friend.

I wanted to ask her to go out to dinner sometime, but I was a little reluctant to ask her for fear that it would spoil our friendship.

When I got up enough nerve, she replied "Yes" with no hesitation. I don't know which of us was the most excited.

Our dinner date took us to Peoria and the Pierre Marquette Hotel. This proved to be the most enjoyable evening that I had spent since I'd returned home. We talked about my learning to fly and my reason for wanting to learn, and she seemed almost as excited as I about it. After dinner, we drove down to the river front and looked at all the boats before returning to Lincoln. It was still early when I pulled up in front of her house so we sat and talked for a while. There seemed to be a peaceful togetherness and sharing between us. When I mentioned again the hardships encountered during the Battle of the Bulge when I couldn't fly out in one of those planes at the field north of Honsfeld, she said, "Don't ever let anyone talk you out of learning to fly." This affected me very deeply. Here was this young lady, nine years younger than I, and she seemed to realize why it was so important for me to learn to fly.

Although we had been seeing a lot of each other, there had never been any bodily contact between us. That night as I sat there looking into her eyes, I sensed a desire for something more. I wanted to hold her and kiss her, but I feared that such a move would end this deep friendship. I finally gathered enough nerve to lean over and kiss her lightly on the lips.

There was a look of surprise on her face, then she put her arms around my neck and kissed me back. I had been kissed many times but never like that. It was not a wild passionate kiss but a kiss with the promise of the sharing of heart and soul. We held each other so tight that it was almost painful. At that moment, I knew that I wanted to spend the rest of my life with this wonderful young woman and share all the good and the bad, the happiness and whatever the future should bring. (This desire later came true.) We both realized that we had found something rare and precious in addition to our deep friendship.

We kissed each other good night and I wondered how we were going to stay away from each other. We couldn't get married until my divorce became final and I knew that my folks would not like the idea of my remarrying. I also knew that she would get the same objections from her family. Things would not be easy for us.

275

When I returned to my room that night, I could hardly believe that I'd found someone this soon that I wanted to spend the rest of my life with. With the problems that I'd had with my wife and the divorce, I had almost given up finding anyone that I thought I could share the rest of my life with.

I thought that maybe there was something wrong with me, something that I'd been through during the war that had rendered me incapable of feeling love. Now I knew this wasn't true. Just one little kiss from this young lady changed all of that. My heart beat faster whenever we came close to each other. All the horrible visions of war disappeared when we were near. She was like magic in my life and I think I was the same way in hers. It was amazing that one little kiss could change two lives so completely.

The next morning, when I picked her up for breakfast and to take her to school, we were a little uneasy with each other. I looked her directly in the eyes and asked, "Are you having any regrets about what happened last night?"

"Oh no," she said. "It's just that something has changed. I have never had this feeling before."

I said, "I think I'm having the same feeling as you. I think we are in love with each other!"

We finished our breakfast. Just sharing a meal and being close and talking to each other gave us a feeling of peace. I had never in my life had such a tranquil feeling of peace. We were actually sharing our lives with each other. I let her off at the collage and then went on to work. When I walked in, Vince looked at me and asked, "What happened to you? You look like the cat that ate the canary!"

I answered back, "Things are going right for a change."

That evening I went to see my two girls and stayed to play with them until Vada was ready to leave. When I stopped in front of her house to drop her off, she asked if she could ride on out to the airport with me. She wanted to see me fly and then she would walk back home. I told her that she could go with me but that she was not going to walk back home. "I'm only going to fly for about an hour and then I will drive you home."

As she sat there watching me, even my flying seemed to go better. Everything just fell into place. When I finished my flying and had my log book signed, I asked if she would like to have dinner with me.

"I would love to, but I feel bad about you buying my meals all the time. Besides, I don't want to go in to eat." We decided to just pick up some sandwiches and drinks at a drive-in and find a quiet place to eat them. We bought the sandwiches, then drove out to the park and sat there talking and listening to the radio while we ate.

Our conversation touched on about everything, such as my experiences during the war, my marriage and about how home-sick she had been. She looked into my eyes and said, "Since I met you, I haven't been near as lonesome and homesick. I feel much more content now."

I told her that I was feeling more at peace with myself now that I was with her, than anytime since I had returned home from the war. I went on to say, "I need you. I need someone to understand and love me."

Looking directly in my eyes, she said, "I need you just as bad as you need me! I don't know what is going to happen but I do know that I want you to be a part of the rest of my life."

Here was this young lady who was nine years younger than I, and she was much more mature than anyone that I had known in my entire life. She seemed to fill a void in what had seemed to be an empty life.

We sat there holding each other and kissed. Outside of a few kisses, there had been no physical relations between us, but in these kisses, we felt a burning passion inside. We knew that part of our love would be just as great as what we had already experienced, but we didn't want a relationship based on sex. I'd already had that.

With my mornings starting with breakfast with Vada, my work, and spending time with my girls, time just seemed to fly by. Life seemed to have regained purpose for me. Now when I gave Vada a ride home in the evening, she would usually take her books with her and go on out to the airport with me and study while I was flying. After that, we would go out somewhere quiet to eat. One nice thing about this was that I had so many area friends in the food and tavern business, we received special treatment almost every place we went.

We would just share a meal and talk and we never ran out of things to talk about. I told her about my family and a lot of my war experiences that I'd never been able to talk to anyone about before. After living with my wife who was cold, selfish and had no emotional feelings for me, I never realized how much I was missing by not having someone I could talk to. I was just another thing that my wife used for her personal satisfaction.

When we would finish our dinner, we would head back to Lincoln and go to the park. There we would sit and talk in private, sitting close to each other in a kind of intimacy that I had never known in my lifetime. When I kissed her, she would close her eyes and put her arms around me and tell me that I made her feel safe and secure. As for me, all the bad war memories seemed to melt away into space during those times.

With the kind of intimacy we shared with our hearts and souls, it seemed we had become one emotional being. I had never before known the peace of mind that I had at that time. We would have to pull away from each other at times like that, as we were afraid that our passions would lead to a physical relationship that neither of us wanted at that time.

On one of these occasions, we took a breather and got out of the car and walked around for a few minutes. When we returned to the car, we sat apart from each other to settle down somewhat. As we talked, she mentioned that she had a three day break from collage coming up and that she would sure like to go home for a short visit. I told her that if I had my license I would be able to take her home and she could stay overnight and I could fly her home the next afternoon. She thought that it would be wonderful.

I thought about how I could manage this without my license, and decided that if I could find someone with a license who wanted to build up flying time I would pay for the rental and plane expenses. I told her of my idea and asked her if she was ready to go home. I told her that I would make some calls that evening and see what I could do. By the time we pulled up in front of her house, we were both brimming with excitement about the thought of her being able to make the trip home, as well as me getting in some long, dual cross country flying time. As usual, the kiss goodnight brought that great feeling of becoming one and melting together. I let her out and headed home to bed.

When I got home, I called "Woody," one of my flying buddies who was working on his commercial license. I asked him if he would be interested in making a 500 mile trip by plane if I would pay the expenses. I told him he could be the pilot in command on the way out and I would be coming back. He jumped at the chance.

I said, "Fine, I'll see you at the field at seven p.m. tomorrow night and we'll make arrangements for the plane and the trip."

The next evening when Vada and I arrived at the field, Woody was already there. We made arrangements to rent a three-place plane for the following Friday, Saturday and Sunday. Luckily my instructor was there, so I could get checked out in the Piper Cruiser and shoot three solo take-offs and landings. I would have to have this to receive credit for my cross country time. I managed to get all this done before dark and Vada was getting more excited all the time about getting to go home.

Woody and I went into the airport office where we bought the maps necessary for our flight. We then sat down and plotted out our course on the map and our stops for gas. We wanted to have all this done so we wouldn't have any last minute details to take care of Friday morning. The days seemed to fly by and before we knew it, we were at the airport at 6:30 a.m. on Friday and ready to go.

We climbed into the plane and Woody climbed up to cruising altitude, lined up our course and we were on our way. Even though I was not doing the flying, it was still a wonderful feeling. Our first fuel stop was at Ottumwa, Iowa, and we all made a pit stop and then we headed for Missouri Valley, where we refueled again. Our next stop was Norfolk, Nebraska, our final destination, and even with the two fuel stops, the trip had taken only a little over four and a half hours. Almost unbelievable.

Vada's' folks were right there at the airport to meet us. Vada had tears in her eyes as she hugged and greeted them. They gave Woody and me a ride into town to our hotel, but Vada and I had decided to say nothing of our relationship for a while. She told her folks the truth, that I was the husband of the woman that she babysat for and that I wanted to build up flying time, so I had given her a ride home.

Saturday morning, Woody and I got a ride back out to the airport and sat around "shooting the bull" with the local pilots and looking over the planes. We discovered that they had a "loaner" car that we could have the use of until Sunday noon, so we now had a way to get around and see the town and the surrounding country side. The time went by real fast and before we knew it, it was time to attend a home-cooked dinner that we had been invited to by Vada and her folks. There we met her two sisters who had also been invited. The home-cooked meal was a great treat and the company, enjoyable. When Woody and I left, we told Vada's folks to have her at the airport by 1:00 p.m.

Woody and I fueled up and checked the plane over in preparation for the flight home to Lincoln. When Vada arrived, she informed me that she was kinda scared and wanted to ride in the back with me, so Woody got to fly back. I didn't mind not getting to fly because, sitting in the back with Vada, the noise of the plane gave us an opportunity to talk privately for hours. After traveling over 1000 miles in only three days, we arrived safely back in Lincoln. Having breakfast with Vada the next morning, I saw the contented smile on her face, a result of her visit to her folks. This gave me a wonderful feeling as I dropped her off at the college and proceeded on to my work. Vince, my boss, continued to tease me, wanting to know why I was looking so happy. I guess, finally having found someone who cared for me and that I cared so much for must have made a great difference in me.

As time passed, my days at work, seeing my girls and Vada, all became routine and I was getting in flying time almost every day. Time was passing at an unbelievable rate. On September 30, 1948, I planned to get checked out in my own plane. I was going from a four cylinder J3 Cub with a 65 horse-power engine and a cruising speed of around seventy miles per hour to a nine cylinder Consolidated Vultee with 450 horsepower and a cruising speed of 147 miles per hour. This plane would stall (quit flying) at the speed the J3 cruised at, so I was very excited. I had a total of 48 hours flying time and I figured it would take me at least three hours to get checked out.

My instructor, Stan, had me sit in the plane, close my eyes and touch each instrument and control as he called them out. There must have been over fifty of them. After that, we did a walk around, checking all the control surfaces, oil and fuel. He told me that on this R-985 engine, I would have to pull the prop through at least six times before starting the engine.

I climbed in the front and he climbed in the back and I used the "wobble pump" to bring the fuel pressure up to three or four pounds, opened up the throttle about 1/10th, set the prop in high pitch and the oil cooler in open position with the carburetor air on cold, set the flaps up and put the fuel mixture on "full rich," all the while working the wobble pump to keep the fuel pressure up. With the switch on "both," I flipped the spring loaded starter switch and the powerful engine roared into life. After the engine started, I sat there until all the instruments were in the "green," then set the propeller in low pitch and taxied to the end of the runway where I did my mag and static check. I lined up with the runway, checked to be sure all the trim tabs were set at zero, then advanced the throttle slowly to the stop. As the motor "revved up," I was pushed back in my seat, and at the same time, the tail came up.

Stan said, "Ease back on the stick, keeping your air speed around 95 to 100 MPH." When I looked at the instrument panel, I saw that we were climbing at a rate of almost a thousand feet a minute. Almost unbelievable.

We left the traffic area to do climbing turns and stalls with the engine both off and on. As we returned to the field, he instructed me what to do. We did three take off and landings, then landed and he climbed out of the plane. As his feet hit the ground, he said, "Now I want you to do three take off and landings by yourself."

What a thrill and in my own big plane! When I had completed these, I landed and shut down the plane. He signed my log book and said, "You are now legal!" The total time for the check out was thirty minutes. I was so elated that I wouldn't have needed a plane to fly. I was walking on air!

That evening, after visiting with my girls, I started to take Vada home, but she said, "I want to go out to the airport with you to see you fly in your own plane." I was only too happy to comply. When we arrived at the field, she went with me as I did my walk-around check of the plane, then she returned to the bench by the airport office. I checked and found that I had enough fuel for about three hour's flying time.

I was feeling mighty proud of myself. Here I was, getting ready to take off in my own plane and sitting there watching was the most important lady in my life. There was not much daylight left and since I wasn't checked out for night flight, I went through the start up procedures and taxied to the end of the runway for take off as fast as possible. To feel the acceleration from that big old nine-cylinder engine shove you back in the seat was quite a sensation. I went right by where Vada was sitting and I could see that she had her hands clasped over her ears. She removed one of them long enough to give me a wave.

I was getting very busy by this time preparing to do landings and go-arounds without stopping. With this plane, it was almost like being a jumping jack with the cranking down of the flaps and then cranking them back up again. My flying demonstration over, I landed, parked the plane and went through the shut-down procedure. Vada came over to the plane and helped me put on the canopy and engine covers.

By the time we got back to the car, I think she was just as excited about all this as I was. I said, "I think we need to go out and celebrate this occasion. Let's drive over to Poplar Acres and have dinner!" As we started for dinner, she looked at me and said, "That was sure loud. As a matter of fact, it was so loud that I covered my ears with my hands, but the bench and the window behind me still vibrated. It kinda scared me." I told her there was nothing to worry about and that noise was perfectly normal for a big aircraft.

When we got to Elsie's Poplar Acres, she provided us with our own special booth and I ordered a drink and our meal. I was still having a little trouble getting settled down after getting my check out in my own plane. Weather permitting, I would have enough time in by the week-end to get my license. I would take my solo cross country and be ready for my license exam.

I told Vada that with the exam out of the way and with the speed of my plane, we could fly non-stop to Norfolk after work on a Friday evening and return to Lincoln in time for work and school early Monday morning. I was closer to what I wanted as far as flying was concerned, than anytime since I had returned from the war. Little had I thought that I would be able to buy my own large Air Force plane. I think you could have looked the world over and not found two happier people.

As we pulled up in front of Vada's home, the goodnight kiss and just holding each other a few moments was the end of a perfect day. Even though we both went to our own rooms in different homes, we were still together in our hearts and souls.

Time passed swiftly and Saturday, the 3rd of October, 1948, I was prepared to take my cross-country solo. I had decided to fly out to Norfolk, Nebraska just to see how long it would take in my own plane. Vada went out to the field with me and I made arrangements for one of the guys to take her back to town after I left. I thought she was going to crush me to death as she hugged me while kissing me goodbye. She was crying and telling me to be careful. She said, "I don't want to lose you." As I circled over the field to pick up my heading, I could still see her standing there waving.

I climbed to about 8000 feet, trimmed the plane and sat back and relaxed. The air was like glass. I was flying V.F.R. (visual), so I had to keep checking and double-checking my ground checkpoints. In only three hours and fifteen minutes, I was sitting on the ground at Norfolk, Nebraska. I could hardly believe that it had been so simple.

One of the guys there at the field gave me a ride to town and I rented a room at the hotel. I called Vada's older, married sister to just say hello, but she invited me out to their place for dinner. She wanted to know why I hadn't brought Vada with me. I had to explain to her that I only had my student's license and couldn't carry passengers until I received my regular license.

All of her children were excited about having someone visiting who was a pilot. I told her husband that if he would drive me out to the airport, I would show the kids my plane. When I mentioned this, there was no way he could get out of taking us to the field. It was sure a great hit with the kids. I let each one of them sit in the plane while I explained how everything worked. When he returned me to the hotel, he told me that if I would call him, he would take me back out to the field in the morning.

After I had fueled up the next morning, I went to the weather station (it was nice to have it handy there on the field). The weather wasn't all that great from Norfolk to Lincoln with a ceiling of only 5,000 to 6,000 feet, but this would make for a fine V.F.R. flight. I took off and climbed to an altitude of 4,000 feet, set my heading and headed back to Lincoln. Due to the low ceiling, I couldn't take advantage of the winds aloft. That meant I would be bucking a twenty-five-to-thirty mile head wind all the way back. Even though I had the plane trimmed on course, the air was rough and I had to stay at the controls all the way home.

When I finally reached Lincoln and started my let gear down, I circled the field to check the wind sock and saw Vada there with a married couple, Galen and Sharleen, who she'd gone to school with. She had talked them into bringing her to the airport so she could watch me come in.

I landed and pulled my plane up to my tie-downs and went through the shut down procedure and locked the controls. Even with the head wind, it had only been exactly four hours since I'd left Norfolk over 500 miles away.

The prop had hardly stopped spinning when Vada came running over. My feet had just touched the ground when she threw her arms around me and kissed me so intensely that I thought she was going to devour me, while all the time telling me how worried she had been. She was very happy and I think that she really had been worried about me.

They all helped me tie down the plane, and since it was near dinner time, I asked Galen and Sharleen if they would all like to have dinner with us. We went to Poplar Acres again, and as usual, we had a wonderful meal. During the meal, I told them that with my cross-country completed, I was going to try to take my exam the next week.

After finishing our meal, Galen and Sharleen went on home and Vada and I drove out to the park where we sat and talked for a while. I could hardly believe the peace of mind I experienced just by being close to such a wonderful person as she. Just sitting there holding hands seemed to make everything OK. Even after we parted, it seemed like part of us was still together. I was sure that we could be exquisitely happy spending the remainder of our lives together.

The day of reckoning (my license test day) finally arrived, Friday, October 8th, 1948. That afternoon at one o'clock I would know if I would be able to keep the promise I made to myself that horrible, snowy, miserably cold day during the Battle of the Bulge. That was the day, out-numbered by the enemy, I didn't know if I would be able to stay alive from one minute to the next, let alone keep the seven men with me alive.

I arrived at the Tremont Flying Service where I was to meet Mr. Orin C. Vice, the federal flight examiner. One hour later, I walked out with a temporary pilot's license that was good until I got my permanent license from the Federal Aeronautics Administration. (I still have that license to this day, almost fifty- six years later.) Stanley Bright, my instructor, was also there. He wanted to see how I had done and to take the examiner and me out to eat, since I was the last civilian that he would instruct. He was returning to the military as a civilian instructor.

Arriving back at the Lincoln airport late that afternoon, I found all my friends were out there to meet me. They were a great group of people. Most important of all, Vada was there. Her happiness for me was unbelievable. I could now legally carry passengers, so I asked Vada if she would like to take a ride.

She replied, "Yes, but I'm a little scared." Everyone told her not to worry because with all of them watching, I wouldn't dare let anything go wrong. I put her in the rear seat, checked her seat belt and everything, then took off and flew over Lincoln and the Christian College. Returning to the field, I ask her if she would mind if I made a low, fast pass over the field, and with her consent, I came down to about 100 feet and zipped across the field at 210 MPH. This was a real thrill for both of us. Climbing back up, I entered the traffic pattern and landed. As I helped her out of the plane, she had a big smile on her face and she hugged and kissed me right in front of everyone and told me that it had been one of the greatest thrills of her life.

I had started my first flight lesson on July 10, 1948, and had received my license on October 8, 1948, with a total of fourteen hours dual flying time and forty-four hours solo, in just three months. I had also been checked out in my own high-performance plane. I had achieved the goal I had set for myself during the winter of 1944 and 1945 while I was in Europe.

By this time, my life had stabilized to the point that I could see that there was going to be future for Vada and me. I also wanted to use my achievement to do something for my country and for the community that I lived in. There were few other countries where this would have been possible.

To be able to use my flying, Vada and I joined the Civil Air Patrol (civilian branch of the Air Force). We would also be able to help the National Civilian Defense Department. I was given a rating of captain and a title of operation officer, and could wear the Air Force uniform. Vada was an observer and had a lot of first aid training. Over the years, we searched for lost children, plane crashes and escaped prisoners, as well as working with civil defense on many of their problems. With all of this, I felt that my time in flight training was not wasted and most of these problems proved to be very interesting.

Vada wasn't too enthused about the flying missions but she loved the first aid phase of the operation. She was part of the ground support team attached to the ambulance division, which we could direct to the crash scene from the air.

I was working and Vada was still going to college and we were seeing a lot of each other. On a Friday, the 17th of October, I picked Vada up from college and asked her if she would like to go home. She said, "Of course, but don't you think it is a little late to start?" I answered, "Not if we start right away." That was all it took. We hurriedly picked up a change of clothes and headed for the field, and within a few minutes, we were headed for Norfolk, Nebraska.

This time the weather was against us. There was a limited ceiling so we had to buck a head wind all the way out there. We didn't get there until thirty minutes before dark. I got us a ride and dropped Vada off at her home and I went on to the hotel.

The next afternoon, I went by the Vada's' house and told her that I was going to the field to check and gas up the plane. Her folks said that they would take me out. When we got there, her mother wanted me to take her for a ride, so I took her up. When I got the plane leveled out, I let her fly it. She did a good job.

When we landed, I told Vada that we should start back early Sunday afternoon because we could run into another head wind. She was ready. We hadn't been able to be close to each other since we arrived because she still hadn't told her folks that we were going together. It sure had been lonesome for me in that hotel room.

Sunday, when her folks took us back out to the airport, I checked the weather and found that it was going to be beautiful all the way back to Lincoln. We climbed to 10,000 feet, lined up on course and two and a half hours later, we were parking the plane at my tie downs in Lincoln, 500 miles away.

We were starved for some time together and couldn't wait to hold each other. I just hoped we could subdue our passions until my divorce was final. It was getting more difficult all the time to keep from giving in to those physical demands that our bodies were making on us. Due to my former marital problems, I could only think that if we gave in to this urge and let sex play a greater part in our relationship, we would both lose in the long run.

We began to spend a lot of time with Galen and Sharleen. They had both finished college and he was the minister at the Rossville Christian Church. They gave us a lot of support and were very understanding. I'm not too sure that we would've been able to hold out if it hadn't been for these two wonderful people, but hold out we did and before long it was time for Vada to go home for Christmas break.

She was still keeping our relationship a secret from her folks but I thought that she should tell them. She said, "If I tell them, they will make me stop seeing you and I'll have no place to go. I couldn't live with you in Lincoln until your divorce becomes final. If I did, I would be kicked out of school and anyway, I don't think we should live together until we are married." I had to agree with her. We had a beautiful relationship and something like that would ruin it.

When she had gone home, I was able to fly out and see her quite often. She would meet me either at June's or at the hotel. When we met in the privacy of my room at the hotel, it was very difficult. Of course, she would have to sneak in and luckily, she was never caught. When we would have to be apart, we would both listen to the same radio program at the same time every night and think of each other. It was almost like being together.

When it was time for school to start again, she was short on money so she decided to skip the next semester, but did come back to Lincoln to work and save her money. She had a full time job at the Lincoln Inn on old Route 66, working for Mrs. Buckles. Her tips there were great. In the meantime, I found a small apartment over a garage with an alley entrance to the garage. For what it's worth, we had privacy.

Meanwhile, my job with Vince, whose business had increased by leaps and bounds, now required two more men to help me. Every third week we took turns working the night and weekend service calls. Of course, if Vada wasn't working, she could ride along with me on these calls. After working the night and weekend shift, I'd be off from Friday noon until Monday noon. This worked out great for me, as it gave me a lot of time to spend with Vada. If she could get off, we would go to Chicago, and by plane, almost any other place we wanted. Of course, by this time, my pay had increased greatly. All we were waiting for now was for my divorce to become final.

I still saw my girls almost every day. On the 4th of February, my divorce became final, thank heaven. Galen wanted to marry us in his church, the Rossville Christian Church, so we set the date for the 19th of February, 1949. For a time it looked like this wasn't going to happen because the marriage had to take place in the same county where the license was acquired, but things worked out and when we arrived at the Rossville Christian Church, Minister Galen was there to greet us. We already had our three witnesses, Robert and Marge Buchanan and Galen's wife, so it was on February the 19th, 1949 that Vada and I were joined together in Holy Matrimony. We could hardly believe that we were finally married.

After the ceremony, we left on a short honeymoon. We arrived at our hotel and had dinner and retired early. When we got into bed, I said, "I love you!" She put her arms around me and said, "I love you too and my final gift to you is my body. You already have my heart and soul." With that she kissed me very, very passionately. That small spark that had been so difficult to hold in check until we were married, suddenly blazed into a white hot flame that bonded us together into one spiritual being forever.

This launched us on the road to a wonderful marriage lasting fifty-five years, during which we shared everything with each other. She seemed to understand me and was able to comfort me and ease my mind of all those horrible memories of combat that I'd gone through during WWII. I, in turn was able to love, comfort and cherish her for the remainder of her life.

On August 5, 1958, I was able to help her through the worst experience of her life. She gave birth to a beautiful girl, Melinda Sue, who lived only a very short time.

Later, after fifteen years of marriage, she presented me with a wonderful son, who proved to be one of the greatest joys of our life and bonded us even closer together. I don't think a day passed without us telling each other how much we loved each other.

We had been married fifty-five years when on the 6th of December, 2002, God took her hand and led her home to heaven. There is now another angel in heaven. Although her body is gone, the memory of that angel still lives on in my heart and soul and there it will remain forever to help me over the bad times that I know I will have. Although there is a terrible empty spot, those wonderful memories of the times we shared will never go away and will never cease to comfort me. I thank the Lord for letting Vada share those fifty-five wonderful years with me before calling her home.

The memories of those fifty-five years of marriage is yet another story.

THE END

Printed in the United States
47854LVS00004B/274-297